THE GREAT DIVIDE

THE
GREAT DIVIDE

A Walk Through America
Along the Continental Divide

STEPHEN PERN

VIKING

VIKING
Published by the Penguin Group
Viking Penguin Inc., 40 West 23rd Street,
New York, New York 10010, U.S.A.
Penguin Books Ltd, 27 Wrights Lane,
London W8 5TZ, England
Penguin Books Australia Ltd, Ringwood,
Victoria, Australia
Penguin Books Ltd, 2801 John Street,
Markham, Ontario, Canada L3R 1B4
Penguin Books (N. Z.) Ltd, 182–190 Wairau Road,
Auckland 10, New Zealand

Penguin Books Ltd, Registered Offices:
Harmondsworth, Middlesex, England

First American Edition
Published in 1988 by Viking Penguin Inc.

Copyright © Stephen Pern, 1987
All rights reserved

LIBRARY OF CONGRESS CATALOGING IN PUBLICATION DATA
Pern, Stephen, 1950–
The Great Divide.
1. Continental Divide Trail—Description and travel.
2. Pern, Stephen, 1950– —Journeys—Continental
Divide Trail. 3. Walking—Continental Divide Trail.
I. Title.
F721.P47   1988   917.3′04927   87-40433
ISBN 0-670-82100-4

Printed in the United States of America by
Arcata Graphics, Fairfield, Pennsylvania
Set in Times Roman

For my mother and my father who,
in their separate ways,
made me.

Thanks

America was fun, so to the nation as a whole – thank you. Most of the people who helped me directly are mentioned by name in the text, but of those who aren't, Pat and Ellie Imperato, Carol Beckwith and Landis Smith in New York, Gay Sutherland in California and Tom Smith in Montana showed me especial kindness. I would also like to thank Wasatch Publishers, Inc., of Salt Lake City, Utah, for permission to quote from *Wind River Trails* by Finis Mitchell.

Writing the book, on the other hand, was hell. Without the help of Jan Collins and Laurence Bristow-Smith I doubt if it would have been published. For coaxing the words themselves beyond the strict confines of the trail I have Connie to thank, though already I'm approaching a different story. I must proceed with this one.

Contents

PART III Colorado

PART IV Wyoming

PART V Montana

List of Maps

Introduction

A long time before I ever wrote books for a living I was a cowboy. The trouble was that we lived six miles from the nearest toyshop and I was always running out of caps. But we had a stream in the wood at the bottom of our Sussex farm, so when the ammo ran out I became a lumberjack instead. Then either my brother or I would fall in and we'd be wet little boys until we got back to the house. My weakness for streams persists, an imperative if you like, publication at first just convention.

I drifted into travel writing in no other way than by travelling then writing a book about it. The two operations were quite distinct. One, in fact, rather disdained the other, but having endured the writing of a second, then a third book, an understanding of sorts had developed: the traveller travelled, the writer wrote, and that, for the time being, was enough.

But time being is not time becoming. I wanted to reconcile the travelling and the writing. Previously I'd trekked through places where you Picked Things Up (malaria, amoebas, key phrases of the language); where you Ate Their Food, Went On Foot and so on, but it was time to drop the capitals. The next trip would have to be, so to speak, through neutral territory, a journey culturally closer to home, and for a contemplative look at the English-speaking world I opened the family atlas, a volume so old that tea chests – or were they fly specks? – still cluttered Boston harbour. America! I wouldn't get away with capital letters there. But Boston was a bit too neutral. More specks caught my eye, further west this time, a dotted line running south to north up the entire page. Right through the Wild West I noticed. I tipped the atlas sideways. "Continental Divide" it said.

The Divide is the world's longest watershed, the backbone of an entire hemisphere, lord of nothing, servant of the great rivers rising on its flanks – in the United States, the Colorado and the Columbia to the west, the Rio Grande and the Missouri to the east; a winding, looping, swooping crest, here knife-edged, there blunt as a plate. And the names – the dots snaked north for three thousand miles, through New Mexico and Colorado, Wyoming and Montana: Bitteroots, I read, and Beaverhead; Steamboat Springs and Yellowstone; Medicine Bow, the Rio Grande.

At this point it would be nice to say that I caught the next plane to New York. I didn't. I finished the washing up and let two or three years drift by, neat, interlocking years, one thing leading to another – Nigeria, Mali, Sainsburys, India – till rinsed, dried and put away, the past became this present: a walk from Mexico to Canada along the Great Divide.

THE CONTINENTAL DIVIDE

CANADA

WA
OR
CA
NV
ID
UT
MT
WY
CO
ND
SD
AR
NM

MEXICO

N

60

Pie Town
23rd May

286
m

DATIL
MOUNTAINS

Alegros Mtn.
10,244'

60

forget my shorts

Continental Divide

PLAINS OF SAN AGUSTIN

ARIZONA

San Francisco
River

GILA

NATIONAL

FOREST

BLACK MOUNTAINS

SAN MATEO MTS.

meet Dee and
Bonny 20th May

Rio Grande River

25

First atom bomb
exploded 16th
July 1945

Elephant
Butte
Reservoir

SAN
ANDRES
MOUNTAINS

Reeds Peak
10,011'

Gila River

Black Pk. 9,025'
Pinos Altos

Mimbres

meet
Peggy

Silver City
15th May

142
m

Santa Rita

River

90

Lordsburg

90

Continental

Soldiers'
Farewell

180

Rio Grande River

Separ

toad herding

Divide

10

Deming

81

flat sage plains —
the Divide indistinct

Rodeo

PELONCILLO MTS.

ANIMAS BASIN

ANIMAS RANGE

PLAYAS BASIN

Hatchita

11

Columbus

9

NEW MEXICO

MEXICO

EL PASO

Animas Pk.
8,532'

Playas Lake

BIG
HATCHET
MTS.

get
lost

San Luis
Pass

ARIZONA

MEXICO

Antelope Wells
5th May

to Mexico City (eventually)

Miles
0   10   20

0   16   32
Kilometres

Southern New Mexico

XV

Northern New Mexico

xvi

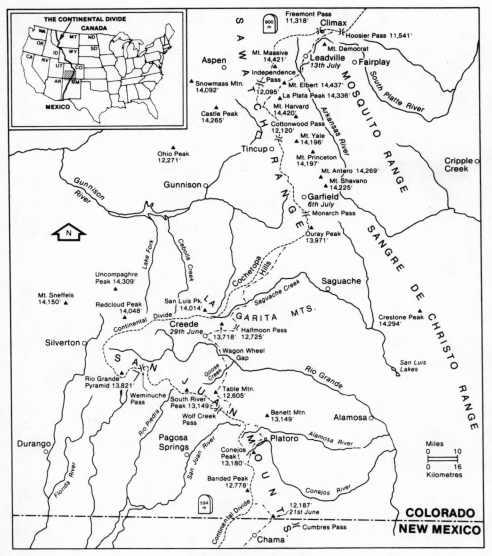

Southern Colorado

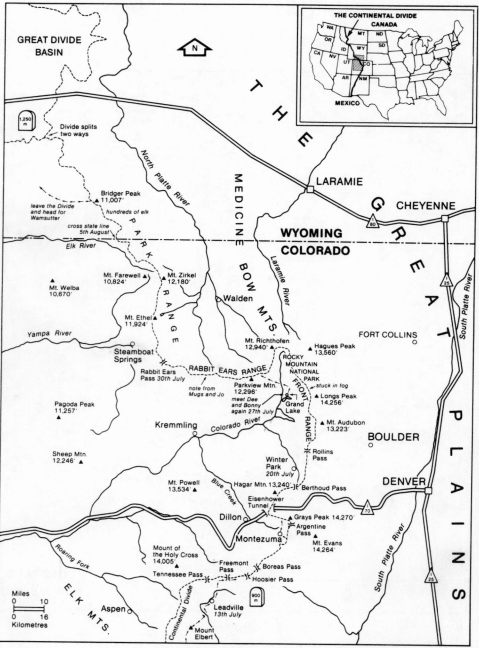

Northern Colorado

The following text labels appear on the map:

GREAT DIVIDE BASIN

THE CONTINENTAL DIVIDE
CANADA

WA · OR · ID · MT · ND · SD · WY · CA · NV · UT · CO · AR · NM

MEXICO

N

1,250 m

Divide splits two ways

THE GREAT PLAINS

LARAMIE

CHEYENNE

80

Bridger Peak 11,007'

leave the Divide and head for Wamsutter

hundreds of elk

cross state line 5th August

North Platte River

MEDICINE BOW MTS.

WYOMING
COLORADO

Elk River

PARK RANGE

Mt. Welba 10,670'

Mt. Farewell 10,824'

Mt. Zirkel 12,180'

Mt. Ethel 11,924'

Walden

Laramie River

Yampa River

Steamboat Springs

Mt. Richthofen 12,940'

Hagues Peak 13,560'

FORT COLLINS

ROCKY MOUNTAIN NATIONAL PARK

25

South Platte River

RABBIT EARS RANGE

Rabbit Ears Pass 30th July

note from Mugs and Jo

Parkview Mtn. 12,296'

stuck in fog

Longs Peak 14,256'

Pagoda Peak 11,257'

meet Dee and Bonny again 27th July

Grand Lake

FRONT RANGE

Mt. Audubon 13,223'

BOULDER

Kremmling

Colorado River

Sheep Mtn. 12,246'

Winter Park 20th July

Rollins Pass

DENVER

Mt. Powell 13,534'

Blue Creek

Hagar Mtn. 13,240'

Berthoud Pass

70

Eisenhower Tunnel

Dillon

Grays Peak 14,270'

Argentine Pass

Roaring Fork

Montezuma

Mt. Evans 14,264'

South Platte River

Mount of the Holy Cross 14,005'

Freemont Pass

Boreas Pass

Tennessee Pass

Hoosier Pass

900 m

25

ELK MTS.

Miles
0   10
0   16
Kilometres

Aspen

Continental Divide

Leadville 13th July

Mount Elbert

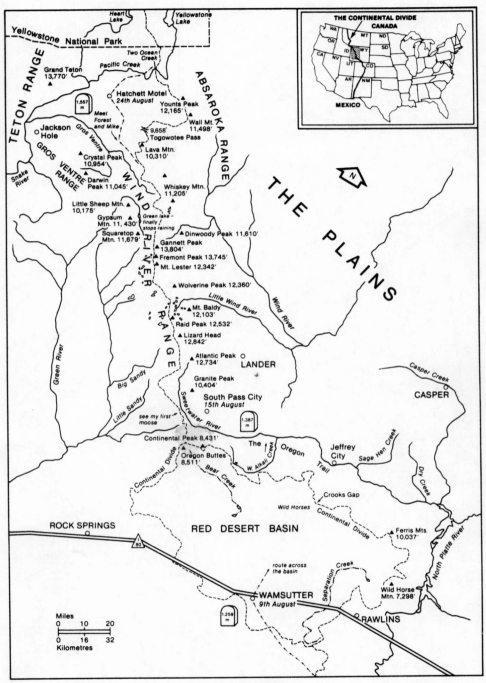

INSET:

THE CONTINENTAL DIVIDE

CANADA

WA MT ND
OR ID SD
CA NV UT WY
CO
AZ NM

MEXICO

MAP LABELS:

Yellowstone National Park

Heart Lake
Yellowstone Lake
Two Ocean Creek

TETON RANGE
Pacific Creek
Grand Teton 13,770'
1,557 m
Hatchett Motel 24th August
Younts Peak 12,165'
Wall Mt. 11,498'
Meet Forest and Mike
Jackson Hole
9,658' Togowotee Pass
ABSAROKA RANGE
GROS VENTRE RANGE
Gros Ventre
Crystal Peak 10,954'
Lava Mtn. 10,310'
Snake River
Darwin Peak 11,045'
Whiskey Mtn. 11,205'
N
Little Sheep Mtn. 10,175'
Green lake finally stops raining
Gypsum Mtn. 11,430'
Squaretop Mtn. 11,679'
Dinwoody Peak 11,610'
Gannett Peak 13,804'
Fremont Peak 13,745'
Mt. Lester 12,342'
WIND RIVER RANGE
Wolverine Peak 12,360'
THE PLAINS
Little Wind River
Mt. Baldy 12,103'
Raid Peak 12,532'
Wind River
Green River
Lizard Head 12,842'
Big Sandy
Atlantic Peak 12,734'
LANDER
Casper Creek
Little Sandy
Granite Peak 10,404'
South Pass City 15th August
CASPER
see my first moose
Sweetwater River
1,387 m
Continental Peak 8,431'
The Oregon
Jeffrey City
Sage Hen Creek
Continental Divide
Oregon Buttes 8,511'
W. Alkali Creek
Oregon Trail
Dry Creek
Bear Creek
Crooks Gap
Wild Horses
Continental Divide
Ferris Mts. 10,037'
ROCK SPRINGS
RED DESERT BASIN
North Platte River
80
Separation Creek
route across the basin
Wild Horse Mtn. 7,298'
WAMSUTTER 9th August
1,259 m
RAWLINS

Miles
0 10 20
0 16 32
Kilometres

Wyoming

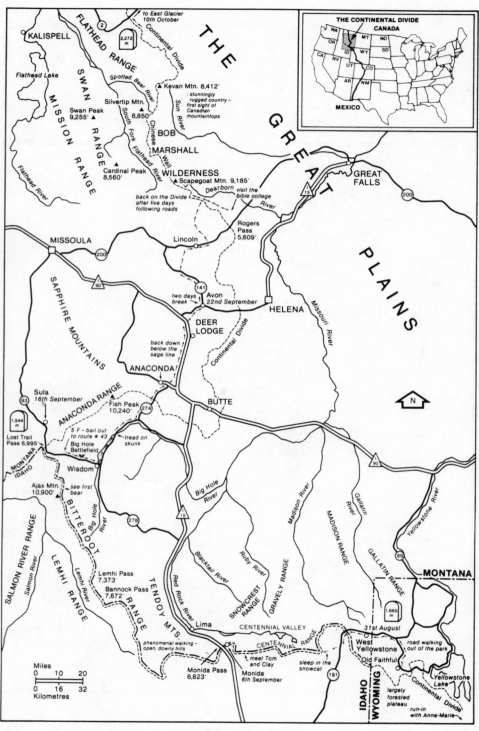

THE CONTINENTAL DIVIDE
CANADA

MEXICO

KALISPELL

FLATHEAD RANGE

to East Glacier
10th October

Continental Divide

2,272
m

THE

Flathead Lake

SWAN

Spotted Bear River

Kevan Mtn. 8,412'

Silvertip Mtn.

8,850'

South Fork Flathead River

Chinese Wall

BOB

MARSHALL

WILDERNESS

MISSION RANGE

RANGE

Swan Peak
9,255'

Cardinal Peak
8,560'

Flathead River

Scapegoat Mtn. 9,185'

: stunningly
rugged country –
first sight of
Canadian
mountaintops

Sun River

Dearborn River

back on the Divide
after five days
following roads

visit the
bible college

GREAT
FALLS

15

200

G

R

E

A

T

MISSOULA

200

90

Rogers
Pass
5,609'

Lincoln

141

Avon
22nd September

two days
break

HELENA

Missouri River

P

L

A

I

N

S

SAPPHIRE MOUNTAINS

DEER
LODGE

back down
below the
sage line

ANACONDA

Continental Divide

Sula
16th September

ANACONDA RANGE

Fish Peak
10,240'

274

BUTTE

N

93

1,944
m

Lost Trail
Pass 6,995'

MONTANA
IDAHO

5 F – bail out
to route # 43

Big Hole
Battlefield

Wisdom

tread on
skunk

90

Ajax Mtn.
10,900'

see first
bear

BITTERROOT RANGE

Big Hole River

Big Hole
River

278

15

Blacktail River

Ruby River

Madison River

Gallatin River

MADISON RANGE

Yellowstone River

89

GALLATIN RANGE

MONTANA

SALMON RIVER RANGE

LEMHI RANGE

Salmon River

Lemhi River

Lemhi Pass
7,373'

Bannock Pass
7,672'

TENDOY MTS.

Red Rock River

Lima

SNOWCREST RANGE

GRAVELY RANGE

1,665
m

31st August

phenomenal walking –
open, downy hills

CENTENNIAL RANGE

CENTENNIAL VALLEY

meet Tom
and Clay

Monida Pass
6,823'

Monida
6th September

sleep in the
snowcat

West
Yellowstone

Old Faithful

191

road walking
out of the park

Yellowstone
Lake

largely
forested
plateau

run-in
with Anne-Marie

Continental Divide

IDAHO
WYOMING

Miles
0   10   20

0   16   32
Kilometres

Montana

XX

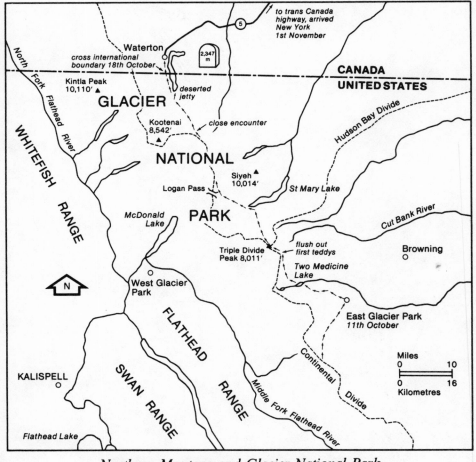

Northern Montana and Glacier National Park

PART I

Getting There

1 Heathrow

The message at the Heathrow check-in was brief: I'd left my boots behind.

But Connie was already speeding across London in a taxi, hoping, presumably, that I'd at least got the right airport. She came running up to the barrier, red laces trailing from her arms, hung the boots round my neck, and laughed a second goodbye. She's from California, we met on a boat, and she reappears in a few pages' time, though by then I'd left my precious notebook in a phone booth. Needless to say, I didn't get it back and the next seven months passed in some suspense lest the same fate befall its replacement. As a form of insurance I took to copying out field notes in full, though in the end I was to mislay very little, except on one classic morning in New Mexico when I'd been walking for two hours before I realized I'd forgotten my trousers . . .

The plane took off. I dozed, woke up feeling grubby, and landed in New York.

2 New York

Luggage speaks louder than words, and, still in the immigration queue, I was feeling self-conscious about mine. It looked unconvincingly new, plus I had too much of it. Also my haircut embarrassed me. I could feel my ears sticking out.

Pudgy fingers reached for my passport. Lips moved.

"How long you wanna stay?"

"Er . . . " I was furiously dividing 3000 miles by three miles an hour – what's that in days? – and wondering what to add on for bad weather. Basically I hadn't a clue, didn't even know what the distance really was, but I did know that the standard visa was for only three months so, ". . . six months," I said.

Bonk! "Have nine," said the immigration man. "Always meant to get out west myself."

Feeling a lot better about my ears I pushed the gear clear of the desk, but the man reached forward to pluck at my sleeve.

"Say," he said. "You English always backpack in suits?"

The jacket and the tie were for a talk which I had been invited to give at the Explorers Club of New York, a distinguished institution, similar in many ways to the Royal Geographical Society of London. The notepaper describes club headquarters on East 70th Street as "The World Center for Exploration". I strode to the dais feeling wise.

The talk – about a past walk in East Africa – went well, and an invitation to attend the club's 79th annual dinner delayed my departure from New York. It was held at the Waldorf-Astoria.

There were roughly two thousand guests (the list ran to six closely typed pages) and for my benefit my host had underlined the most famous names. He had put little notes in the margin – "science writer" (Asimov, Isaac); "former head of the CIA" (Helms, Hon. Richard); "head of Occidental Petroleum" (Hammer, Dr Armand); "president of National Geographic" (Grosvenor, Gilbert); "well-known restauranteur" (Bruno, John) and so on. Abelson, M. to Zern, Ed. – this was a glittering occasion. A fanfare announced the food.

The hors-d'oeuvres included Beaver and Bear and Moose Mousse and Manta Ray wings. I chose Picadillo of Hippopotamus, but was disappointed when it came. It looked just like Chicken McNuggets. In fact, everything did. The President rose to speak, his subject, "The Explorer at Risk". What was this man selling? Cannibals? I picked idly at the Tiger Lily Buds on my plate. Was this joke food some kind of sacrament: this is the body of The Wild, eat in remembrance of me? And what was all this about risk? The main problem for most of the other speakers seemed to be a shortage of cash for their next project. The programme said we were there to honour courage and human curiosity, but we seemed instead to be feasting a myth: that only certain people discover the world, reveal it and peel it for others to gobble up.

3 Food

I caught the Greyhound bus to a place called Hancock, Maryland, and rang my father. He is English but had remarried and now lived six miles away across the Potomac in a place called Berkeley Springs. Meeting your father in the foreign country of his new wife should be worth more than these few lines, but the whole thing was surprisingly normal. The phone booth in Hancock is where I forgot my notebook.

I got a new one in the local Berkeley Springs supermarket, threw it in with my fourth trolley-load of shopping. I hadn't bothered to figure calories per day for this trip, but tipped stuff off the shelves because I liked it or because it was cheap. As for weight, I avoided tins but otherwise would carry as much food on this walk as I could, though safely back in my father's barn I began chopping soap bars in half; I commandeered kitchen scales and prepared little ounce packets of salt; I cut the margins off maps, the labels off clothes, my nose off to spite my face. I knew perfectly well that these obscure little ounces aren't really what matter on a hike. It's your basic clobber – boots, wet-proofs, stove and bag – that grinds you into the dirt and I'd already bought mine, total weight with the camera and so on in the region of forty pounds. Assuming seventy pounds was about my limit, I had thirty pounds free for renewables – the food, fuel and maps I was planning to dump in advance along the yet to be determined route. The Route. Like "Explorer" and "at risk", the route was a retrospective fabrication. Looking back on the walk, it's impossible to believe that most days I didn't have one, that I really made the whole thing up as I went along. So the route could wait, but the calculations I was making as rain dripped through the barn roof could not.

Thirty pounds of renewables would last me – be generous – ten days. And how far could I walk in a day? Not just any old day, mark you, but a day after day after day type of day – say, fifteen miles? Times ten. I had a range of 150 miles. In the event the gaps between supply points varied – some stages of the journey were half this distance, others were over 200 miles – but I was working with ball-park figures. (Having heard this expression I couldn't remember the English equivalent.) I was also working with doubt. Three thousand miles (it turned

out to be two and a half thousand in the end) all in one go seemed
rather a lot, more, in fact, than I could imagine, so in Berkeley Springs
I only bought enough food for the first third of the way. If after that
all was still well I'd hitch-hike to the nearest big city – probably Denver
– hire a car, and restock to the Canadian border.

After two days of weighing and spooning, I'd lined up eight identical
ten-day food packs, except that I had no packaging. English check-out
girls are usually till-deep in cardboard, but in America you get brown
paper bags. The cartons themselves are trashed.

"Where?" I asked Linda at the Berkeley Springs Mart.

"In back of the store," she said.

A heap of sauce-stained pulp was smouldering in the drizzle. I
prissied around for several minutes, trying not to get dirty and wet.
Then I changed gear and burrowed in. Wiping ash and soggy cardboard
down the legs of my jeans, I threw eight empty cartons into my father's
pick-up and went back for a bath.

4 Maps

America is very, very big – eighty times the size of England if you
include Alaska – but the standard maps are rather small. To cover the
Divide from end to end takes 291 separate sheets, and since they aren't
printed on Kleenex tissues I'd have to be selective. The counter staff
at the US Geological Survey building in Washington were unfailingly
patient as I called for and rejected sheet after sheet.

"Don't need that one," I'd mutter, "the ground's all flat. Hilly bit
here though – ah, sorry, the Divide only knicks the corner."

I kept having to go off for a coffee and a think. The overall plan
was to follow the Divide as closely as possible, but the small print –
the cliffs, the glaciers, the waterless stretches – was confusing. Injury
or bad weather might also force detours, and my eventual selection,
especially for New Mexico, was pure guesswork. Maps for Colorado,
Wyoming and Montana were easier to choose because there I'd be
mostly on public land – generally National Forest Service land – and
if you need to examine a million acres at a glance a Forest Service
map is just the thing. The scale is small, a half inch to the mile, but
at a dollar apiece forest maps are a godsend to the poor. Despite all

this I left the map office with a cardboard tube the size of a drainpipe under my arm.

A queue in plastic raincoats was standing outside the White House. Pale hands swam in see-through pockets. I decided not to linger and slushed past the main gate, heading out to Dulles airport to pick up Connie.

I'd been assigned the car – a VW hatchback – as a courier, desti-nation Newport Beach, California.

"Some guy relocating," the delivery agent had said. "You drive stick shift?"

I nodded as he took my deposit. "Eight days to deliver, call if it dies. We start you gassed, you finish gassed, 'kay?"

"'Kay," I said.

He hadn't asked why I wanted the car so I didn't tell him, but the plan was to ignore the route manifest and leave food boxes cached from mid-Colorado to the Mexican border before going on to make the California delivery. I hadn't told the agent about Connie either – "No hitchers, no passengers," he'd said, but she lived only ten miles from Newport Beach so I'd rung England to offer her a lift. We drove back to Berkeley Springs, loaded the food, waved goodbye to my father, and set off.

5 California

It was raining again. Pittsburg flashed by; coffees on the dashboard near Indianapolis; eats in Kansas City; a night, a day, cramped sleep short of Denver; dawn touching the Rockies. We slipped into the city for breakfast and planned the next move with a teaspoon.

From the scale of the roadmap the plastic spoon was ten days' walk long. By turning it end over end down the map we picked seven more or less equally spaced locations on or near the Divide, and in three red-eyed days had dumped off all the food bar one box for the start down on the Mexican border. No one had refused us. We left boxes at cafés, a couple in shops, two at forestry offices, one in a garage. All that remained was to deliver the car to the coast and bus back to New Mexico. The start point of the walk – the actual dot on the map

– was to be Antelope Wells, an isolated customs post fourteen miles east of the spot where the Divide crosses into the States.

Five days after leaving Berkeley Springs we stopped. I sat in the car while Connie ran across the road for cigarettes. Beside me was a place called the Bath Mart, displaying individually designed fittings – taps, towel rails, bidets, bogs. The smoked-glass shop-front was lettered in gold:

THE BOTTOM LINE
IS
INTEGRITY
COMMITMENT
SELF-EXPRESSION

We had arrived in California.

A week went by in about two minutes flat. It was time for the bus. Connie and I sat on a tree, the branches coaxed low by sea winds. I was feeling extremely English, fidgeted, and read the side of a carton which had spilled from a nearby bin. "Lucerne Two-Ten Milk", it said, then underneath:

Dear Safeway Customer,
    We hope that you enjoy the contents of this container.
    I'm new on the job and would like to receive your comments on this product or any of our other Lucerne Dairy Products.
    Just drop a line at the address below,
    Sincerely,
Gottlieb Ribary,
Milk dept mgr., Safeway Stores, Oakland, Cal.

As we walked towards the bus station I composed a reply:

Laguna Beach
4th May

Dear Gottlieb,
    Thank you for your letter. I was rather sad today. It really helped.
    Yours,

6 The Texan

I changed buses in San Diego and found myself beside a Texan with pink legs and a bicycle for which there was no room. I knew he was a Texan because he told me. The bicycle would be put on the next free coach.

"Goddamn fuckin' driver," said the Texan. "How come theah ain't no room? Fuckin' bike's worth five hundred fuckin' bucks."

The Texan bit his nails all the way through the first three towns, but he gradually calmed down. Within two hours he was rebounding a monologue. His opening line was pretty good.

"Ain't killed nobody in five years," he said. "Nossir, ain't no one died because of me in one long time."

I didn't know quite what to say, but the Texan seemed fairly self-contained. His remarks were made at intervals of roughly fifty miles. The next came as we whistled through El Centro.

"Evah go south, don't weah no yella suit," he said. "Yella's big trouble in Mexico. It's what theyah hoods all weah." Luckily most of my stuff was dull green, I told him, and in any case I wasn't going more than a token step south of the border.

We reached Yuma just after sunset. The Texan frowned.

"Know what a gargoyle is?"

"A what?"

"A gargoyle. Gargoyles're why I'm on this fuckin' bus. They fly round heah at night."

I fought down manic laughter. "Gargoyles fly round heah at night?"

"Right. Don't nevah ride this freeway after dark, not on no bike. You godda be so goddamn careful" – he leaned towards me – "because gargoyles ain't the only thing. Bigfoot's out theah too."

Bigfoot!

"You got any Bigfoot in Europe?"

"No," I said. "But there's a whole stack of gargoyles."

"No kidding?" said the Texan.

He got off the bus in Tucson, Arizona, though not before he'd mentioned that he wanted fifteen children. He also wanted to go fight the commies in Central America.

"Them fuckin' people think they own the fuckin' place," he said.
"We give them fuckin' money, fight their fuckin' wars and they still
screw up. Yeah, I'll be fuckin' down theah you betcha."

But not down theah just yet, however, because the Texan was
actually en route for his mother's house, his wife having kicked him
out of their flat in Los Angeles. He said he'd soon find another girl.

"Young and dumb. I'll knock her up, divorce her, take the kid back
to LA. My Old Lady theah'll have me back when she sees I got a
kid." It seemed a remarkably long-term plan. As he left the bus I
asked him his age.

"Nearly twenty," he said.

7 Desert

I was dropped on the freeway halfway between Lordsberg, which was
small, and Deming, which was even smaller. Both were a long way
away.

I felt like a bug whose stone had been suddenly lifted. Perspective
had vanished, the pimply hills between freeway and horizon could have
been minutes or long days away. I looked down. An ant was pitching
through the broken tarmac at my feet. It disappeared under a Baskin
Robbins popcorn carton which came skittering along in the slipstream
of trucks rolling east towards Texas. The waxed cardboard made a
poor football, but I dribbled it down the exit lane till it fell between
the bars of a cattle grid at the start of state route # 81. The Mexican
border lay sixty miles to the south.

I waited three hours for my first lift, part of the time squatting
behind a spindly bush, though there were so few cars that the lack of
cover didn't matter. What did was the fact that I'd unhitched at last
from the world of freeways and drains.

Along came Greg in a Mustang. As I got in I asked him if traffic
was always this light around here.

"Yeah," he said. "Ain't nowhere much for it to go." He turned the
airconditioner on to full blast. "Got a copper smelter near Playas, a
few people left at Hatchita, and that's it. Antelope Wells where you're
goin' ain't no more'n a fence an' a phone."

The scenery through the windscreen wasn't too lively either – all sage brush and free-range beer cans. I asked Greg why the empties were mostly on our side of the road.

"Shift workers going down to the smelter," he said. "Never save none for the way back."

"Right," I said. These "rights" and "I guess nots" creeping in weren't premeditated, but they did at first rather linger in the mouth. "Funny place for a smelter, though," I added.

"Yeah," said Greg, who worked on a ranch. But it was a funny place for just about everything – beer cans, barbed wire, the odd water pump, nothing looked comfortable on this broiling plain.

Greg dropped me beside a reef of old fridges and drop-bellied trucks. "Hatchita," he said. Something thin, loose and bent shook in the wind and a ball of brown weed tumbled over a cracked concrete forecourt. A sign propped in a tyre said "Gone Bust – Moved up a Block", which is where I found Mrs Been. I think that was her name. Her place stocked groceries and gas – nothing fresh, not that I wanted lettuce. I went straight to the fridge for a Coke.

"Used to be upwards of a thousand people around here," said Mrs Been. "Only about fifty left." She said all the beef came from feed lots in Georgia these days. The open range was just a tax write-off. I popped the Coke can and Mrs Been mentioned her sons. They were both left-handed like me. One worked on a road crew in Albuquerque and the other was down at the smelter. Yep. Both left-handed. You know what the chances of two left-handed sons is? But just then a lorry stopped and Mrs Been said I'd better go ask, because that would be about my only chance of a lift out of town. Town? But America doesn't really have villages. Missed out the middle ages completely.

The lorry driver's name was Ed Payne. Ex-armoured corps. Brought back a wife from Germany and they now lived in El Paso, Texas. No kids. Ed had a load of fresh tar for the road.

"Be paved clear to the border one day," he yelled over the gears. "County's way of spreading loose cash. Gets worked on one year, the next it don't."

Ed took me fifteen miles. There were no bends. Tiny black specks became roadmen with rakes and Ed said that was as far as he went. "Last thirty's all dirt," he shouted. "Send me a postcard from Canada."

The next vehicle had five people squashed in the cab and a load of beehives in the back. I climbed aboard and shut my eyes tight against the dust. I flicked them open to check on the hives – I'd not had the wit to enquire if they were loaded, though it did occur to me to tap on the cab and ask what the fare was back to California, or New York, or anywhere cooler than this. Eventually the vehicle swirled to a halt and I flopped out.

Twin splodges of colour were fluttering against the blue sky, the Stars and Stripes on this side of a cattle grid, the red, white and green of the Mexican flag on the other. A single roadsign stood between them. "New Mexico State Line," it said. "Mile Zero."

Mile zero!

But my spirit was running about like a lost dog. I'm always anxious at the start of a trip – not the catching of the plane but the real start, when the last car door bangs. It's like falling out of bed in the night, and like most bedroom floors Antelope Wells was a pretty arbitrary spot. 31° 20′ north – that's where I was – and 49° north is where I was going.

PART II

New Mexico

---

1 Antelope Wells

The plate-glass door of the US customs post threw back an unpromising reflection – five feet nine of pigeon-chested Englishman, examining himself with familiar feelings of inadequacy. The ten-day stubble chirruped a faint "caramba", but the rest was distinctly unmacho. Navy-blue trousers of a light cotton material were rolled above knees which might well have been surgically sharpened. From this spindly platform what looked like twin broomsticks plunged into clumsy leather boots. "Wild and Wonderful" screamed the bright yellow T-shirt, a souvenir of West Virginia. New Mexico's catchphrase was "Land of Enchantment". It didn't look it.

To the east I could see the Hatchita Mountains, like low hot cows in the haze; the exhausted snake uncoiled in the west was the line of the Animas range. That was my first objective, the point fourteen miles distant where the white frontier posts climbed up and over the snake's long back – the precise spot where the Divide crosses the US border. Precise spots would become less important to me as time went on, but just then they were highly significant. I would follow the crest of the Animas north for the first forty miles, a rough forty miles, followed by an easy hundred across rising plains to the first food pick up in Silver City, where Billy the Kid used to live till he ran off to shoot people professionally.

A lanyard shivered in the wind, clattering against the metallic flag pole at the side of the customs building. No one seemed to be in. Twenty yards away, through a loose wire fence, the other mast was clattering too, with a different sound though because it was wooden. Leaving my pack, I teetered over the cattle grid and walked towards a group of four men. They were leaning on a car bonnet in the shade of what looked like an adobe shoebox. Untended power lines trailed from the roof to disappear through a hole in the wall, followed, as I approached, by a scuttling lizard. The men wore cheap jeans and check shirts.

"Buenos tardes," I said.

Gold-flecked smiles broke out.

"You goin' to Mexico City." I wasn't sure if this was a question. "Te gustaras mucho Mexico."

"Si," I said. "Gracias." I hadn't spoken Spanish for nine years.

"Where you goin' right now?"

"Canada," I said.

"Ah," they all said together. "Canada."

"You have any car?"

"No," I said. "I'm walking. Want to come?"

They laughed. "No passeporte," said Señor Casillas. He was the customs official. "No visa so no chance to cross. You have any food?"

"Dried stuff," I said. "Tea, soup, rice, things like that."

"No beanses?" asked Señor Casillas. "No meat? You need sontheen now you go head to tell me. Sontheen to eat you need it I have son sardines to help you."

I could hardly refuse such kindness and was groping for an excuse – more weight was the last thing I needed – when a distraction appeared in the shape of a six-legged mongrel, hopping along with its tongues hanging out and its back tail wagging like fury.

"Look, look," cried the Mexicans, stamping their feet. "Los peros estan haciendo amor!" They certainly were. The roars of laughter and encouragement diminished as I stepped back over the cattle grid to the cool, lime-green structure that was the American half of Antelope Wells.

Cupping my hands to reduce the glare I again peered through the plate-glass door, and this time I caught a glimmer of life. Quite a large glimmer. A lady in tight black trousers was stalking a fly. Her pistol jutted from a mattress of hip, and the nametag on her shirt said "Ruby". The fly was still buzzing gamely, but with only a calender, a clock and two vinyl chairs for concealment the creature was doomed. It ended up smeared down the side of a cabinet and Ruby hung up her swat.

"You want some water?"

"Thanks," I said, turning to the drinking fountain.

"That'll be too warm," said Ruby, taking a bottle from the office fridge. I told her why I was there and she asked me to sign her book, a record of all the hikers who'd started for Canada from Antelope Wells. I was the only one that year.

"You've left it a bit late," she said. "Six months from now'll be winter, maybe even earlier this year. It's been a real strange one so far – had two feet of snow a couple of weeks back but we'll be up to a hundred degrees real soon." It felt as if we already were.

Ruby's partner came in from one of the two mobile homes at the rear. His name was Ed. He had friends in England, civilian employees of the navy, he said, but he couldn't recall their names. Came over every year to visit their relatives in Deming. Ed had himself been stationed at Antelope Wells for five years.

"I'm ruined for elsewhere after this," he said. "The other ports're jammed up with traffic and drunks, but all we have here is good, clean people coming through. No drunks, no hop heads, no smugglers. Just nice ranch people and I like it. I have my family up in Deming. They like it too." Ed looked up at the clock. "We close at four," he said. "Gonna have to lock you out."

And that's exactly what they did. I had hoped they'd invite me to supper.

I licked chocolate from the wrinkled foil round a packet of biscuits and felt slightly sick. I hate leaving places. Lukewarm water dribbled from a tap at the side of the now deserted building. I'd half-filled the water bag, shocked at the extra weight. Stupefaction set in, the surrounding country so uniformly enormous that it hardly seemed to matter in which direction I went. North, south, east or west – who cared? No houses, no hedges, no rivers, no fields – there was nothing to break the monotony. Just a flourish of weeds round a leaking tap and the rest was simply Out There.

I needed something to dispel my inertia. There was a phone booth against the outside wall – a perfectly normal, everyday booth with aluminium sides and "TELEPHONE" in blue at the top. I just wanted to pick up the receiver. It was something familiar to say goodbye to. Hell – I was about to walk three thousand miles. I wanted champagne smashed over my pack. Ruby could have done it, and Ed could have cut a ribbon or, or . . . a do-it-yourself send-off is an empty affair. In the end I just picked up my stuff and went, though that sounds a lot slicker in words than it was in practice.

I had two separate pieces to carry.

The camera bag was a standard, rectangular shape, with a long zip round the lid and it weighed exactly twelve pounds. Inedible and valuable it would still weigh twelve pounds at the end. It was to function as handbag, dashboard and desk – notebook and maps, compass and camera, lenses, binoculars, cassettes and film all to hand at the twitch of a zip – though initially the bag was a bloody nuisance because I hadn't worked out how best to sling it. For the first three weeks of the walk I looked like a badly tied parcel.

The rucksack went on my back – not much choice about that. The problem was to get it there. With ten days of food and a full waterbag my Berghaus weighed sixty-five pounds. Including the camera bag, what I actually set off with on that first leg of the walk was well over half my own body weight; and getting half of yourself strapped on to your back is awkward until you get the knack. I did it with the help of some kung-fu style grunts and the customs shed window ledge. The hip belt snapped shut and I drew in the slack. I felt like the sheriff in "High Noon". Do not forsake me, oh my da-arling. Now, just check m'gear. Hmm. Good, yes, fine, damn. The alarm clock had stopped. I rushed back into Gary Cooper's office and slammed the door.

Without an alarm clock Canada might as well have been Mars. I'd never get there in a million years because I'm such a terrible getter upperer. I can, and often do, sleep for eleven hours at a stretch, but that regretful, self-knowing yawn of mine simply won't do on a hike. If you can set off at dawn, and walk for, say, half of a fourteen-hour day, you give yourself seven hours' leeway. A later start doesn't of itself make you slower, but it cuts down your freedom to respond to things on the way – the heat, for example, or the view, or people or storms or just thinking your thoughts on a hill. But without an alarm these free hours would all dream away. I checked the time through the plate-glass door and reset the hands. Five in the afternoon; May 5th. Banging and shaking the brown plastic clock I stumbled off down the road. It was nothing like "High Noon" at all.

2 Zero Plus Four

I'd seen a windpump glinting two miles away west over the scrub, and as I left the dirt road a final shake brought the obdurate clock to life. "Thank you," I muttered, greatly relieved, "thank you very much," and, breaking into song, walked straight into a cactus. God it hurt. I had bayoneted myself in the shin.

It was really no more than a scratch, the slightest of excuses to stop, but I grabbed it with both cheeks and sat down. Not to walk is such a relief, especially in the first hundred yards. I hardly moved for five minutes, absorbed, as one is in this lacklustre mood, by the utterly commonplace – in this case the blood skittering down my leg, a thick, scarlet oil enfolding each hair shaft before bursting on to the next. The thickened blobs slowly grew wrinkles. They winked in the sun like the skin on cold cocoa and soon only dark flecks were left on the trail leading down to my sock.

Small weeds blushed in the deepening light – Milk Vetch, Desert Parsley, Yarrow, a fine down of shadow streaming over the dry, cracked earth. My boots scrunched on, swerving to avoid scattered outposts of Yucca, the cactus which had cut dead my song. Yucca looks more like a hedgehog than a plant, but like most desert flora its main battle for survival is fought underground. Creosote, for example, poisons the surrounding earth against competitors, while Mesquite sends roots diving right out of sight – eighty, ninety, one hundred feet down – to tap sources of deep fossil water. Yucca does the complete opposite, relying on a very shallow root mat to draw in the slightest penetration of moisture.

Most green plants transpire by day (allowing carbon dioxide in, permitting water vapour out) but this sort of slack-jawed behaviour would very soon shrivel, then kill, a cactus in the heat of the desert. To minimize the loss of water vapour, cactii keep their pores shut until nightfall. But the chemical reaction that turns carbon dioxide into food only works in daylight. Since, to conserve water, cactii take the gas in at night, they need a temporary storage system. Instead of inflating themselves like barrage balloons, they lock the carbon dioxide chemically, a reaction triggered by the evening drop in temperature and reversed by the rising heat of dawn: the greater the cool-off occuring at night, the more carbon dioxide stored. Which is why cactii do so well in deserts.

The windpump I'd seen from the customs post door was now a towering tin daisy. The holding tank beside it, about seven feet high, was set on a concrete base. I rapped, but it sounded empty.

Windpumps had, until then, been as remote to me as the Queen. I had seen them flash by from train windows and cars and sometimes blown up in films, but I had never actually touched one. The pylon clanged thinly as I climbed the metal rungs to a platform below the fan. The brake was on. At close range the blades looked enormous, twenty-four galvanized petals, all exactly symmetrical; a shivering turbine which rattled as the wind shook the vane. "Samson" was stencilled in black on the fin, then "Stover Mfg & Engine Co, Freeport, Ill, USA". It was such a simple machine. All you had to do was to plop grease on the bearing, oil the shaft, and open a tap in the pipe to the tank, which, as I had thought, was dry. I could see down onto

the scum inside, bleached twigs and the husk of a dead bird gummed
to the concrete. I lit a cigarette. On walks I get through about ten a
day. I generally smoke them half at a time.

Hillocks warped, then buckled the plain. I was aiming for a gap in the
treeless slopes and walked for about one more hour. When I hit a dirt
road running through the gap I decided that I'd come far enough. Four
miles behind me the customs posts glowed like gulls on a sunwashed
sea. Antelope Wells, at 4658 feet, was the lowest spot I touched for
the next two thousand miles.

I stripped, my clothes like salty blooms on the spiked wands of
mesquite around me. My T-shirt was drenched and so were my
underpants and so was the waistband of my shorts – a heat map of my
body in cotton. Delicious cool patches were spreading as the sweat
dried out on my skin. I slipped rubber flipflops onto my feet and,
brushing aside stones and a few confused ants, I eased the foam mat
from its straps. Subduing the roll with a boot at each end I sat down.
Then I stood up, fingers locked behind my head.

"I've begun," I yelled at the stubbly hills. "I've bloody begun!"

It was warm, it was dry, and still a good hour before sunset. I wasn't
in the slightest bit hungry, but I thought I'd better eat and swivelled
round on my backside to get at the pack.

The Berghaus had two outside pockets, one soft as a sausage and
stuffed full of tent, the other awkwardly ribbed by the stove. I wriggled
the stove bag free, drew open the string, and pulled out the reflective
heat shield. It was made of tin foil and I stuck it on my head for a
laugh while I assembled the burner.

Pumping away at the fuel bottle I became rather self-conscious.
What if somebody saw me, squatting naked out here on the range? I
had nothing on but the flipflops and this childish tin hat: worse, I had
no car. Nakedness was odd, an eccentricity perhaps, but no car was a
downright perversion. According to Ed, back at the customs, walking
was something that regular guys just didn't do.

"We don't get pedestrians down here," he'd said, "leastways not
Anglos. See a guy on foot in this country it's ten to one he's a wetback
– an illegal alien to you."

The tin foil bobbed about behind the mesquite as I slipped on a
spare pair of pants. The chances of a car coming by were remote, but
the pants made me feel less vulnerable; I also took off the heat shield.
I twirled the stove's built-in flint and a squirt of petrol thumped into

flame. Ten seconds later came the roar of vapourized fuel through the jet.

The stove was a neat bit of gear. It could bring my one-litre pot from room temperature to boiling in under four minutes, which, at this early stage, was actually a little too fast: I was still conducting the menu with a spoon when eruptions of steam told me that something could by now have been ready. I threw in some sugar and a teabag and went back to the pantry.

I'd spared Señor Casillas the full details, but on that first afternoon there were twenty-seven items of food in my pack. They fell into three main groups: boring things; nice things; and salt. Included with the salt were boullion cubes, vitamins, dried onion, bacon bits and curry powder. The boring things were retextured protein and potato flakes, oats, instant rice, dried milk, soup powder, noodles, dried vegetables and wheat thins – a type of dry biscuit. The nice things were honey, jam, peanut butter, Snickers (similar to Mars Bars), granola bars, mixed nuts and raisins, beef jerky, muesli, Tang orange drink powder, cigarettes, sugar and tea.

I kept all the food in two nylon bags, a big one and a small one. The small one held enough for three days. It came out at every halt. The big one contained the rest and it came out only when the little one needed topping up. Almost everything I carried had a bag, and the bags also had bags, stuffed one inside the other like a set of Russian dolls. My kitchen at home tends to look like a civil disaster, but on the trail I'm obsessively tidy, mainly because if I weren't I'd spend half the time looking for things. If the mundane jobs can be reduced to a drill done by numbers, you can preside over, say, tea-making, in body, while your spirit drifts off on its own.

I regarded the first few hundred miles as a practice run for the Rockies a month ahead; everything would find its place before long, even the camera bag. Eventually I'd sense that something was missing even before I knew what it was – perhaps by the changed contours of the pack or by the subconcious memory of routine imprecisely followed. Until then I would have to concentrate and be careful: it's not much good to discover that your compass is missing twenty miles from where you last used it.

I tipped salt, a boullion cube, bacon bits, dried onion, dried vegetables, rice and noodles into the pot, gave it a stir, and let it simmer while I put the stuff away. Then I ate it, straight out of the pot. I had half a granola bar for pudding, by which time more water had boiled and I threw in another teabag. I drank the stewy tea until dark. It had been a long day. It had started next to the idiot Texan, and now I was here. Content.

But not for long. I woke up at midnight, scrabbling for the water. I couldn't find it, so I scrabbled for the torch instead. I couldn't find that either. I got up, shook the rucksack, tipped out the camera bag, knelt on a stone. Ouch. It was a small, round stone and it was under the mat. I lifted the mat. Grabbed the stone. Switched it on. Found the water.

After two or three nights I had narrowed the cause of the midnight thirsts to the noodles. Connie had seen them on offer in a Denver supermarket, and we'd bought eighty packets at thirty cents each. There'd been no time for field trials, but I reckoned I had a bargain. There were five flavours – Prawn, Chicken, Beef, Pork, Vegetable – with a succulent photograph on each packet. I assumed there would be dehydrated bits of prawn and so forth mixed in, but the reality was sachets of additive powders, inserted like free gifts into otherwise identical packets. The thought of them still gives me heartburn. Next day I deflowered each separate packet, threw out the sachets, and scrunched the pasta into a single, space-saving bag. From then on unflavoured Ramen noodles went into at least two pots of food every day.

My first supper had been fairly typical. It had, in fact, been utterly typical. The truth is that every one of my main meals for the next five and half months was exactly the same. I don't bake, stir-fry or grill on the trail. I boil water; add food; and eat. Bung-it-in, get-it-wet, get-it-down. The aim, with an absolute minimum of delay, is to stop feeling hungry, though here in the desert my appetite was dulled by the heat. I wouldn't start to feel the usual hiker's pangs until the air cooled off as the Divide rose into the Black Mountains beyond Silver City. By then I was sleeping with the waterbag well within reach. The torch I kept in a boot by my ear. I kept my penknife in the boot too, handle up, to be grabbed in case of small emergencies. The sleeping bag had a large hood to hide in in case of big ones.

I'm not actually into knives – a carpet-knife blade is all you need on a hike – but some of the cutlery you see on the trail is amazing. There's always a sort of "I'll show you mine if I can see yours" session with people shaving hairs off the backs of their hands and going "nice blade" and the other guy goes "yeah, good balance" as if he were about to Davy Crockett you into a tree. It's quite incredible to watch this sort of thing, but what's even more incredible is that I do it along with the best of them. I don't carry a sheath knife myself, but I nearly

always go through the hand-shaving ritual with the knives of people
who do. Since I met so few hikers – one couple in the whole of New
Mexico – my hands on this trip stayed hairy. The other thing I'm
averse to is hats, which is why my nose already looked like cat meat,
though the rest of me was quite brown.

3 Morning One

I was up, packed, and ready to move by six-thirty, except that I'd
made too much porridge. Waiting for it to cool I watched hares slip
away through the scrub, their delicate ears capillary pink in the sunrise.
Then I went too, with a last glance at the ground where I had made
my first camp. Like a good boy-scout, I left nothing behind but my
thanks.

The jeep track I now followed ran beside a dry wash overrun with
mesquite and cactus. The water was way underground, but in an
otherwise very dry region the slightest source of moisture had an
immediate and dramatic effect. And, as elevations – and rainfall –
gradually increased, so the character of the vegetation would change.
Here below 5000 feet I was in the Lower Sonoran Life Zone – an
average of nine inches rainfall a year, frost absent or rare, mesquite
and creosote the typical species. But already the land was rising. A
black hawk slopped air with its paddle shaped wings, holding course
for a distant terrace of hills: Upper Sonoran, 5000 to 7000 feet above
sea level, twelve inches of rain (increasing with altitude), sage, juniper
and piñon pines the dominant species. What comfort I drew from these
facts! Without a name a plant remains just a plant, an anonymous
stitch in a carpet, but, knowing the names, patterns emerge. Absences
and changes, variations in style feed the eye.

I glanced at the map. Contour lines whirled down the middle of an
otherwise blank sheet of paper, the Animas flats west of the Divide,
the Playas basin to the east. The longitudinal squall separating the two
was the line of the Animas range, a series of dry, rubble-shouldered
hills to which the ground was gradually rising. I scuffed at the first
small stones. They were pinkish and dusty, which is about as far as
my geology went without having to look them up. According to my
rock book the Animas themselves had erupted thirty-five million years

ago. There were tables with emergent life forms in the margin to show when that was – well after Viruses by the look of it, but before Flowering Plants. Perhaps I got that wrong because dinosaurs wearing "Age of Reptile" T-shirts had wandered into my brain, clumsily barging aside my attempts to see the eroded hills as volcanoes. The book diagram was no problem to handle – schoolboy facts, safely second-hand, rarely are – but the knowledge that I was happier with a diagram than with uncharted reality bugged me. In some ways all this walking was a bit of a pretence.

I was to spend a good deal of time in New Mexico trudging over volcanic rock. From Silver City, where my first food box was waiting, to the second pick-up in a small place called Pie Town, I would be crossing the compacted ash of the Black Range. On stage three – Pie Town to Interstate 40, where Connie and I had left food at a place actually called Continental Divide – the horizon was broken by the distant cone of Mount Taylor. But stage four, the run up to the Colorado state line, would be different. No volcanics there but sedimentary escarpments, bone-white and pink, the desolation enhanced by scattered hogans of the Navajo Indians. I'd written to the tribal council at Window Rock and had been given permission to cross the reservation, though the Jicarilla Apache, who share the San Juan basin, had refused me wayleave for their section, still 400 miles to the north. I'd sort that problem out when I got there, but right now I was watching six cream-coloured dots streaming south over the plain. Pronghorn antelopes don't shift into top gear until they're doing fifty miles an hour – the Mexican border, still just in sight, meant nothing to them.

I should have stopped to rest sooner that morning, but didn't. I'd got a bad dose of the NFEs. NFE stands for Not Far Enough – the irresistable compulsion to go on and on till you ruin whatever you're doing. In this case it was wading through sage, but it happens with many other things – tightening a bolt is a classic example, though painting, writing, correcting a child are all susceptible. The solution, of course, is knowing when to stop.

A man, a mere dot, free on landscape, should perhaps think only of the wind in his hair, of what lies beyond the horizon. But he doesn't. He thinks a great deal about food; thinks even more about rest; thinks, naturally enough, of sex. From time to time he glances up to assess the view. But what really gnaws at him, gives him ulcers almost, is his obsession with going far enough; with, he can still hear his father saying it, not slacking when no one is looking.

But conscience can be an over-rich fuel. When I did bring myself to halt on that first morning it was already approaching midday. I was contouring north to strike the Divide at a place called San Luis Pass, but a slim pool dappling gold-yellow gravel had been too inviting to resist. I was in, as they say, like Flynn, rinsed all my clothes, and as I lay drying naked in the sun, I wondered why I was so bloody silly.

I could hardly believe what I saw. How could this have happened to me – to one who had done so much walking? Had I not spent years in the African bush which so resembles this part of New Mexico? Yet here I was by this nameless pool, not twelve miles into three thousand, and look! – I already had blisters.

It wasn't the boots, that was for sure. The replacement soles were still a bit stiff, but the uppers were like doe skin inside. And it wasn't fair wear and tear. Twelve miles was just pathetic. No, the blisters were caused by neglect. I should simply have dealt with them sooner. Damp, sweaty skin is highly susceptible to friction, and the answer, in these hot, dry conditions, was clean, dry socks not once a day but every two or three hours. From this very moment on I would pour sunshine and foot powder into my boots at every possible halt. I would pummel my socks and pick off the burrs. I would fluff them, I would bounce them, I would sing them encouraging songs. Footcare had re-entered my life.

Meanwhile I had to deal with the immediate problem. The Denver noodle bargain had left just enough change for a custom-made pharmacopoeia, bright red, with "First Aid" on the front in crisp letters. I extracted a packet of Spenco, another of Connie's suggestions and blew her a long-distance kiss. Spenco is a non-stick frictionless dressing, awkward as blancmange to get hold of, but with a patch slapped over each punctured blister my feet healed up in a week. I was to race through oceans of powder, to write off twelve pairs of socks on the long haul to Canada, but those two sharp warnings, delivered still in sight of the Mexican border, did an absolutely spot-on job. Though the soles of my boots would wear down to wafers, the two little blisters of San Luis Pass were the first and the last of the trip.

I had been saving since lunch time for a ceremonial piss, planned for the crest of the pass. I was going to direct a stream of my own personal urine precisely onto the watershed. I would watch it divide, flowing east, flowing west, two momentous trickles, messengers to the far distant seas bearing the news that I was, at last, On The Continental Divide.

But the pass turned out to be an indistinct dip, which I quartered in vain for the exact spot. It could have been anywhere within a half-mile stretch. Eventually I just had to let go, and instead of a knife-edged parting of the flood, what I got was the usual discoloured froth and a plate-sized damp patch in the dirt.

I pressed on north, up to my armpits in scrub. It had all looked so easy, back on my kitchen table. The patron saint of hikers was probably killing himself – fifteen miles, two blisters, and now I was stuck in a thicket. I extracted a thorn, sighed, and looked for an easier route.

It is possible – in theory – to trace the Divide without deviation, but in practice (and by mid-afternoon on May 6th I'd had plenty) it isn't. The simplest thing would be to work out a route by road. I could do that and never be more than thirty miles from the watershed. Yet rolling down a highway for week after week seemed a pretty bleak prospect. I needed to strike a balance, to admit impracticability, if not defeat, when I had to, while resisting the temptations of tarmacadam until absolutely necessary. But absolute necessity is a flexible concept. It depends on how tired and how thirsty you are: today's jungle is tomorrow's highway.

Temptation in the wilderness was to become almost a daily affair. It wasn't so much the devil taking me into the high places – I managed that fine on my own – as him trying to lure me down. Occasionally he succeeded and there were times when I was too soft on myself. But there were many more when, scarcely summoning the energy to unhitch the pack, I knew I'd pushed myself to the limit.

4 Tea

A house and a shed stood in the hollow below me, the bungalow roof of white-painted tin, the slat-sided barn a dull red. There was no garden, but a windpump rose over cottonwoods shading the creek. I could see the silver blades turning.

A man was shaking out hay for three horses beside the barn. I shouted hallo and a dog jumped through the wooden railings. It growled and the man told it to shut up. He seemed about the same

age and size as me. He reached for the stained plastic bucket beside
him and hooked it over his arm.

"Buenos tardes," he said, though he didn't look at all hispanic. His
eyes were too grey, his skin too pale, quite white under the brim of
his hat – a hat I actually liked, more of an old shoe than a stetson,
black, with a tide-line of sweat round the crown. His boots were pretty
old too, worn down at the heels where his jeans were beginning to
fray. The sleeves of his check cotton shirt were buttoned above hands
ingrained with dirt. The man's name was Steve Gilson.

"Thought you was Mexican," he said when I asked if I could go on
over the land. His voice had a resonant, trailing quality, not deeply
pitched, the vowels hooped into a gentle twang. "You come up the
draw past Culberson's?" I had seen only one other building that day,
so I supposed that I had.

"Anyone there?"

I hadn't called in, but there'd been no vehicles or livestock around.

"Probably gone into town," said Steve. "We're all part of the same
concern. Just changed hands and ain't restocked yet. Easy time for the
mounts."

"D'you actually use them?" I asked.

Steve must have thought me a moron, but he didn't show it.

"Yeah, we do," he said courteously. He broke open another bale.
"We have a vehicle for transportation to town, but you seen this
country. All rocks. Can't cut cattle out on wheels around here."

I kicked the last of the hay down the stall. "That'll do," said Steve.
"Come on up to the house."

Despite the horses, this was not Ranching As I Knew It. Where was
the bunk-house? The cattle-trough one dunked into? The longhorn
skull over the gate? There was no gate. Steve passed the bucket
through the railings.

"Hope the pistol didn't alarm you," he said.

"What pistol?"

"That there in the bucket." The revolver was black, its ivory handle
yellowed with age. "We geta lotta illegals crossing the border down
here. They walk up through the mountains, same way as you.
Majority's friendly, but there's always a few looking to pick something
up. They're needy guys most of them – no money, no shoes – but I
guess you gotta protect your own."

The front door of the house opened directly to the main room. It
was totally bare.

"Only moved in last week," said Steve. "Been down in Texas for a year but we heard about this job and came back. This here is my wife."

I'd seen Grace through the window as we approached. She'd been holding a rifle. She wondered if I'd like some tea, then hesitated.

"I seen on TV the English drink tea hot," she said, taking a large pickle jar from the fridge. I sank two pints and asked how the fridge worked out here.

"We got a small genny," said Grace. "Comes on at night. Radio works off the car battery, but it's bust."

It was restful in this bare house. Coming indoors had been like switching off loud music. Inside, it was still as a chapel. On the table top there were only the large pickle jar and some wet tea bags throttled on their strings; in the main room just four packing crates and the rifle propped in the corner – nothing to play mind games with except Steve's boots in the middle of the floor. Freemen of the house, I reckoned.

I stayed for an hour, chatting about land and cows. The ranch covered eight hundred square miles, of which Steve personally managed seventy. He called them sections, the boundaries corresponding to the exact square-mile grid system on which much of the west was surveyed. All boundaries – private ranch, public national forest, township and county – conformed to this disconcerting grid, though actual fences were thankfully thin on the ground. Straight lines are so unconvincing: according to the map, the Land of Enchantment was the exact shape of a box, though being a big one perhaps such conventional limits didn't matter. The forestry maps, overprinted with the grid, looked like huge crossword puzzles, filled in over the years by the Homestead Act.

The Act of 1862 awarded quarter sections – 160–acre squares – to any individual able to pay the nominal fee, build a homestead, and occupy the plot for five years. Over one and a half million patents were filed, but a single cow would need two or three quarter sections of this desiccated land for its bare subsistence, and livestock needs water too. Homesteads without it were useless, so the possession of a key well conferred control of the surrounding territory by simple default. Vast holdings were built up in this way, though the federal government, through its various agencies, remains by far the largest landowner in the west. New Mexico was atypical in this respect. Apart from the Black Mountains north of Silver City, and the Zunis beyond Pie Town, my route through the state was almost exclusively across private land. No one bothered me though. Steve was telling me the best route to take over his patch.

"Stick with the wagon tracks north," he said, "and you'll drop off into Deer Creek. Stay with it till you head out over the saddle, and somewhere in about fifteen miles you'll hit the old OK Bar ranch. Might see a mountain lion if you're lucky, but don't tread on no snakes."

My eyes were downcast for the first mile or so, but it wasn't because of the snakes. As I was leaving Grace had asked me if I were a Christian. I'd laughed and said, "No, not full time." There'd been an awkward pause. Grace had been looking for a tract – from St Matthew she said – to help me on my way, but her bible was still packed in a crate.

"Oh well," she said. "You're educated more'n us anyway."

The blush must have glowed right through my beard. I felt about two inches tall – itchy and useless as I walked past the cottonwoods and picked up the track into the hills.

5 The Animas Mountains

I lost the trail within half an hour, ate, slept, and the following morning did exactly what Steve Gilson had told me. I dropped into Upper Deer Creek.

The canyon sides were of friable, mauve-coloured rock which scrunched under my boots and cascaded in pieces over the edge. So did I. The bush I had clutched as I felt myself slipping came straight out by the roots. I hit the stream bed feet first and was promptly knocked flat by the pack. I felt like a half-grated carrot. There was blood all over the place. I picked out the worst of the embedded gravel and swabbed myself down. Having stitched up the rips in the back of my trousers I had a brew and limped on. I could feel the skin prickling and growing tighter as the scabs began to form. They dropped off after nine days.

Hot, empty hills crowded Deer Creek on both sides. The rivulet shrivelled and died, curling off the rocks in straight-sided scales of white clay. Twigs lay where the water had left them, the unburied dead of past winter rains, stranded, entangled, stiffened with scum and with brittle horsetails of grass. The midday heat twirled like a forgotten record, my boots going bop, scratchy bop, scratchy bop as I trudged up the withered channel. I went wrong a couple of times, turning back from blind gullies in sweaty frustration, but my third try took me high on to a saddle which I assumed was the one that I wanted. The view was superb, valleys whizzing off in all directions, red cliffs tumbling into silent canyons, black vultures pinwheeling in the sky.

I consulted the map and checked off the salient features. Yes, good, fine. Should reach the old OK Bar Ranch in what? – two hours at most. It took the best part of two days. I was, of course, on the wrong saddle. For the past three miles I had been walking east instead of north, but getting lost creeps up on you slowly, as, little by little, you bend the world to your expectation, until you have completely remoulded the landscape. If the map says "let there be mountains", you will see them wherever you look. If it indicates a small stream, great rivers will instantly shrink. Never mind about compass bearings – you can always dismiss them with old chestnuts like "magnetic rocks" or "must be my watch". You don't have a watch? Then the pack frame will do. Meanwhile the hills are just waiting. Sooner or later the excuses peter out; the facts rear their ugly heads; you stop, and instead of your cheerful "nearly there, chaps" out comes your first "where the fuck am I?"

I decided to carry straight on and swung down through a dense stand of juniper to a trickle of water below. I drank and moved on, lowering myself from boulder to boulder and swearing loudly at the thorns. I become overwrought when I'm lost. I'm off course, I'm not where I should be, my neat little world collapsed. Instead of being where I actually am, I project myself to where I am not. The result of all this was a discordant blob, grouching his way down the canyon. It took me roughly three hours to emerge, at a canyon junction beside Walnut Creek.

I wasn't sure which the walnut trees were, but scrub oaks and cottonwoods grew thickly on both banks. I dug out a hollow in the gravelly stream bed, threw off my clothes, and lay down. Cool water washed over my body. I knew where I was now. The nibbled remains of a cart track ran alongside the stream. I was happy again. I shut off the stove and lay back with a potful of food. A bat was twitching through the trees. Twice in the day silver jet planes had winked high overhead, miles too far away to be heard. There had been silence now for twenty-four hours. I couldn't remember when I had last been alone like this. I recorded the fact in my notebook, tucked the camera bag under my head, and slept.

6 Geronimo

In close-up, the Winning of the West is exactly what the movie men say it is – a story of individual courage, tenacity, vision, greed, etc. But a long shot shows something else: that two-thirds of present-day America was acquired at the stroke of a pen. Actually three pens – possibly the three largest land deals in history, made not with the original owners, of course, but with the Mexicans, the Russians and the French. The price list was this: $15 million for the Great Plains (Louisiana Purchase, 1803); $15 million for the Southwest (Treaty of Guadalupe-Hidalgo, 1848); and $7.2 million for Alaska ("Seward's Folly", 1867) – a sum total of $37.2 million for roughly two million square miles. 2.9 cents an acre. So much for the west. Back east it was harder – a million dead and wounded in the Civil War for starters.

The 1848 sale of the Southwest hadn't been entirely voluntary but the presence of ten thousand US troops on the streets of Mexico City speeded the exchange of contracts nicely. Unfortunately the soldiers had all gone back home before it was realized that nowhere in these new territories was there an easy passage for a transcontinental railroad. So an additional strip was purchased along Mexico's northern border, a deal negotiated in 1853 by James Gadsden, diplomat and railroad executive. This area – The Gadsden Purchase – was what I crossed in the first week of the trip. It included Antelope Wells and the Animas Range, and the Peloncillo Mountains away to the west, as well as the flat, dry plains which the Southern Pacific was eventually to traverse.

But if the rail engineers were content, the US Cavalry was not, because lurking about in the newly acquired hills were some serious military problems. The worst of these claimed some five hundred lives and took thirty years to settle. His Apache name meant "One-Who-Yawns", but the Mexicans called him Geronimo.

The Apache Indians were plunderers, wolves among pueblo-dwelling sheep, though not wolves only for fun: squeezed into an unpromising land by southward-moving Comanche, the raid was an integral part of Apache economic life.

Fast moving, flexible and secure in their mountain retreats, the Apache were hard to combat. Mexican forces would occasionally surprise and kill small groups, but their patrols were generally ineffective. By the middle of the nineteenth century the state government of Chihuahua had dropped the signally unsuccessful shoot-on-sight approach and were trying a version of hearts-and-minds. A sort of Apache-Geld was offered each year in the form of trade goods and drink in the hope that, given enough loot, the recipients wouldn't bother to steal any more. But, over on the western side of the Divide, the state of Sonora was still offering bounties for Apache scalps: 100 pesos for a male, 50 for a female and 25 for a child.

This state of affairs was of no great concern to Geronimo, whose homelands were 150 miles north of the border, when, in 1850, at the age of twenty-one, he joined a band of Mimbreno Apache and travelled south for the annual tribute. Following the long mountain corridors, the Indians moved down through the Peloncillo range until they reached Janos, about sixty miles south of Antelope Wells. There they made camp and were feasted for two days in the customary way.

Unknown to the Chihuahuans, the military governor of Sonora was also heading for the rendezvous. His memory of the expedition was clear:

> There is a small town named Janos, in Chihuahua, near the eastern boundary of Sonora [he later told an American friend] where the Apache have for several years been received and provided with rations by the government of that state, although the same Indians were at that time in open war with the Mexicans of Sonora. Not being able to comprehend the virtue of a policy which feeds Indians in one state that they might prey on and destroy the citizens of another, I concluded that my duty was to destroy the enemy wherever I could find him. Acting upon this decision, I waited until the allotted time for the Apaches to visit Janos to obtain their regular quarterly rations and, by forced marches at night, succeeded in reaching the place just as the carnival was at its height. We killed a hundred and thirty . . . principally women and children.

Among the dead at Janos were the mother, the wife, and the three small children of One-Who-Yawns.

"I stood until all had passed," he recorded, "Hardly knowing what I would do. I had no weapon, nor hardly did I wish to fight, neither did I contemplate recovering the bodies of my loved ones. I did not pray, nor did I resolve to do anything in particular, for I had no purpose left. Finally I followed the tribe . . . "

The survivors escaped north through the Animas mountains and back into the Gila Wilderness. Four months later Geronimo returned to Mexico with a band of Chiricahua Apache, attacked the Sonoran town of Arizpe, and set off what John Clum, agent at the San Carlos reservation, later described as the most humiliating military campaign in American history.

For the next twenty-five years Geronimo took his revenge. In 1863 he looted and burned the north Mexican town of Crassanes. In 1865 he cut a swath clear across Sonora to the Gulf of California. Naiche, youngest son of Cochise and a long-time friend of Geronimo, made this distinction: "Geronimo killed Mexicans because he liked to see them die. Americans were killed only as part of raiding to get supplies, and to prevent them from telling the Army where we were."

North of the border Geronimo remained a minor figure until the death of Cochise in 1874. From then on he became the focus of opposition by the Chiricahuas to attempts by whites to pen them at San Carlos, an arid region along the lower Gila river. Even the US Army took a dim view of the place. Cavalry Lt. Britton Davis called it Hell's Forty Acres, a gravelly flat, dotted here and there by the drab adobe buildings of the agency. Scrawny cottonwoods marked the waterless streams. Dust-laden winds swept the plain. In summer 110° in the shade was cool weather. "At all other times," wrote Lt. Davis, "flies, gnats and bugs swarm in millions." In summer, he noted, most of the flies disappeared, "leaving, evidently, for the mountain resorts".

Davis also reflected on the mood of his 600 charges.

"Everywhere the naked, hungry, dirty, frightened little Indian children, darting behind bushes or into wikiups at the sight of you. Everywhere the sullen, stolid, hopeless, suspicious faces of the older Indians . . . you felt the challenge in your marrow . . . "

It is surprising that Geronimo agreed to live at San Carlos at all, and when in 1875 all other reservations in Arizona and New Mexico were abolished and the sometime-warring occupants concentrated there together, he broke out. It cost $12 million in military expenditure to get him back. His depradations were reported in the *Silver City Enterprise* under headlines like "Murdering Redskins" and "Demon Apaches". On April 20th, 1883, the paper reported that: "A man named Mason, near Camp Rucker, Arizona, was attacked by a party of Indians but escaped to the underbrush, where he lay concealed.

One of the redskins more daring than the others followed and Mason with his trusty '.45' converted, and will send the scalp with ears attached to the Young Men's Christian Association of Boston."

The *Tucson Citizen* demanded war – "steady, unrelenting, hopeless and indiscriminating war, slaying men, women, and children . . . until every valley and crest and craig shall send to the high heavens the grateful incense of rotting and festering Chiricahuas . . . " – this in response to an incident near Silver City in the spring of 1885. A band of 100 Chiricahuas was reported to have attacked a ranch three miles out of town, and the *Enterprise* carried the following report from "a citizen who is thoroughly conversant with the Indian situation":

> Some twenty of us saddled up and rode over. Arrived there, a sight presented itself that drew tears from the strongest men. In the house and around it was one large slaughter-pen, blood and brains on the walls inside and on the posts and ground outside; large streams and splotches coagulated on the hard dirt ground; bunches of hair and bits of human flesh in every direction. Lying in the midst of this were the bodies of two men, two women and six children, all cut and slashed and bruised till but their raiment reminded us that they were human beings. Outside the door on a sharpened wooden peg used to hang meat was impaled a babe of six months, the peg having passed through its body and six inches beyond. On a hillside covered with loose rocks we found a child uninjured. When the Apaches attacked the house he escaped, and lying down, witnessed the massacre. Uninjured did I say? Yes; but what the day before had been a bright, intelligent boy was today a gibbering maniac. We took him to the house and he laughed in merry glee over the corpses of his parents and playmates, and to this day he remains the same.

The citizens of Tombstone, Arizona, were petitioned to sponsor-a-scalp, and they raised a fund to pay out $250 each for the heads of "hostile" Indians. The sum of $500 was offered for the delivery of Geronimo himself, dead or alive, at Silver City. The bounty was never claimed though, because, as an Albuquerque paper put it: "On September 4, 1886, Nelson Miles, a general officer representing the Army of an industrial nation of millions of people, accepted the surrender of a beleagured band of Indians – Geronimo, sixteen other warriors, fourteen women and six children." Wearying of the constant chase, and promised his life if not his freedom, Geronimo had given himself up.

He was exiled first to Florida and then to Fort Sill, Oklahoma, where he lived as a farmer for the last twenty years of his life. He sold autographs for ten cents at a time and his photograph for up to two dollars at the fairs and expositions to which he travelled, but he was never allowed to go back to his native Southwest. At the age of eighty-one he contracted a fatal bout of pneumonia and he died at Fort Sill on February 17th, 1909. Marion Morrison, better known as John Wayne, was two years old at the time.

7 Ted

It was dawn-cold down in Walnut Creek. I woke on that third morning of the walk to what sounded like squirrels with coughs. Sleeping outdoors is a good way to watch animals – bodies in sleeping bags don't seem to bother them. I stuck out my head to face four rather beautiful mule deer. They were standing under a tree about ten yards away, their uncertain breath misty on the still air. They looked at each other, coughed again, and trotted away. There is something intangible about deer. I can't really describe it. They make me yearn.

An hour and a half up the valley I came to the ruins of a cabin. An actual log cabin! I was temporarily thrilled. Behind the crumbling chimney was a stack of barbed wired, coil long rusted to coil; a rotted saucepan; fallen timbers. The place was called Lawhorns Ranch. The Lawhorns must have had a hard life here. You could see where they had dammed the stream to make a water tank in the rocks, and some of their handcut fence posts were still just about standing upright. How many hours of effort did each of those twisted posts represent? Too many. The family had long gone, maybe to California. This little canyon was, after all, only a few miles south of what had once been a main route to the west, a trail blazed in 1846 by a battalion of 400 Mormons. They'd enlisted en masse for the Mexican war to fund the migration of their co-religionists to Utah. Jumble sales probably hadn't been invented.

"History can be searched in vain for an equal march of infantry," their commander wrote of the eleven-hundred-mile march to the sea, "half of it through a wilderness where nothing but savages and wild beasts are found, or deserts where, for want of water, there is no living creature." The Mormon battalion finally reached the Pacific in January 1847. "Marching half-naked and half-fed, we have discovered a road of great value," concluded Colonel Cooke, and they had. Twelve months later the California gold rush was on, and by 1849 tens of thousands of people were following Cooke's trail west. I wondered how many of them had camped in this very canyon, silent now but for a scuffling ahead which stopped me dead in my tracks. A long, furry tail unfurled itself over the rocks.

I sank to the ground, unstrapped the pack, and slipped forward. Four ginger creatures were snuffling along with their tails straight up in the air – rubbery snouts, foxy bodies, little monkey hands rummaging into everything in sight. Perhaps they were looking for insects. They were having a pretty good time about it – shinning up trees, falling off rocks, jumping on each other from great heights. I would have liked to join in, but the breeze shifted, they caught my scent, and vanished over the hill. They were Coatimundis, Mexican cousins of the Raccoon – quite rare north of the border.

The trail straggled forward across the Divide, dipping into a wide bowl of grassland; faint whisps of cirrus were blowing up from the south. I saw the OK Bar ranch far ahead – actually more cottonwoods and a windpump, but that, I knew, stood for a house. The language of a landscape is pretty easy to pick up. Broken tiles littered the ground. They looked like smashed flower pots – an image of childhood, I realized. I hadn't seen a clay flowerpot in years. Trees were nudging the bare rafters. The building was raised on a low platform of stone, sprouting tufts of grass which pulled out of the cracks as neatly as dirt from finger nails. I rounded the corner and there in the shade was a mule. Someone said "Hi"; we shook hands; and I realized that nowhere since landing in New York had I met anyone with bad teeth. Ted's were a disaster.

His father had tended stock fences in the area for over thirty years, and apart from a spell in the army that's what Ted had done too. He'd come down from his camp miles back in the hills to rendezvous with his wife. It was Mothers Day and she was bringing the kids and a picnic.

"Should be on her way over from Rodeo right now," said Ted. "That's the place where we live at. Wasn't but a gas station when I was born, and it ain't all that much more now." He moved the mule further into the shade. "Too rough for vehicles further on," he said. "Darned near too rough for the fencin'. Gotta bust rock to get it set in."

He rubbed his head through his cap. "Used to make all the fence posts myself, juniper mostly, but lately there ain't no timber big enough left. Stretchers and stakes is all metal these days."

The voice had that same, whimsical lilt as Steve Gilson's, easy on adjectives, very long indeed on the pauses. When he spoke Ted seemed to be humming along to a tune in his head. He said a lot of local people had found work at the smelter.

"Makes it easier getting jobs out here, though. No one to do them. Ranching itself ain't changed much. Switched from Her'furds to mixed breeds that take to the climate better, but the stock's still darned near as wild. Round up's the same – branding, injecting, and worming in spring, trucking them out in the fall. Takes a month to work right over this place."

Ted reckoned the hills carried three head per square mile, but down on the flats you couldn't run but one steer per section. He didn't know England, he said, but he'd spent seven days in Australia on R and R from South Vietnam. I pictured him bashing in posts for the week across the Nullabor Plains.

"I'd like to live out there too," he said. "Shoot, some of them places're more'n two hundred miles between towns. We got big country here, but it ain't nowhere like theirs."

How could you have your wife drive forty miles just for a picnic and still think the place was too crowded? But, compared to the Nullabor Plains, it was. For what the statistics are worth, the average population densities are these: Australia, six per square mile; New Mexico, thirteen per square mile; England, nine hundred and thirty.

Ted's wife and father-in-law turned up in two separate vehicles. "Case'n one of them breaks down," he said. He kissed the kids, warned them not to drown in the water tank, and disappeared towards the old ranch house with his wife. Which left me with Mal, the father-in-law. He popped a beer and talked rattlesnakes.

"Saw two of them devils right there by the car," he said. "Seven feet long and thick as your thigh. Didn't have no gun at the time so I just set tight in the truck. I'll tell ya, rattlesnakes is one thing they got here that's bigger'n in Texas." He sighed. "That's where my wife is, goddamnit. Just cain't figure out why. Kids're growed up. Pension comes through. Trailer home's fixed up real nice. I guess she just don't want to move. Look at that."

An old battery lay under a bush. "Real strange what people throw away." Mal discarded his beer can and threw the battery into the pick-up. "I got copper and lead, shit, hundreds of pounds of it waitin' back under the trailer. Found a welding torch on the Hatchita dump last fall. Made me a Her'furd bull outa bits of this an' that. Holds a glass ashtray between his horns. Got a pretty good jacksaw too. Made all the cupboards and fitted the trailer out real good. But she still wouldn't quit Texas. Too goddamned cussed to move."

8 The Flats

The following days were a trial. Heat scrambled my brains, sage ripped at my legs, and I longed for the sun to go down. It was the cool of first light that I relished, the dilute hour of freshness before wasp-tongues of sweat were again rasping my skin. There was one spell of delight, however, on the shallow saddle of Whitmire Pass.

Except in the gardens in California, I'd pretty well missed spring this year. New Mexico was already looking like loose hay so to suddenly come across a patch of Gold Poppies was a lovely surprise. They looked like a flock of canaries. But the shrivelling green of the sage flats returned as I re-entered the Playas basin.

Sage. *Artemisia tridentata*. Otherwise known as Mugwort. Sixteen or so varieties, *tridentata* the most common. How I hated the stuff. It wasn't even the sort you could cook with, no relation at all to the garden herb; a complete and utter waste of space. I was to walk through hundreds of miles of it, some up to my knees, some over my head, though on average it came to mid-thigh. Little twigs of it were always poking up my shorts or snagging me in the bootlaces, but what I grew to dislike most was the unremitting quantity of the stuff. Below the 7500 contour it seemed to cover the entire state. I was too high for it in Colorado, but in southern Wyoming there it was again; I even walked through it for a week in Montana. By then it had flowered, though you'd hardly have noticed because even the blossoms were boring. Sage is an invader plant. It smothers over-grazed range. Cows won't touch it, so once the grass has been eaten off the young shrubs grow undisturbed. The only value it does have is as browse for wild animals: I tried it myself a couple of times. It tastes of aftershave.

The Playas basin sage was not only irksomely dense, but was too low to throw useful shade, so at the noonday halt on day five I resorted to the tent. The pegs pulled straight out of the sand but by draping the fly-sheet over the camera tripod I rigged up a wigwam and crawled in. The humidity which built up under the nylon fabric was worse than the direct heat outside it. I crawled out, gasping. Lethargy struck. I tried sucking at the mess of a chocolate bar but gave up and threw it away. The very thought of food made me feel sick. What I wanted was water, torrents of it, but I had none. I packed up my gear and slogged on, scanning the flats for a glint of windpump through the haze.

I struck graded dirt and turned north. It was more like an airstrip than a road but gave me a vanishing point and regular telegraph poles – a whiff of creosote every 265 steps. It was very boring.

Then I saw a galvanized stock tank – my biggest thrill of the day – but it didn't look too promising, the knobbled earth round it trampled and bare but for bleached wafers of dung. I walked slowly towards it. It was quite a low tank and by now I could see over the rim. No sign of anything yet. I tried to swallow; couldn't; got nearer and nearer; assured God I'd be good for ever and ever; but still nothing. Well shi – I was just about to turn away when I saw dappled light on the tin. Three miraculous inches of slime, algae and bugs at the bottom. Absolute bliss.

Suffused with sweet tea I sank on to the mat and a nightjar fell out of the sky. It took off again and was racing, flick-flack, through the sage, twisting and dipping and sweeping and swooping before tumbling back to earth. The stars began to come out. I saw a stick of red lights flashing on and off to the south which at sunrise next day turned to mute shrieks of white. These lights were the hazard beacons on the smoke stack of the Playas copper smelter. The complex was about five miles away, a ship in an empty ocean, a long, white sigh drifting east from its funnel. I love the sensation of freedom and power that walking across empty landscapes engenders. Out here you knew that whatever happened you'd see it.

By midday I had crossed the first tarmac road of the walk, county route # 9, linking Hatchita and Animas. Something like a fuel spillage seemed to be evaporating ahead. It looked like silver paper. It was in fact a trailer park, laid out in shimmering lines, a squared grid as divorced from the landscape around it as a chessboard is from a home.

I reached the road running up to the trailer park from the smelter
and kicked an old tin, half-buried in sand, off the verge. A small
Exxon truck overtook me and turned to cruise slowly along the first
row of trailers. It stopped. A dot jumped from the cab, dragged a hose
across the road, returned, pulled a lever, and waited. I covered another
two hundred yards. The hose went back on the truck, the cab door
fluttered stiffly, and the dot disappeared. The truck cruised out of sight
and tumbleweed blew down the road.

I was deciding which of the trailers to try for water when I saw a
fat man in shorts. He was hairy and white and was hacking away at
some rabbitbrush, his sweaty T-shirt transparent against his paunch.
His wife was in the trailer. She was pregnant.

"That's my fifth boy on the way," said the man. His name was Pat.
"Had all the others back east. But if this one ever needs to say where
he was born he's gonna need a map."

"Back east" was a mining town in Pennsylvania. Pat wanted his
brother to come out and join him.

"Good money at the smelter," he said. "Brother could find a used
trailer easy. He'd have it paid off in three months. Still says he ain't
coming though – not till you get rid of them injuns he says. Hell, I've
been here three and a half years and I ain't seen no injuns yet. Too
goddamn deserted."

Why had the smelter been built in such an isolated place?

"You ever been to Pennsylvania?" asked Pat.

"Driven through," I said.

"Well, we got laws about pollution in this country and you go to
Pennsylvania you can see why. Out here they got laws too. Only thing
is, ain't no one around to apply them."

The Divide swung away to the east in a huge and irrelevant bend. It
had lost its command of a landscape now flowing smoothly under
my feet, a treeless, shrubless, biscuit-dry plain which I was roaming
unfettered and free. But the first of the five interstate crossings on the
journey was only ten miles ahead. Across that I'd be following dirt
roads all the way into Silver.

A branch line had been built from the smelter to Deming, now forty
miles to the east, and I walked along the empty rails for four miles.
Vehicle ruts ran either side of the track, then a fence, then twin slices
of desert. The land on the left was a mirror image of that on the right.
My abiding impression of New Mexico was of these unbending lines.
I always seemed to be walking towards the point of convergence, to

the retreating centre of a circle, the tiny point into which the world vanished or from which it streamed out towards me. New Mexico's trick was never to let me quite get there.

The branch line was so easy to follow that I should have covered the four miles in little more than an hour. In the end it took three. I got held up by a posse of toads.

They were actually Texas Horned Lizards. It was their circular bodies and bewildered expressions that made them look so like toads. They had very short tails and instead of toady warts were covered in spines; they were camouflaged a splotchy grey-brown and only gave themselves away when they moved. The first one shot out from under my boots, its thighs working quadruple time, its stumpy tail wagging furiously in the air. Up popped another. Then another. I am but a lonely toadherd, yodle-ay yodle-ay yodle-ay-ay-oo – soon I was driving a whole flock up the track. They had evidently burrowed up from below, and, trapped in a four-foot-wide world, could have run to the end of the line – as far as New York if they'd wanted, though they wouldn't have seen much on the way. I decided to rescue them, dumped the pack and lassoed the nearest with my T-shirt. Its spines got caught in the cloth and Wild and Wonderful West Virginia went tearing off up the track, little legs going ten to the dozen. They got muddled up, the creature tripped, and I caught it. The spines turned out to be harmless. I unhooked the lizard and popped it under a shrub. It dived headfirst into the sand and, shovelling itself underground with quick, sideways movements, was gone.

Something winked as it sped along Interstate # 10, heliographing the course of the still invisible road. The highway had whispered all night – my sixth from Antelope Wells. "Chocolate milk," it said, "doughnuts and microwaved burgers."

It was right. Bowlin's Continental Divide Trading Post had them all. It also had postcards and key-rings and fluffy pink dogs and dolls of all nations and teacloths and tomahawks and nothing at all of the land within – at a guess – a two-hundred-mile radius. Bowlin's was a log cabin-style rest stop. A hopper of free ice cubes stood outside in the sun and beside it was a notice which said "GAS SKIPS WILL BE PERSECUTED".

I lay full length on a bench, bun in one hand, Coke in the other, and belched in outstanding contentment. The traffic hummed past. Eventually a large truck rolled in for gas. I contemplated it idly. It was decorated with the sort of pictures that tattooists do. The brakes hissed. I could see the driver up in the cab, shifting his weight as he reached for his back pocket. He slicked the comb through his hair, opened the cab door and jumped down.

"Morning," I said as he clumped past me to the door. He turned and looked at the pack.

"Don't give no rides," he said.

I felt smug. "I'm not hitching," I said.

"How the hell you get here then?" asked the trucker, and I told him. "No shit?" he said. "You wanna Coke or something?"

We both had coffee.

"Your lorry looks nice," I said. It was black and silver and vulgar. Lots of tooth, tit and claw. Green dragons and cobras writhed over the mudguards, and there were nude cowgirls on the flaps. They had sheriffs' badges on their nipples.

"That's a two-thousand-dollar paint job sitting out there," said the trucker. "Won me eleven trophies so far. See them doors? That's 'Death Dealer' this side, and the 'Sun Goddess' on the other."

He was proud of that truck. Ted, with his dreadful teeth, had been proud of his fences; Ed, back at Antelope Wells, had been proud of the nice, clean ranch people that came through his checkpoint; the Texan had been proud of his bike; and good old Gottlieb Ribary had obviously been proud of his milk. What was I proud of? Well, I was quite proud that the trucker had bought me a coffee.

9 The Plains

I reached Silver City on 15th May, but I took a short break on the way. North of the Interstate I'd passed more cottonwoods clumped round windpumps, the isolated ranchsteads looking as if they'd been assembled in kit form, except they were all the demonstration model. There was none of the muck or the weed-ridden scrap that you find around English farms, no tractors or ploughs and no smells but sage dust in my nose. Sometimes I'd see a pick-up trailing across the range, or a few plastic toys on the porch of a house, but generally the ranching scene seemed static, until, a day north of Bowlin's, I called in at a place for water. The man restraining the dogs asked me in for a coffee and I ended up staying two days. His name was Buck Adams.

I slept through most of the first day – I was a lot more tired than I realized, and the combination of a shower, a pillow and Patsy Adams' steak and beans knocked me out till Buck got back from work the following evening. He was a machine operator at a large copper mine under the Black Mountains.

"Forty miles away in a straight line," he said. "You can see the tailings from Soldiers Farewell."

"What's that?" I asked.

"A hill on our ranch," said Buck. "You passed it back down your road. Best landmark between here and Texas. It's where the old Butterfield stage trail crossed over the Divide and the escorting soldiers changed over. Eastbound went on to El Paso, westbound headed for a cantina called Mud Flat Bar. Patsy's grandfather got shot in the leg there one night and it kept him off a horse for six months. He got married while he was recooperatin' and along comes Patsy's uncle and her dad. You got that much history on your place in England?"

The Butterfield line was the first transcontinental stage service. It ran from St Louis to San Francisco. The inaugural run, in September 1858, took twenty-four days. Eleven years later, in 1869, a ceremonial gold spike was driven into a final rail tie and the Butterfield line was out of business.

Even more short lived was the Pony Express service which had also drummed past Soldiers Farewell in its sixteen-month dash into history. Though only one dispatch was ever lost, the Express bit the dust in 1861, dry-gulched by telegraph wires. The backers lost two hundred thousand dollars.

"Shoulda kept the film rights," said Buck as we walked out to the barn. There were chickens clucking around green bales of alfalfa, an anvil on the floor, and thick leather chaps slung over a beam.

"Keeps the mesquite outa your legs," Buck told me. We'd stopped beside a rack of eight saddles. "This here's over fifty years old. Belonged to Patsy's grandfather that got shot. The ranch went to her uncle, but he died so we're caretakin' till the family decides what to do. There's thirty sections all told. Living in it for one family but not for us all. It'll probably wind up getting sold and we'll go back to living in town. Todd ain't gonna like that, but our other two kids're living there already as it is."

Todd was eighteen, just graduated from high school in Silver. He didn't smoke but he chewed tobacco. His brand was called Redskin. It came in little round tins and looked like snuff. He shoved a fingerful under his lip.

"I suppose you'll be going to college soon," I said.

"Tryin' to," said Todd.

"What d'you think you'll study?"

"Prob'ly baseball. Cochise over near Douglas has a programme in rodeo and baseball both. I'll do that if I can. If I can't then I'll just play baseball."

A friend of his had arrived from town, and they went off to hunt snakes. Todd kept the rattles in a jar. He also had a collection of flaked arrow-heads which he'd found at various spots on the ranch.

"Usually where the Indians made camps," said Patsy. "Some of them're real pretty. Keep a look out as you go up the draw. You wanna watch for Javelinas too. The boars're meaner'n hell. We'll see you in Silver day after tomorrow." She'd offered me their place in town for the night.

The Indians – Mimbreno Apache in the region of Silver City – made their arrow-heads not only of stone but had used native copper as well. They found it growing in fern-like crystals at locations along the base of the mountains. I could see the hills now as a distant smudge, the tree-peppered slopes rising to a dark band on the northern horizon. A white slash in the haze was the spoil heap from the mine, almost a separate hill in itself: once the source of a few crystals of copper, Santa Rita del Cobre is now one of the largest open-cast pits in the world. The hole is a mile across and over a thousand feet deep. If you stand at the top and shout, the people at the bottom can't hear you. It gets bigger by an average of 37,500 tons of extracted ore per day, which in the forty-eight hours that it took me to reach Silver City, had become 640 tons of pure copper. Whether that was a roomful or a houseful I didn't know, but I forgot to ask.

10 Silver City

The road into town was almost empty. Little birds flew in and out of the trees each time a car went past. Then they flew back.

The town limits sign said 9500 feet, which surprised me till I realized that the 9 was upside down. The population was 7551: Silver City was easily the largest place I walked through on the entire two-and-half-thousand-mile journey. (It wasn't three thousand in the end.) I passed an orange windsock and a hangar and some cocky little planes parked out in the sun. Then came a gas station, straggling mobile homes, traffic lights, and I was slipping down a familiar channel – McDonald's to starboard, Dairy Queen to port, a bank, a drug store, each marooned in an ocean of asphalt. I docked at the Sonic Drive-In. A youth in a customized pick-up roared in beside me. He wound down his window.

"Order of French Fries," he yelled at the intercom grille.

"Order of Frendge Fries," came the tinny reply.

The youth looked at me, picked his nose, and wound his window back up. His muffled car radio announced seventy-eight and cloudy. I took off the pack and decided to have French Fries too.

"Could I possibly have French Fries too, please?" I asked the loudspeaker.

"Frendge Fries?"

"Yes, please."

"What?"

"Yes, please."

"Uh huh." Short silence, then, "Booth two? Are you Australian?"

I spent the night at Buck and Patsy's house – purple and green painting of Patsy's dad's boots on the wall – then I went to pick up my food from the forestry office. The ranger's name was Scott. He was collating information for an officially proposed Continental Divide Trail, and so we went over my route from Antelope Wells in some detail. He explained, as far as he knew, what the Divide was like ahead: a steep pull up to Pinos Altos, the old gold mining settlement just north of the town, then over the Pinos Altos ridge itself and down to the Mimbres valley. That led back into the Black range where the trails were a bit overgrown – budget cuts, Scott said – and the last seventy miles were across open range land to route # 60 and Pie Town.

"Looks like you've done about 140 miles so far," said Scott. "How far you doin' a day?" We measured it off. It varied between seventeen and twenty-four miles, eleven on the day I got lost. Scott's radio crackled. It was the Mimbres valley forest guard.

"I got a hiker comin' your way," said Scott. "Doin' the Divide."

The reply was muffled by static, but "Lotsa snow . . . twelve-foot drifts . . . " came through loud and clear. Scott turned to me.

"You're gonna have lotsa snow. Twelve-foot drifts."

This information was official, therefore infectious. The forest guard had told Scott. Scott had told me. I was worried. I didn't think to ask when the snow had last been measured. By the end of the trip I would have.

Scott unlocked the shed in which, seventeen days earlier, Connie and I had left the stuff. I'd arrived exactly according to plan. This rather depressed me. Plans take the edge off life. But I was soon back in the swing of things with spontaneous smears of honey and jam all down my legs. I made a complete horlicks of sorting out the new food box and started again, this time very slowly. I checked everything off with a list. Maps, batteries, matches, dish cloth, biro, soap, foot powder, freezer bags, film, tape, bit of candle, food. Finally I decanted two litres of kerosene into my aluminium flasks. I was to go through this routine seventeen times altogether: this first transfer took two hours, but the last one – in East Glacier, Montana – was over in just twenty minutes.

There was one food pick up job, however, that I actually got worse at, something I dreaded each time I got to a town. It had to do with the stove. The main fuel was kerosene, but I used short squirts of petrol to preheat the burner – a shot-glass-full every ten days. I kept it in a specimen bottle. But gas stations don't sell such tiny amounts, as I realized when I crossed a nearby garage forecourt. So I waited by the Coke machine, and along came a man in a Dodge. He pulled up by a pump – leaded, but I didn't care. I had to time this just right. The guy had nearly finished. The nozzle hiccuped, and, as he turned to hook back the hose, I materialized, bottle in hand. What I needed were his drips.

The reaction was always the same – the incredulous stare, the slight reddening, then, "Sure, sure, where's your can?" Up came the specimen bottle. Now for the mid-air refuelling sketch where the guy ends up with petrol all over his pants and me going "whoa, whoa, that's plenty," and fetching an armful of towels. I'm not a charity case though. I straighten up, throw out my chest, and look the guy square in the eyes. But how exactly do you offer someone thirteen cents? Gas was a real dilemma.

So were post office opening hours. I hadn't only to pick up my mail: at the end of each stage there were films, tapes and used maps to post home; sometimes spare clothes to forward; and, of course, letters to be sent. The trail was like a roulette wheel, I the hapless ball. The wheel spins, I clatter round, the wheel slows. I am approaching a pick up spot and a post office. The wheel stops. And goddamn it, I've landed on a Sunday yet again. The prospect of a bare post office

flagpole was spur to some prodigious bursts of speed on my way north
to Canada.

The last building on the way out of Silver was a garage. On the wall
in big red letters was "WE CAN WELD ANYTHING EXCEPT A
BROKEN HEART", which was a pity because I met one five miles
further on up the road.

I was just short of Pinos Altos, the small settlement in the hills
above Silver, when I saw the distant figure. The gap between us closed,
me plodding uphill, the other person's knock-kneed stride swinging
downhill. I realized it was a woman. Coming right down the middle
of the road. Traffic swerving badly both sides. I put on a slight swagger
– she must have seen me by now – and I stopped breathing through
my mouth. She was bound to ask about the pack: seventy pounds, I'd
tell her. Heavy? No, ma'am, I hardly notice it now. And no, ma'am,
not from Silver. From the border. Yep, entirely alone. To Canada,
ma'am. Pretty fit, yeah. Girl now sidles to roadside, rips off clothes,
and ecstatic moans reverberate through the forest. Then: I guess I gotta
pull my boots on again, ma'am. So long then, stranger. So long, ma'am.
Clip clop, clip clop, clip clop . . .

My actual "hello" came out in a rush, with an ear-to-ear smile to
cover the lungful of air I heaved back inside me. But the great grin
froze. In her grimy white boots, the woman was half a head taller than
me, and heavier by at least twenty pounds, most of them slopping over
the waistband of her jeans. She had knotted her denim jacket, leaving
her puckered midriff bare. This was cooling for both of us. She was
probably forty, certainly not a hiker, and . . . perhaps her car had a
flat?

"Hot day," I said. "Had a punc . . . ?"

But she was frowning, swaying ever so gently.

"BAAArp!"

It was a belch of quite staggering proportions. I winced as the fumes
drifted over my head and was about to move on with a "nice to have
met you" when the woman seized my wrist.

"You got ten dollars?" she said.

Oh shit.

"Er, well I'm doing this really long hike and . . . "

"I have," she said. "Ten dollars is all he give me, the fart. Christ
my hair's in a mess."

It was. She tucked a lank strand behind her ear. Another car swished
past.

"Jacket's OK like this, ain't it?"

But she scarcely paused.

"What the fuck'm I asking you for? I can wear what I goddamn want. Last thing he says is to do it up normal – I says do yourself up you fart. Fat shit thinks I'm his wife. But I ain't nobody's wife. I take this little ass where I want." She laughed.

"I been three years with that son of a bitch. But I still do my drinking in town. So what? Sheriff always brings me back nex' day. Did this morning. Drops me off and I walk in the house. An' what does that fat shit say? Out! He says – Marie, you're leavin'. Didn't know if to shit or go blind. He gives me the ten dollars, says call up a cab an' just git. I says fuck your cab, mister, I'm goin' right now an' I walk straight out the door. Wassit to town? Three or four miles or somethin'?"

By this time I was trying unobtrusive little movements to ease my captive wrist. But she suddenly jerked my hand against her thigh.

"I'm quite a little cowgirl, you know!"

Oh God.

"Feel that?"

Oh God, oh God.

"That's a dollar in quarters for the juke box. I gotta a singing trial comin' up in Silver nex' month an' I gotta practise. You like Country an' Western?" She did a couple of unsteady dance steps and flicked her thumbs. I got my hand back. For one awful moment I thought she was going to sing.

"Well," she said. "Glad I ain't humpin' all that stuff. You take good care now. I gotta get my ass into town."

11 The Black Mountains

Pine cones lay all over the road. The air smelt tangy and fresh. I could see back for miles, the sackcloth of desert now frayed by a velvet of trees. I was to see a great deal of forest on my walk through the States – too much some days – but at least it was never in rows.

I had a bit of trouble deciding where to turn off the road – the map was unclear and tarmac is so easy to walk on – but a guy in a red pick-up put me onto the right trail. He was parked at the spot where it branched off the road and led into the forest, a six-pack of Coors beer on the front seat beside him, a copy of the state *Gazette* spread across the wheel. His name was Tony.

"This'll putcha straight over the Pinos Altos ridge and down to the Mimbres river," he said. He offered me a beer. "Used to backpack in the service. Done my time in the navy. Wacha call them things? – hundredsa planes? Yeah, aircraf' carriers. Met lotsa your guys. Liverpool, Portsmouth – went all over. Hey, you want this paper? Got all the huntin' seasons in here – sep'rate dates for all the game. Black Bear's just startin' up now. You packin' anything yourself?"

"No," I said.

"Not even a .22 for squirrels?"

"No."

"What if you see a bear?"

"A .22 wouldn't help," I said.

"Ain't livin' off the land then?" said Tony.

"No," I said. "I'm not."

He took a slightly disapproving pull at his beer. I was to meet a good number of Tonys during the next five months. In fact I wondered if they hadn't all known each other, back in the service. I quite liked most of them. Guys with dreams on their sleeves are usually pretty harmless.

The alarm clock went beeb-beeb in the chill of an 8000–foot dawn. The sky looked like a bit of old shirt caught up in the trees. It was far too cold to get up, so I went back to sleep.

I woke up with a start. Something had pounced into the clearing. I could hear it scrabbling about in the pine needles. It was probably just another deer. I wondered if it would cough like the others had done, but, popping open my eyes, I realized that it probably wouldn't. Coyotes howl, don't they? This one was virtually sitting on my head – easily within spitting distance, except that I was suddenly rather short of spit. I'd never seen a coyote before. It was about the size of an alsatian dog, with a thick, grey pelt and slightly puzzled eyebrows. It raised a foreleg, sniffed, and, still puzzled, trotted away. Perhaps I should have invited it to breakfast.

Wild turkeys were gabbling as I ploughed up and over the timbered ridge. Everywhere there were trees, mostly ponderosa pines. Mature trunks loomed skywards, the flaking bark cinnamon red, while at boot level seedlings, like dishevelled squabs, wobbled free of the pine-needled ground. The Divide dropped back to 6500 feet round the head of the Mimbres valley, open parkland studded with piñon pines. Smaller and darker than the ponderosas on the higher slopes, the piñons resembled lollies on sticks. The vegetation changed so satisfyingly with altitude. It was like being in a department store – ground floor for range grasses and sage; second floor for oak, piñon and juniper; third floor for ponderosas; then douglas fir; and – top floor – dark candles of englemann spruce.

The Gila National Forest covers roughly 5000 square miles. It runs clear from the Rio Grande to the Arizona state line. The map alone is the size of a table cloth. Spreading it out I had in my lap an area larger than southeastern England, though because there were so few roads, and virtually no buildings, it was difficult to appreciate how big it really was. Only when I began to count the overprinted sections – each one a mile square – and got to sixty, then eighty, then a hundred, did it mean anything at all. To be attempting these huge tracts on foot seemed no more than pleasant fantasy. I'd stare from the high points in the forest as if from a plane window, disassociated utterly from the remote dot down there that was me. Then the trees, like clouds, would close in.

The outer ridges of the Gila were forested right to the top, but, when there was one, the view to the east was vast, an ocean of trees, shoaling here and there against outcrops but thinning, as the foothills descended, to pale oaks, brittle scrub, and, eventually, to the bleached sage of the desert. The Rio Grande itself, forty miles away, was a flat brown gleam in the haze.

Such a huge expanse was almost too much to take in, though forty years earlier – on July 16th, 1945 to be precise – a sudden flash on the far horizon would have provided a sharp point of focus, followed, perhaps, by a faint rumble. In the deserts beyond the Rio Grande is a place called Oscura Peak. It's where the first atom bomb went off. Up here the white-barked aspens were just breaking bud, the newly hatched leaves like buckets of tears sparkling high in the trees.

I followed the Divide along the main ridge of the Black Mountains for thirty-five miles. Progress was slow. The snow was no problem – from a distance I'd mistaken it for litter among the trees – but picking up the faint path again on the far side of a drift wasn't easy. Scott had been right about the budget cuts. The trails hadn't been cleared for years. With the exception of a set of hoofprints pressed into the soft forest floor there was no sign that anyone had yet attempted to get through here this spring. Perhaps it was two or three horses ahead – I'm not much of a tracker, but I could see that the riders must have been very patient. Awkwardly placed drifts had forced them off the ridge again and again; branches that merely required me to duck had meant niggling detours for them. The exceptionally heavy snows that winter had brought down a great many trees.

This was an official Wilderness Area – no vehicles, no roads, no commercial extraction whatsoever. The trees were allowed to live out their natural span – they grew, they died, they fell over; and sod's law dictated that, if they possibly could, they'd fall straight across the trail.

The death scene of a big ponderosa is a protracted affair. Extracts were scattered all over the forest. Very few of the dead trees were cleanly broken, most having keeled stiffly against a neighbour. Some of the leaners would sway in even quite moderate breezes, squeaking like bedsprings but enticingly hard to pinpoint. When I did spot the giveaway movement it was always with a slight sense of collusion. Eventually the surrounding rigging would give way and, though I never saw this actually happen, a leaner would topple, its shattered arms hammering into the ground to prop the trunk in a grisly press-up. From my point of view these splintered barricades were the least amusing trees in the forest – wildly frustrating to wriggle through – though once properly down they weren't so difficult to cross. In time they'd become really pretty, the upstanding grain a countercurrent to the tide of decay. Slowly, slowly the wood was digested. Sometimes I'd speed things up with a kick, watching heartwood soft as couscous shred under my boot. I tried not to disturb the knots though, often all that was left to see, a poignant line of bleached tally bones on the sunless floor of the forest.

The horse tracks grew steadily fresher, and on the fifth morning from Silver City I passed a khaki-green cobble of dung steaming under a sunbeam. I was north of the Wilderness area now, looking down on a glade of large ponderosas. Three horses and a mule were grazing between the trees, and beyond them was a green tent. There was gear all over the place – axes and hammers and ropes and boots and saddle blankets and skillets and all sorts of food and a tube full of rolled-up maps. Presiding crosslegged over all this was a guy called Dee Fogelquist. A broken girth lay across his lap.

"How are ya?" he said, flicking the hair out of his eyes as he looked up. "Seem to rip some goddamn thing every day. Keep havin' to deadhead through the brush an' everybody's tired out so we're restin'."

"Everybody". I liked Dee. His wife Bonny emerged from the tent with coffee.

It was a long, happy afternoon. We lay in the grass and just talked, Dee mostly about his hatred of the mule, Bonny about how Dee would just have to make friends with it. They too were headed for Canada, the first (albeit honorary) hikers I'd run into. I met no more for six hundred miles.

12 More Plains

It took three more days to reach Pie Town, easy walking over treeless range land. Passing close by a house, the first for eighty miles, I stopped and asked for water. It was a fairly isolated place – the cattle grazing so far off in the distance that you knew they wouldn't have names; an airstrip; and, beside the house, a TV satellite dish. Melody, aged nine, said it received nineteen channels. I was impressed but she wasn't. It was, she sighed, supposed to get twenty-four.

Her mother asked if I ate beans. She was Mexican, and her husband managed the ranch. When I asked her how big the place was she just waved her arms at the horizon. A round trip to the nearest shop was two hundred miles, she told me, so the great slab of cheese she passed out of the window was a pretty generous donation.

I ate it the following night, on the plains of San Augustine. Choosing a place to sleep – "campsite" is too formal a description – wasn't usually much of a problem. All I needed was a body-sized bit of ground. I'd snuggle up against a fallen tree trunk or into a slight hollow, fitting much like a milk chocolate into its hole in a tray. Sometimes I'd make a mistake, pick a wrong-shaped hollow and spend an uncomfortable night, but at least it *was* a hollow, an actual location, uniquely, though briefly, my place. Perhaps I over-exaggerated topographical minutiae to the extent that my little nests existed as distinct locii only in my head, but there was always some kernel of attraction, some irregularity which had fixed my attention and suggested a halt. The plains of San Augustine were, however, unblemished, a perfect white string with no ends, flat as a pancake, utterly treeless, houseless and – for once – sageless. There was nothing to bring me to a halt so

I made for the only object in sight, a windpump two miles out of my way. Such was the price of a home.

I was loping north with wolfish vigour, nothing to impede my progress, holding course by the peak of a far, far distant volcano. Things were going very well, the pace efficient, unforced and fast. Full of self-congratulation I set off next morning at the usual early hour, scarcely acknowledging the farewell wave of the rag fluttering from the ladder of the windpump. Six miles later I reached the dirt road leading to Pie Town and stopped to put on my shorts. I couldn't find them. A rucksack is a very small world, but the search took half an hour, about one minute of which was a proper hunt for the shorts and the rest a futile rummage to save face. I did not go back for them – they are probably still out there, flapping happily from the windpump – and I covered the next 250 miles in my rolled-up long trousers. By that time it was June 5th and I still hadn't passed a clothes shop, so I took a trail break and went off to find one.

Meanwhile, I'd reached Pie Town, population: the signboard didn't say; elevation 8112 feet – open range land until 1916 when it was opened to homesteaders. The local ranchers had watched them coming in along highway # 60, one – Anne Cleaveland – expressing the misgivings all must have felt.

"Country's too arid for single section farming," she wrote. "Thirteen inches of rain at most, nearly all of that snow. And the moisture and heat don't come together. When it's hot, it's dry; when it's cold, it's wet – we're lucky to get two months good growth a year. One section will not support over sixteen head, and how many people will sixteen head support? It just can't naturally be done."

She was right. Sage-flooded fences stitched the range, a ruined cabin every few miles. Highway # 60 was a backroad. Through traffic uses route # 66 nowadays, 100 miles to the north, and no one makes pies in Pie Town anymore. Not that I cared very much – I'd walked a ridiculous thirty-three miles that day and all I wanted to do was to stop.

"Lucky you got here though," said Emily, who was looking after my food box. She ran the truck stop. "Me and my daughter're going into Albuquerque tomorrow. Gonna pick up a wedding dress. I'm getting married next month."

"June bride," said an old chap in the corner.

I looked out of the window: an incinerator, dust, darkening sage, matchbox houses scattered through it. No verge. Just broken tarmac, then gravel, then weeds. No wonder Americans have make-believe weddings.

"June 18th," Emily was saying. "We're flying to Vegas."

Nothing much was moving next morning except dogs and dead cotton-wood leaves. The post office looked a bit like the Alamo – a defeat, but the flag was flying. There was none of your satinized aluminium here. It was all nails and old bits of wood. I sat outside on the stoop while the postmistress looked for her glasses.

"England?" she said. "Twenty cents, ain't it?"

"Forty," I said.

The mobile library pulled in. The wheels made crunchy sounds as they rolled across the gravel. I should have taken more interest – the library had pulled up right beside me – but I wanted to get on with my letters. A few ordinary-looking people came and went, nothing very distracting. I went back inside to leave a forwarding address. Next stop was Continental Divide, a strip of gas stations and motels where the Divide crosses route # 66. About six days from here, I reckoned.

I stood in the doorway, yawning. After yesterday's marathon I didn't feel like going very far. In fact I didn't feel like going at all. Pick-ups came and went. Men with immobile faces dropped women in badly cut slacks. The library only called once a month.

Then a long stick of shadow came swinging across the road. That was unusual. I'd become accustomed to people who waddled, people who swaggered, people whose thighs rubbed together; but these legs, thin as flamingos, moved well.

The man himself was about six feet six inches tall. Not a stitch of polyester on him. Just bare, bony legs, loose cotton shorts, a caftan, no socks, and no car. He certainly wasn't the sheriff. Though his hairline had receded to headphone position a tight pony-tail hung to his waist. The tanned forehead could have been a cathedral, the eyes a couple of bishops, brilliantly blue in their niches under the dome. His name, he said, was Shine.

"Shane?"

"Shine."

He exchanged his books and we walked out of town together.

13 Shine

Shine was a difficult guy to keep up with. It was partly his Maine accent – all Fastin' and Breathin' and Understandin' and Studyin' – and partly his constant halts to exhume jetsam from the sage. Most of it he chucked back – cans, bottles, hubcaps – but he did pocket a tangle of wire. Then he bounded on. The Fastin' had made him strong – nothin' but water for three days now, and tunin' to new energy fields. He was into Breatharianism – vital energy comin' in through the lungs. In fact Shine was into just about everything: literature, levitation, space geometry, vortex physics, harmonics, cosmology, astrology, communication psychology, magnetics.

"But theories are a dime a dozen," he said. "Tappin' cosmic energy fields and so on. Eventually you have to invent and out here I've found I can do that; I can run a wire for miles to pick up on that energy. Doesn't matter if what I make's right or wrong; doesn't matter if it works or not – it's all steps along the way."

By this time we'd done five or six miles and had turned down a sandy track. Beyond an old ranchstead we could hear the din of distressed cattle.

"McGee must be brandin'," said Shine. He'd opened the gate and a girl in her mid-twenties was smiling from the toy-strewn porch. "Beth, this is Steve, and Steve" – he took the baby – "this is Ariel. Liza and Galen'll be around somewhere."

"They're watching McGee," said Beth, and we walked over to the corral.

The calves had been separated from the cows so both groups were bellowing loudly, though the calves were bellowing the loudest. They were being roped one by one, towed forward, and wrestled to the ground. The brand mark was Diamond Bar Zero, the hiss of the irons producing instant billows of thick, greasy smoke. The tang of burnt hair and seared flesh filled the air. The dust and the noise didn't bother me that much – I'd been brought up on a farm myself – but, leaning on the railings, something about this branding party was making me feel very unsettled. It was the Explorers Club Dinner all over again –

a grossly top-heavy performance, eight or ten pot-bellied cowboys branding less than a dozen calves.

Beth was in the kitchen, patting rissoles of fermented beans. She had a fantastic complexion, and beautiful, bare-footed legs. She was fifteen years younger than Shine, which didn't bother her, but when I asked Shine how old he was he hesitated.

"In this body? Uh, forty-two. Forty-two years."

He was in the front room, juggling. His black canvas slippers were, he told me, Tai Chi shoes out of China. There were a lot of good things out of China these days: he and Beth had recently swopped their tepi for a yurt. Shine talked about Asian nomads and harmonic shapes as we walked past the lettuces to see it. The label on the door flap said "Pacific Yurts, Oregon". Shine mentioned the New Mexico yurt franchise, craft fairs, a broken-down van. The air inside the yurt was cool and smelt of new plastic. A few butterflies were fluttering against clear panels in the roof. Shine and the kids said, "Bugs!" and shooed them out.

At supper we joined hands round the table. I do not say grace myself and gritted my teeth, but instead of a prayer Galen – aged four – looked up and said: "Can I do the E?"

When Beth said yes he almost lifted himself out of his chair. He pulled in an enormous breath, held it briefly, then, "Eeeeeeeeeeeee . . . " It came out like a minute tornado. We all did one, down to the last gasp, and flopped, laughing, on the table. I'd been getting a bit fed up with Yurts and Cosmic Energy.

Shine sipped water as we ate and talked about rock climbing. He and Beth had done most of the classic ascents in North America. Like me he'd been born on a small dairy farm, which brought him to the subject of his father.

"An intense man," said Shine. "Always right there, always sharp-focused in Now. 'Now's all there is' – I can still hear him sayin' it – 'now's all you control. There's no yesterday, no tomorrow except in the mind. Now's the real power to what's going on.' "

"What about your children?" I said. "What about a tomorrow for them?"

Shine laughed. "What they're gonna do, what they're gonna think, I have no idea. I don't even know what they'll be needin' twenty years from now. But if they just have the self-confidence to be with nature and their creator and to love their fellow-man it doesn't matter what they do; it doesn't matter what they choose. To love, that's the best thing to learn."

I left the following morning. A few hours beyond Shine's place was another old ranchstead, this one right by the road. I recognized the guy greasing the old windpump as McGee from the day before.

"Figured you'd be coming this way," he said. "Don't get a lot come by. Last two was in March. Sisters. They was facing some real bad snow, so I says why doncha hole up here for a whiles but they didn't hardly stop for a coffee." McGee looked wistful. "Must be someplace by now though, I guess."

14 Pie Town to I–66

Pie Town to Continental Divide took seven days altogether, and I stuck to the Divide the whole way. I saw buzzards in the distance, mule deer and spindly jackrabbits, but the only animal I observed closely was a four-foot-long bull snake, banded yellow and black like a wasp. Bull snakes aren't poisonous. This one was lying in the middle of the road and hissed as I picked it up, but when I got the microphone out to record it, it shut up completely.

A pick-up overtook me and stopped. The driver stuck his head out of the window.

"Saw you aways back," he said. "Thought you was a cow."

He'd seen me as a black dot miles down the road – evidently on foot, therefore a cow – and so he'd saddled up a horse and trailed it out here to catch me. Next day I saw how this catching was done. I could see the dust of another pick-up rattling towards me and waited for it by a fence. The driver's name was William. He stopped, led his horse from the trailer and strapped on his chaps. A denim jacket was rolled behind the saddle. "Wire's down back in the trees," he said. "Manager's bringing in a loose steer."

I looked up to see a horseman trotting down the fence line. He was slowly swinging a rope, the steer keeping just ahead. William eased his horse forward, uncoiling his own lariat as he went. The two white loops looked well as they dropped across the steer's dark flanks. Chatting casually, William and the manager walked the animal towards the trailer. They passed the ropes around the stanchions at the front, nudged their mounts and the steer was aboard. I'd hardly noticed how they'd done it, and the steer hadn't a clue. I love watching people doing something they're really good at.

"Fifty per cent's down to your mount," said William, "and thisn here now's my own. Quarter horse is what he is. Starts looking for cows soon as you get on his back. You don't have to encourage an animal like him to do nothing."

For the next fifty miles I got no encouragement either. I just walked, for mile after mesmerizing mile. When on day three from Pie Town a turkey vulture dropped into a roadside tree I almost resented the intrusion. I wasn't due a halt for another half-hour, but I'd have to stop now if I wanted a picture. I sighed and dumped off the pack. Naturally the vulture flew off, and with it the last of my holiday mood.

I'd been walking for three weeks by this time, and had covered three hundred miles – a half million footsteps, my legs thin metronomes. Tick – raw hips. Tock – raw back. Tick – eyes stinging with sweat. What was that stuff Shine had mentioned about Now being all there is? Now to me was toilsome discomfort. It lasted all day – twelve or fourteen hours – and I did anything I could to avoid it. I'd drift along for hours with my head full of comforting guff, one internal channel running highlights of past love affairs, another showing read-your-stars stuff: What would I be doing a year from now? . . . how far was the next tree?

Thoughts, when they came, condensed round some strange nucleii. Octopuses, for example, though I've no idea why. Tall bit of sage, that. There's an old tyre. Ah yes! Octopi are just like rubber bands. That'll do. Octopi are just like rubber bands. Sands? . . . Glands? Yes, glands. All covered in suckers and glands. I stopped for a brew. Changed my socks. What rhymes with glands? Another half hour through scattered piñons, then, Hands! Hands rhymes with glands. Sexy, flexy. That cheered me up. I actually burst out laughing:

> Octopi are just like rubber bands
> All covered in suckers and glands
> It makes me feel sexy
> To think of those flexy
> Hands hands hands hands hands hands hands hands!

Orqueta, Lobo, Americano, Comadre – the plains had developed a rash. Long-dead sinter cones were strung along the Divide like a join-up-the dots children's game. It took two full days' walking to complete the line.

No more than two or three hundred feet high, the dished crowns and black flanks of the little hillocks were lightly hairy with pine, though the last heap, sixty miles on from Pie Town, was bare. The Divide ran up one loosely cindered flank, half circled the crater, and pitched north down the far side. Cerro Bandera was a small but textbook volcano. It was also privately owned.

"Saw the potential way back," said the guy at the visitors' centre. He'd been operating his "Land of Ice and Fire" for the past thirty-five years. "And now the government wants it."

The National Monuments people were offering compensation, he said, but – and I was pinned to the gift-shop door for nearly an hour – it sounded as if a long court case was coming up. Who'd busted the access through the lava? Erected railings like the insurance had asked? Set up the benches, the picnic tables; built the overnight cabins? Where was the government then? Thirty-five years, he'd been here, and by the time I escaped I felt as if I had been too. But his wife was still bubbly, a real contrast in personality. She gave me a copy of her poems from a pile unsold by the till. The crater and the ice caves loomed over the first few pages – satanic cenotaph, omnipotent furies and so forth – but, as I read on, the poems began to speak. They'd seen the potential too. Still did. She loved him.

I climbed Bandera to catch the sunrise and could see all the way back beyond Pie Town – the volcanic pimples, the pines and the sage, the lava spread out like black toffee. The Spaniards had called the area El Malpais, the badlands, so shattered and raw that they'd had to detour all the way round it.

The year was 1540. Mexico, Peru, the Carribbean overrun, and where could a young caballero go? Northward of course, with Francisco Coronado, chasing rumours of a new El Dorado. A wandering priest, Friar Marcos de Niza, had seen it glittering up there in the waste and had returned with reports of six similar places – the Seven Cities of Cibola, bulging with turquoise and silver. Why shouldn't more troves exist? Aztec gold and Inca silver were flooding back to Spain by the shipful, though having ridden over a thousand miles Coronado and his men had so far found nothing.

But the army was getting warmer, because, immediately below Bandera crater, runs a very ancient roadway indeed – the Cibola trail, linking the pueblos of Acoma and Zuni, the two most sophisticated indigenous settlements ever found in the United States. The Spaniards weren't archaeologists though, and one look at Zuni was enough – "all crumpled together", one chronicler wrote. "There are ranch houses in New Spain which make a better appearance. Such were the curses hurled at Friar Marcos' head that I pray God may protect him."

Undeterred, the expedition trailed on north. They'd been riding hard for six months by now and were bound to find something good soon. But they didn't. A month onto the great plains – they got as far as present-day Kansas City – turned up no more than a few Comanche bands and tedious quantities of bison, "the most monstrous thing in the way of animals ever seen or read about". They shot a few for food and turned back. The first serious attempts to colonize the Rio Grande valley weren't made for another forty years, and Santa Fé, the state capital, was eventually established in 1609. As such, it is the oldest city in North America.

Empty roads give a strange sense of holiday, and at that early hour New Mexico # 53, heir to the Cibola trail, was deserted. But I didn't stop and, ignoring a dirt track criss-crossing the slope ahead, ploughed straight on up through the trees, a half-hour on full revs to burn off the languor of the plains. Blood vessels roaring, I sat on the steps of the hill-top fire tower to recover. A guy stepped onto the catwalk above, yawned, and shouted for me to come up.

The cabin was the size of a cable car, with a map table set in the middle. Despite the heavily overcast sky you could see for miles in all directions – Mount Taylor, an hour's drive to the east; Bandera a dot to the south. The main fire hazard lay to the north, along the forested slopes of the Zunis, a confusion of hogbacks and parallel troughs running up towards route # 66. I would follow the crest line – the Oso Ridge – for the next two and a half days.

"Classic anticline," said Wayne, who was studying geology.

So the universities had broken up! It hadn't even been examination time when I'd left Antelope Wells.

I was still looking hard through the metal framed windows but couldn't see an anticline.

"Precambrian core," said Wayne. "Granites and metavolcanics."

"What, that high bit with the trees?"

"Right. Runs northwest-southeast."

It was obvious when you had it explained: the cigar-shaped core, like a submarine, surfacing through the sedimentaries of the plains. Why couldn't I have seen it myself?

"What you've come through so far's been a mess," said Wayne. "A lot of faulted volcanics and quaternary deposits all mixed up together. But you get through the Zunis it turns out real neat – regular changes, scarps and dips, getting younger as you go north."

I did another six miles that afternoon, picking my way along the slabby rocks of the Oso ridge. I kept stubbing my feet, unused to the irregular surface, pine needles and fragments of crinkly lichen in my socks. The forested ridge was broad and gave little sense of elevations, though sometimes I caught flashes of pink through the trees – the distant escarpments Wayne had described – and, below me on either side of the ridge, a hint of wet, boggy valleys. Low cloud snagged the long ridges and it actually drizzled for an hour, just hard enough for me to break out my wet-proof jacket. I crinkled along, feeling half naked in my shorts, then put the jacket away. This was its only outing in New Mexico.

I lay on a wet slab, permian sandstone as it happened, pulling in the sharp evening air, the sun a red axle sinking inexorably west. Wisps of steam curled off the damp rock and insects flimsy as cigarette ash began to dance. One landed on my arm. I went to brush it off and crushed it by mistake, a kind of small moth I think. A half dozen jays flew up from the darkening valley. They made a clumsy landing in stiff branches on a level with my slab. When I reached out to touch them they squawked and flew away, arms up, arms down, like prisoners doing PT. I laughed as I slid into my bag.

15 Continental Divide

Coming off the ridge on May 30th I lost fifteen hundred feet in altitude and was back into sage brush once more. By midday I'd reached route # 66, striking the highway at a straggle of motels and gas stations actually called Continental Divide. The place looked like a gauntlet of hitch-hikers, each with some gimmick in winking neon to persuade the traffic to stop: electric punctuation on a landscape which itself was wordless.

There were times, here in the New World, when I felt despairingly European. I needed the comforts of history, the muddled adaptations of ancient landscapes. I wearied of relentless utility. For a moment, crossing the motorway bridge, I became a Celt on a hill top. I understood why, when the Romans left Britain, their wonderful roads were ignored. Roman roads were simply objects, vehicles in themselves. But tribal paths aren't like that. They don't have fixed widths, they allow you to stray, they evolve with the people who use them. And this disconcerted me about America: religions, diets, whatever you like – people were forever jumping into vehicles and driving off at high speed. Life here was first established, then lived. Back home it was the other way round.

Gene Gonzales' Continental Divide Grocery (Indian Jewellery Wholesale) was really quite shabby – ordinary strip lights, a glass-fronted fridge, wooden shelves of canned food, TV magazines on the counter – but glancing up at the ceiling I found the comfort I sought. I made two quick guesses – first that Mr Gonzales had built the place himself, and second that it was Navajo. I got five out of ten. It was Navajo, but it had been built by Mr Gonzales' uncle. I'd not seen this construction before – doomed, like Shine's yurt, but of cantilevered logs, rough-cut, knotted and grained; not beautiful, not square, not convenient, not clean, not even waterproof by the look of the streaks down the walls. In Washington I'd done a bit of sightseeing, but this shabby little store, with its funny log roof, struck a far deeper chord than the White House.

Wind teased dust from the dirt strip between the highway and the railroad. Continental Divide had probably been established first as a mile camp. Mr Gonzales led me round to his shed, dropped the chain and jammed the door open with a stone. A spot of rain hit my cheek. I held out my hand and looked at the sky.

"You feel rain?" said Mr Gonzales from inside the shed. He handed me out my box. "Least it is not snowing." His first language was Navajo. "Couple of girls did reach here two months back. They was bad frozen up. They stayed in a motel down the road a coupla days but they did finish their rest and go on."

These must have been the sisters that McGee had mentioned. Canadians, Mr Gonzales said. Short little feet. I wondered if I'd run into them, though an eight-week start and the many possible permutations of route made it seem very unlikely.

"Two guys rode through last year," Mr Gonzales was saying. "Come all the way up from Durango in Old Mexico. They had a fist fight in the bar – can't know why, but they never rode no further. Just arguing, I guess."

The Top o' the World Bar was a three-minute walk up the service road. A few pick-ups were parked outside. Weeds were growing round the door. What was it about bars that made them different from pubs? This one had no windows at all, just a door in blank breeze-block walls. Drinking is like that in the States. It rears awkwardly, less a reward than a pursuit. Americans, I remembered, do not confer. They convene, and their bars reflect this. They are facilities which make drinking possible, whereas pubs are amenities which make it pleasant.

The Top o' the World had no garden of course, not even a tub by the entrance. The afternoon glare mingled briefly with the gloom as I opened and closed the door. I saw impassive faces, all in a row, and loose bodies sacked onto bar stools; two females, artlessly fat; cheap clothes, loose threads – my eyes had adjusted to the pool table moonlight. Outside it was a Monday afternoon. In here time was suspended; a kind of theatre, another make-believe. Pubs aren't make-believe. Landlords live in them, actual people, with kids in bed upstairs; locals moan about closing time and the quality of the beer. But I was romanticizing. All I wanted in here was the phone. It was right by the jukebox so I had to ask Connie to shout.

"Where are you?" she yelled.

"Route # 66 – the guy with the grocery store."

"Sounds like he's happy to see you. I've got to be in Albuquerque next week. You want to take a day off?"

A week would get me to my next pick up point, a small place called Regina, eighty miles short of the Colorado state line and only two hours by bus from the city. By the time I got there I'd be needing a rest, as well as replacement shorts. I was fed up with the rolled-up long trousers.

"Yeah," I shouted. "I'll meet you at the airport."

As I put the phone down I heard a dull thud and turned round. One of the girls had fallen off her stool.

I went back to the shed and began to sort out the food. I was looking forward to seeing Connie.

Mr Gonzales' son sat beside his tape-recorder and watched as I opened the box. He knew that I was walking all the way through the States, though right now I was sitting in an abandoned lot with jam all over my trousers. I felt I was letting him down. I should have been cleaning a rifle or something, telling the boy things he'd never forget, stuff about whuppin' fellas in fair fights and cuttin' the tops off cactii when you're starvin' thirsty – not asking him to pass me a J-cloth. But then he actually lived here. He asked if it were true the British don't have commercials on TV, asked me what music I liked, told me about his sheep – he had four – and mentioned the Navajo farm club he belonged to at school. For a kid of eleven he knew an awful lot about wool prices. He broke off as a freight train went past, clang-clang-clang-clang, vehicles, clang-clang, chemicals, roadstone, boxed crates, clang-clang-clang, Atchison, Topeka and Santa Fé, destinations chalked on box car doors, 123 . . . 124 . . . 125 . . . 126 . . . , then a fat man came round the corner.

"Hi," he said. "My name's Robert E. Sandberg. I'm a radio amateur and for instance I have about 285 various countries all over the world I have talked to and have confirmed on my amateur radio equipment for instance I talk to people in Great Britain quite often, one man in particular I talk to two or three times a week and tonight or tomorrow night if the weather conditions around the world permit I will call him and let him know how you've got along and he can pass the word out that you're safe and you did make it to Continental Divide, New Mexico, for instance and you've covered 400 miles and have 2000 to go."

Mr Sandberg looked at Mr Gonzales' son.

"You want a lift to your grandmother's?"

"Ya."

"OK."

At the post office next morning I ran into Mr Sandberg again. He was sorry he hadn't got through to Great Britain, he said, but he'd be trying again that night. I asked him what radio amateurs talked about over the air.

"Talk about? Uh, we talk about the weather, the types of equipment we have, our families, for instance four a.m. this morning I was talking to a Norwegian lady on Pitcairn Island and she's fine, then I picked up a guy in Missouri asking when the communists are gonna quit Afghanistan which you can't reasonably do if you're transmitting to Russia as he was and I spent six Christmases in Vietnam myself but there's things the Soviets can't talk about then on comes a guy from British Columbia – I've been talking to him for years – he's got eighteen kids and thirty-five grandchildren. Gotta get up there and see what he looks like sometime. Maybe take the camper this summer."

It was time to get going again. I walked down to Sturkey's rest stop for breakfast and stupified myself with a plateful of hashbrowns and waffles. The bill lay in a ring of wet coffee. I lit a cigarette and stared across the forecourt. The plate-glass muffled most of the sounds, but I heard them anyway in my head – mesmerizing familiarity, guys pulling up for gas and doing exactly what I'd do, yawning, slamming doors, scratching their balls, holding dip-sticks away from their trousers; women tweaking their skirts coming out of the rest-room, kids tugging at arms going in. It was so nice just to loll in the surf like this, ignoring, from this cluttered table-top, the escarpment looming beyond the highway. Leaving Sturkey's was like getting out of bed.

I pampered myself for a further ten minutes. I'd planned on only five but was held up in the gents, eavesdropping, as one does, on the comings and goings around me. The outer door let in a draught and the chink of plates. Two sets of footprints crossed the tiled floor and I was privy to the following snippet:

"You wanna poo?"

"No."

"Well try. I'm not gonna stop again."

I delayed coming out till they'd gone.

16 The Navajo

The cliff north of Sturkey's was a palisade of triassic sandstone, horizontally bedded and porous enough to show palmprints of sweat as I climbed. At the top I met a girl called Dolores. She was walking along with a carrier-bag and a four-month-old baby. She looked very poor and spoke hardly any English, but she taught me the Navajo words for "Hallo", and, when she turned off the trail, for "Goodbye". I've no idea where she had come from or where she was going. When I looked back she had become a solitary blip, then she vanished.

In the late afternoon an old truck crossed the plain ahead, trailing behind it its quota of dust. It was headed for an isolated shack. One vehicle, one shack, an immense, bald sweep of bare sage. A landscape too wide for surprises. I saw the dust disperse, the truck door slam, two wagging specks bound up to the driver. The shack door winked open. And shut. And that was Navajo land. Shacks on a landscape. I caught a whiff of dead horse where I halted that night and that was Navajo land too. I wandered across it for the next five days.

Next morning I followed the same line of fence posts for miles. The wire was down so I passed the time by slaloming from side to side. I came to a circular hut of neatly dressed stone, the domed roof again of cantilevered logs, except that the mud plaster had fallen away leaving a lovely pattern of sapphire-blue chinks between the interlocking beams.

At noon I heard a vehicle ahead – stuck by the sound of it. A man in blue slacks and platform-heeled shoes was trying to get it out. His name was Andy Bodie. When he took off his baseball cap to wipe his forehead I saw that he had a short pigtail. The wheels spat sand as he raced the engine again, but my weight on the back made no difference.

"OK," said Andy. "My uncle and cousin'll be over sometime. Let's just get the water off."

Andy's shoes looked a bit out of place as we kicked the two heavy drums off the truck – a mild surprise, not quite what an ordinary American, a United Statesian, would wear in these circumstances. And Dolores, the girl with the carrier-bag and the baby, she had made my mind blink as well. Nearly all the Indians I met did that in one way or another. They gave normality a subtle twist. We'd been rolling the water barrels for about fifty yards when I realized that Andy had two shirts on, both of them normal, long-sleeved cotton shirts, but one buttoned over the other. That weird twist again.

I shivered. Hallo Earth, hallo Earth, this is Moonbase One. Moonbase One calling Earth. Aliens in the airlock! WE HAVE ALIENS IN THE AIRLOCK. Apparently human . . . fooled all the guards . . . oh my God! (sizzle of krypton gun) . . . the shirts . . . they're wearing two shir . . . (Loud explosion. Transmission ends.)

We heaved the water drums upright against a couple of gnarled junipers, the only trees for miles. A rifle hung from the branches of one, a TV aerial stuck out of the other. The cable ran across the dirt ground, past a pair of truck batteries, and under a bright yellow awning. A rickety table stood outside the shelter, the bare boards stacked with unmatched pots and pans, and behind the table was a stove – an old oil drum sawn in half with a rolled sheet of tin for a flue. The breeze fluffed at wood ash round the base of the stove and rustled the yellow tarpaulin. Sky, sage and a yellow tarpaulin – that's all this place seemed to be, the TV aerial in the tree the only visible connection with anywhere else in the world.

Outwardly, the camp might have been set up by a couple of hippies – there were enough bits of junk lying around – but the disquieting, two-shirt twist ran through even that. This was not a substitute house. There were no familiar shrines – a television, it is true, but no book shelves, no photos, no clocks, no house plants, no alternative energy sources. Alternative to what? These people, whoever they were, were coming from a different direction. There were no breatharian diets or fermented bean rissoles either. Andy had offered lamb stew.

The tarpaulin cast a restful glow under the awning. There were blankets and old sacks on the floor. Andy's cousin Kathleen was watching a hospital soap opera from a low divan (there was no other furniture) and her baby was asleep on the ground. She said something to Andy in Navajo.

"She wants to know if you have a camera."

I opened the bag.

"So will you take a picture of Adrian?"

I would have paid to take a picture of Adrian. He looked like a miniscule Genghis Khan, impassive as Kathleen picked him up. She had a post office box number for me to send the pictures to, somewhere not on my map. I reloaded the camera twice, blazing away at everything in sight.

But somehow I missed the mark. When I eventually saw them, my pictures showed only a scruffy old campsite and a load of castoff junk – a muddle of symbols, more mockery than explanation. I heard a tinkle of bells on the wind. Andy's mother was bringing in the sheep.

"This is her place," he said, "that she got from her mother. There's another place northeast of here where we plant our corns, and between them whichever has grass the most we move."

The animals were nibbling their way towards us, the kind of sheep that look exactly like goats. Andy said that they had to be rounded up every two hours or they'd blow themselves out. On this? Even the jackrabbits looked hungry. But I didn't get a chance to take this further because an old lady had ridden up and dismounted.

"That's her," said Andy. "My mother. She's seventy-three years old."

I knew that face. I'd seen it staring from the pages of every book on Indians ever written. I restrained an impulse to dive straight in for the camera and we shook hands. Nan Nez Bah asked, through Andy, if I had eaten, then turned back to the sheep. She just sat on the edge of a battered dustbin and watched them. I watched her. She wasn't just old, she was ethnic. Her clothes were straight from "How the West was Won". When the Navajo were incarcerated at Fort Sumner in the 1860s the women had adopted the Mother Hubbard skirts and blouses they saw worn by the army wives. Nan Nez Bah's generation were still in them. Wide bands of turquoise encircled her wrists, the silver mountings worn paper thin.

"She had that since she was a girl," Andy said. "At the time she first remembers how to herd sheep. And for being such a good shepherder and a nice gal her mother and her father give her these so she can be proud of them. But now all people do is live in houses and speak English and it's very hard for my mother to understand. That's how come it's puzzle for her when she goes to the store and we have to translate most of the words.''

He nodded at the resting sheep. "That's her life right there. That's all she live with – sheep, lambs, nothing else. She cannot even spend a day or two away from the sheep because that's what her life was when she was a little girl and ever since then she's stuck to it.''

I'd been here less than forty minutes: the embedded pick-up, the water barrels, the rifle in one tree, the TV aerial in the other, the arid sweep of the plains; an old Indian lady riding in with her sheep, spinning wool now, crosslegged on the ground, a twist of fleece in her left hand, the rough yarn coiling round the weighted spindle in her right; the hospital soap still going strong in the corner. I wasn't sure what to make of it all. I'm a sucker for ethnicity – old ladies with rifles get my vote every time, especially if they can't speak English and they cook lamb stew out of doors. It's what I call the inglenook syndrome – native is noble; history is good; never mind the worm holes, feel the grain.

And the grain did run deep. Indians were definitely different. But was this good, or bad, or the white man's burden, or what? I didn't know. In the end it was all part of the show, perfect the way it was.

I lay on the ground, chin propped in my hands, watching a dung-coloured bee. I'd stopped beside a dirt road an hour beyond the Bodie's encampment and was having a rest. The wind dropped for a moment and, seizing its chance, the bee zoomed into land, snuffling through a tuft of purple locoweed until its rompers were bulging with pollen. It took off again and was whisked south in the direction of a shallow lake. I'd assumed that the bedrock here was porous sandstone still, but checking the map I saw it was impervious shale. Hence the lake. Then I looked up locoweed in my flower book. "*Astragalus pershii*," it said. "Has the ability to absorb selenium from shale soils . . . loss of stock may result." Shale – Selenium – Nan Nez Bah bringing in the sheep every two hours. I lay in the sage, enjoying the unexpected connections.

A vehicle stopped as I was setting off again and the dust swirled into my eyes. The driver's hair was yellow – he obviously wasn't Navajo –

and he smelt faintly of disinfectant, though I'm not sure if I'd noticed
that before or after he told me what he did. He was the Indian Agency
public health nurse, and his name was Gary. The wind was gusting
hard by now and I tucked myself behind the open cab door as we
spoke. Gary poured himself a coffee from his dashboard thermos.

"No one offered you a ride yet?" he asked.

"Lots of people have."

"So what do you say to them?"

"I say thanks very much. Then we usually chat for a while, and then
they drive off."

Gary sipped his coffee – he didn't smoke – and I answered the usual
questions: what did I eat; how much did I carry; how far did I walk
each day; then, "How d'you afford nine months off work?" he asked.

I didn't mind this question – I'm always curious about money myself
– and was well into my stride, banging on about loans and long-term
savings, before I realized that Gary wasn't listening. He looked more
disappointed than bored. I could see in his eyes that he didn't want
the real answer. He would have preferred me to be adventuring on
the strength of some windfall – a lottery win, an inheritance perhaps,
anything to put this journey of mine beyond his own reach. A clapped-
out truck rattled past and an empty bottle flew out of the window.

"That's the main cause of death around here," Gary said. "Drink
and car wrecks. Same on all reservations. The latest theory on it is
there's not enough zinc in the water."

"That sounds like a load of crap," I said.

"Probably is," said Gary, "but it sounds good and I have to work
here. In any case the Navajo are in better shape than most. They have
more clout than all the other groups put together."

"Why?" I asked.

"Well it isn't money. They've got an oil field but their per capita
royalties are nothing compared to what some groups get. Maybe it's
their numbers – about 160,000 spread through Arizona and New
Mexico – or maybe it's the women. The inheritance goes down from
mothers to daughters." Gary swilled the coffee grounds from the cup
and screwed it back on the thermos. He was looking for something in
the glove compartment. "Thought I might have some stuff for that
nose," he said. I stuck my face into the wing mirror.

"It's always like that," I said.

"You boil all your water?"

"What's that got to do with my nose?"

"Nothing," said Gary. "But if you don't you're at risk from Giardia.

Knocks the shit right outa your pants. Anyway, if you want skin cream there's a trading post at Borrego Pass. People's name is Don and Fern Smauss."

Gary's brake lights came on about forty yards down the road.

"Forgot to warn you," he yelled against the wind. "Don't step into any prairie dog holes. They carry the plague."

Ha ha. I was standing on a dog town right there.

Borrego Pass was another fourteen miles along the Divide. I was tired when I got there, but braced myself at the door: "Vote Dunkin for Sheriff" said the poster. "Veteran World War II". The gas pumps looked like defaulters rigid in the sun.

There was an old trolley-type weighing machine on the stoop with the week's wool prices chalked up beside it. The platform wobbled as I slid the weights along the bar – I'd lost seven pounds since leaving California.

The stack of wire baskets under Dunkin's poster (Dunkin really looked mean; I wondered which side he'd been on) was low so I wasn't surprised as I pushed through the door to see the store crowded.

"Fusht of the mummf," said Fern Smauss, who was eating sunflower seeds. "Welfare check day."

I parked myself on a pile of cement bags, nibbling round the bad bit of a peach. Borrego Pass wasn't good for fresh fruit but it didn't matter. Don and Fern had been here for over fifty years and watching them was an absolute treat.

A trolley jam had developed round the hardware counter as Fern was speaking – a bunch of guys in not much of a hurry, leaning on handles, chatting, chewing gum, pushing back their caps with their thumbs. Then a little old lady pattered out from between the stacks. She glared at the hold-up and trilled something fierce in Navajo. Grinning placidly, the guys dispersed with their trolleys, baseball hats and plump shoulders visible over the aisles as each ambled after a hidden granny. Son or grandson in tow, the little ladies would eventually pop out near the checkout. There were only two tills, both on the one counter.

"You got that, Don?" Fern's spectacles were like old, brown windows. "Four gallons of reg'lar" – she turned to the diminutive, headscarved figure at the counter – "reg'lar, right? Four gallons of reg'lar on Estella's account."

But Don was holding a blister pack of spark plugs up to the light. "One-O-One stroke . . . is that a seven?"

"Four of reg'lar . . . "

". . . seven nine? That should fit a seventy-eight as well. What was that on Estella's account?"

"Four of reg'lar," said the guy buying the plugs.

Fern was on the till nearest me. She punched the buttons with her sunflower seed hand and collected wet shells in the other. Every so often she would swallow prematurely, nudge a packet with her elbow and bark, "Wassat say, Freddy?" at a youth leaning on the counter. I don't think he worked there. It was a busy day and he just happened to be around. Fern must have known everyone in the store from birth. No one actually paid, the totals – "wassit come to, Freddy?" – were just jotted on account cards kept under the till, though one lady got credit for a handwoven rug she'd brought in.

"We're moshly buying wool right now," said Fern. "Later ish lamsh and cowsh." She spat out the sunflower husks. Mr Smauss, she said, had tried to improve the stock over the years by bringing in good breeding rams, but the quality was slipping back. Fern and Freddy worked through a couple more trolleys, then: "Where did you say you were from, young man?"

"England," I said.

"Well my grandfather was from England. He was a convert to the Mormon Church but his uncle was the Bishop of London and he told my grandfather to get out of there so he came to America. The Mormon Church made my grandfather what they call a colonizer – all over Arizona and Old Mexico – but we were driven out by Pancho Villa. You heard of him? Then my father settled near here just after I was born so I've lived on a reservation all my life. And I can tell you this welfare programme has ruined our Navajo people. They used to be an industrious people. They used to weave. They made beautiful silverwork and they had herds of fine sheep, but now they don't hardly have any. They don't want to do anything but ride up and down in cars."

Weren't the welfare checks going straight into the Smauss' tills?

"It's business," said Fern. "But it's not the right kind of business. We believe in doing what our heavenly father wants us to do – God, if only you know who I mean – and what did he tell the people? He told them to go out and earn their bread by the sweat of their brow. That's what the Lord told Adam, wasn't it? Well our Navajo people aren't earning it by the sweat of their brow. They're just getting it for nothing and we don't like it."

I asked Fern if she actually felt herself to be Navajo.

"No," she said. "I'm just a white girl that's lived with them all her life. But it's true I don't feel comfortable with a bunch of white folks around. Only white guy I've ever lived with is this one." Don peered over his glasses and did a little whoop. "We've been married fifty-five years."

I didn't walk much further that evening but unrolled the mat in a clump of piñons and read the *Navajo Times:* births, marriages, deaths, Jumbo Toilet Tissue $1.98. It was cold. Blowing steam off my tea I lay in my bag and watched the stars coming out. I was about halfway across the reservation. I'd covered about 430 miles by now and May had slipped into June. When I set off next morning I noticed that the evening primroses, so fresh and white when I'd set out from the border, were dying.

The Divide dipped out of the haze and into an oil field. For the first mile the smell made me want to throw up, but I got used to it and quite enjoyed the sight of the dozens of pumps, quacking up, quacking down like mechanical ducks. The brown-stained dirt road led past a shed where guys in overalls and work gloves were cleaning a truck. Most had thick, black braids hanging out of their plastic hard hats. The radio was tuned to a Navajo station. The manager offered me a sandwich and we chatted for about half an hour – a bit about the oil field (it had been running since 1928, employed fourteen men and produced 1000 barrels a day), and quite alot about the "Benny Hill Show".

"Benny Hill is networked in England?"

The manager sounded surprised.

"It's an English programme," I said.

"Yeah, I know, but that kinda stuff really gets put out over there?"

"Nationwide," I said.

"Jeez," said the manager. "Maybe that's how come it's shown over here. I mean you never get that much, er, that much on an American show."

The road became sandy-white once again. Distant escarpments rose, sphinx-like through the haze. I was overtaken by an orange school bus. The driver waved, the kids waved, I waved. I saw it again, miles away, making stops all over the landscape.

Next day I saw a dark lump two miles off and changed course to take a look. Two miles wasn't far any more. I ducked through a fence, hit a path not much used, and looked up.

Car stickers and T-shirts and re-enacted gun fights notwithstanding, out here in the west history skated on pretty thin ice, a franchised posse, flabby with national honour. But at Pueblo Pintado the ice simply gave way. This wasn't just another log cabin ahead, nor the vaingloriously trumpeted site of a sordid massacre. No franchises, no car parks. Just lizards and spiders, and the ruins looming out of the sage. I'd been expecting broken adobe; collapsed timbers; perhaps a few rusty tin cans; but close to I saw walls three stories high. They were built of cleft sandstone slabbed row upon row, a skin of extraordinary beauty. The casements and portals threw unblemished shadows. Even the sockets where floor beams had rested were still perfectly aligned. The sky said nothing; the wind whispered unimpeded across the vast, dry sweeps of sage. This beautiful ruin had been abandoned long before Columbus was born. There were no signboards. It had nothing to do with the United States whatsoever.

The ruins fell away at a steady three miles an hour; the detour had cost me six miles. On a journey like this everything had a value in miles. However I tried, there was no escaping this insidious economy.

The landscape became a confusion of mudstones and shales. Residual hills, flat-capped, salt-white, broke the northern horizon. The eroded gullies which furrowed the plain were dry as a bone. There had been no running water for the last 200 miles; I'd squat to drink from broad, shallow pans, shoulders hunched as I watched sediments settle in my cupped hands. Fluctuating and desolate, these lakes had no life of their own. They came and went with the rains, the protruding tips of drowned grasses waving from the sticky margins. Sometimes I'd see long-legged birds, hear the dee-dee of a killdeer over the wavelets, but that was all. The wind moaned constantly, my eyes red with the dust. I'd tighten my chest and send globules of phlegm spinning into the sage, satisfyingly viscous as they dangled, glistening, in the sun.

Somewhere out here a line had been drawn between the Navajo and the Jicarilla Apache, not that I gave a toss where it was. I'd not seen a soul now for two days; it was almost dark; I felt dreadful. Perhaps I'd had too much sun. I flopped down where I was and hoped I'd feel better in the morning. I was summoning the energy to assemble the stove when a dog came bounding through the scrub, leapt the rucksack, and licked me right in the face. Fuck off, dog – I'm ill. Another dog jumped on my legs, and a few moments later I was being stared down at by a man on a horse. He was an indian, but not a Navajo.

I enjoyed this subconsciously acquired knowledge. You don't have to think why you know that someone is French, for example, or German or English or Dutch – you just do know, and this guy's face didn't fit the Navajo template I'd unconsciously established in my mind. Which meant he was a Jicarilla, and the Jicarillas had written to say they had no plans for hikers – i.e. keep off the reservation. But Alvarido had just trotted over out of curiosity. He'd seen me an hour earlier, he said, but he'd been checking his stock and he knew his dogs would find me when he sent them off to look. I was swaying on my feet through this preamble, but perked up slightly when he mentioned his daughters. He had six.

"They can forget being Apache no more," he said. "Sent them all to school in Santa Fé. Do the hair, I tell them, make the tribal fiestas – that's OK, but leave it there. These reservations're like safari parks. You stay, I tell my girls, you gonna rot in perfect security."

This was interesting stuff, but I had to sit down again. I used the dogs as an excuse, squatting on my haunches and making a fuss of them both to hide how grotty I felt.

"Too rich," Alvarido was saying. "We got too much money for a small tribe. We don't work. We don't have to. We're just like the Arabs. Junked cars, empty bottles – that just about says it all."

Despite the daughters I was sincerely hoping that he wouldn't invite me back to his house. I didn't want to be ill in front of his entire family, not having claimed I was walking to Canada. But I'd have to watch that. Public images tend to foster private delusions, and while in New Mexico – hot, flat and dry – I might get away with delusions, high in the Rockies – cold, slippery and wet – I would not.

But by dawn I had recovered. The night had been slicingly cold and for the first time I woke to find ice in the waterbag. I set off at six, nearly trod on a badger, and by eight was sweating up to the lip of a wooded escarpment. Having spent the past six days crawling across the king-sized double bed that was the San Juan basin, I was now overlooking the gap between the mattress and the wall. The rocks, untucked here and there, had, so far, been more or less flat, but the forested hills rising ahead were the first hints of the real mountains to come, though not, as yet, major crests. The faulted valley at my feet would channel me north the remaining eighty miles to the Colorado state line where the climbing would begin in earnest. Right now I had to descend. Regina, my fourth food pick up point, was the gas station on the county road running through the scrub below. I planned to leave the pack there for a couple of days while I took a break in Albuquerque with Connie.

17 More Food

I spent what was left of the afternoon talking to Virginia, the lady who owned the gas station. Every time a customer came in she'd say, "Know what? This boy's walked clear from Old Mexico!" and I'd bite hard on my Good-n-Fast sandwich. When she went over the road to fix something for George I had the place to myself. George had had a stroke and couldn't do much anymore. Later on he shuffled over and sat in a chair with his mouth open, but I couldn't understand what he was trying to say. Nobody really spoke to him: it was "Hi, Virginia, how's George?" and she'd say, "Not bad today," or, "He's doing OK." I liked Virginia. I spent the night in her barn.

The morning sun threw my shadow across the steaming road. There had been a tremendous rainstorm during the night, and the Albuquerque bus was two hours late due to flooding. When it finally turned up it was full. I sat on the floor, talking to a data processor most of the way, but she had a seat so I got a crick in my neck.

Sitting on the floor was a good way to get rid of my apprehension though. Cities are handy for buying shorts and so forth, but they aren't environments in which I feel naturally comfortable. I always brace myself to some extent as I approach one. But Albuquerque looked OK – a low, sprawling place, pseudo-Spanish in style, mostly painted light brown. I was looking up camping shops in the *Yellow Pages* when a guy came waddling across the bus station concourse. He introduced himself as Jinx.

He said, "Hey man, you're travellin'."

Full marks, Jinx.

"The Good Shepherd Mission's cool if you need a place," he continued, "but, dig man, you gotta look needy. So you leave your stuff in a lock-up here." I hadn't heard anybody say "dig man" in years. "And man, you goin' to the Rainbow Gathering? Like no one organizes it but this year it's in Michigan, July 4th through 6th. Everyone campin' out – coke camps, dope camps, smack camps, whatever. You gotta quarter for some coffee? Yeah? Thanks man. Here, leave you this. Yeah! It's a credit card number. Belongs to a friend of mine. It's cool – he don't mind me using it so you just . . . hey man, where you goin'? . . . hey don't forget now . . . July 4th through 6th . . . ''

I caught a bus to the Coronado Shopping Center, bought a pair of shorts and put them on. Connie was due in the morning, but I didn't bother with the Good Shepherd Mission because a lady at the forestry office, where I'd gone for more maps, invited me back for the night. Her name was Jan and her husband's name was Paul. Since I had a few hours to spare next day they suggested that I take the cable car up to Sandia Peak, overlooking the city from the east, but I missed my chance because I fell asleep in the public library. I was woken by the guard only an hour before Connie's plane was due in and yawned all the way to the airport. Jan and Paul had kept me up until three.

They began the evening with a blank sheet of paper on the supper table. By ten it was covered in pencilled circles: me; them; lots of their friends; their friends' friends; their friends' friends' friends, and so on. But no, this wasn't pyramid sales. This, Steve, was an Opportunity To Succeed. This was Amway Corporation, makers of quality home and personal care products. Thousands of them. The catalogue ran to 200 pages. Amway was to industrial chemistry what *Readers Digest* is to literature – utterly, utterly cosmetic; but by midnight I had become, on paper at least, Amway's latest recruit. A Direct Distributor. Nine more like me and Jan and Paul would become Ruby Direct Distributors. When we ordinary DDs started recruiting our own groups, Jan and Paul would be Pearl DDs. Then Emerald DDs; then Diamond; then, even, Double Diamond. Silk, satin, cotton, rags – Amway was like the Crusades. There was even beatification – look at this, Steve. Paul was flicking through the annual report. It read like a manifesto: Dick and Bunny, previously policeman and homemaker; Chuck and Jean; Frank and Rita – all of them now Crown Ambassadors. And that's Enterprise II. Only five feet shorter than a commercial yacht; first-class all the way. Lookit – Dick and Joyce, previous occupation missionaries: "We thank God every day for our lives in Amway." And – I couldn't resist this one – next time you have a cookout remember this: Amway sold enough aerosol oven cleaner last year to clean up after a barbeque of 75,000,000 steaks. Eaten too much? Need the bathroom? Worried about leaving a pong? Don't be – enough Quiet Breezes' Fragrance Cartridges were sold last fiscal to freshen every home in the state of West Virginia. Enough DrainMate to unclog . . .

God I was tired . . . enough Wonder this, Magic that – I had to go to bed. I dreamt that I was back on the Divide, trapped by rising tides of TriZyme presoak detergent booster. What could I do? Keep going, keep going. Stick to the backbone.

Connie said I'd lost weight. I said she had. We both felt awkward. Being in a motel didn't help, so we left. Connie made a couple of phone calls, I hired a car. We drove up to Denver, roared round a supermarket, turned a motel room into a shambles of empty packets, and, leaving a large tip for the cleaner, hit the road with eleven food boxes sorted and stacked in the boot. Three thousand miles and eleven days later we were back, my chain of supplies complete to the Canadian border.

Thursday, June 16th, one-thirty in the morning. I crept out of the room, but as I got into the taxi I saw a little white face at the window. Kleenex time.

I'd picked up a copy of the *Albuquerque Tribune* at the bus station, but I couldn't really concentrate. I was thinking about the miles that Connie and I had covered – hour after hour at a steady seventy – which I was now about to walk. In Wyoming it had still been snowing. I turned a page – more headlines, nothing very interesting, then:

ARIZONA BOY DIES OF PLAGUE.
A five-year-old boy from the Arizona part of the Navajo reservation has died of Bubonic Plague. In addition to the Arizona case a total of seven plague cases have been confirmed in New Mexico this year . . .

Sorry, Gary!

Sunlight was streaming through chinks in the roof of Virginia's barn. I stuck my head under the tap and went into the office. The stool by the till was empty, but a cigarette was still smouldering in the ashtray.

"Just been to fix coffee for George," she said as she came in. "I was wondering where you'd got to." I explained about making the food drops. The next one was at a place called Creede.

"Creede, Colorado? That's some way."

I hadn't thought much about a route yet, though the eighty miles left up to the state line would be fairly easy. I'd worry about the mountains when I got there.

"They expecting you?" asked Virginia.

"Who?"

"The people in Creede."

"Sometime, I suppose, but they don't have a set date."

"So what happens if you don't show up?"

"They'll probably use the food themselves," I said.

"I mean what happens to you. If they don't know when to expect you how do they know if you're OK?"

It hadn't occurred to me that I wouldn't be OK.

"Well Colorado isn't New Mexico," said Virginia. "I'll be worried."

18 Regina to the State Line

I'd nagged at my legs for seventeen miles and was sitting in the dirt feeling sore. Everything ached. Everything jarred. Everything was a pointless bloody hassle. I stared morosely at the ground. For the past eleven days I'd had people around me; things to read; action, reaction, distraction. Now I hadn't. It took two or three days to get back into my stride, heading always north, the swelling plains wearing dark caps of pine. In place of sage, short grasses stirred in the breeze, and, on the second morning, white topsails of snow broke the horizon.

I passed several lakes – real ones at last, iris and sedges clogging the shallows, and, for the first time, mosquitoes. Insect repellant never seems to work on me. It's much like superglue – infallible till you actually use it – but to my amazement this stuff really did the trick. The mosquitoes were like kamikazis on short strings, jerked to a halt within an ace of striking home. I taunted them for the next two and a half months, till, grounded by the first autumn frosts, they left me alone.

On the third night north of Regina I slept in a junk-filled canyon. Abandoned diggings peppered the slopes and the stream bed was full of wrecked cars. The morning sun crept down the canyonside, catching willow fluff on the warm air. A grimy dog started to bark. It was chained to an empty oil drum beside a notice which said "Keep Gate Closed – Anamels inside". The gate was of course wide open, and just behind it was a shack.

The old man on the porch was called George Carillo. He was sitting on a cast-iron bedstead, knuckles clasped round one knee, morning light streaming over the railing. When I asked him for water he unhooked a crutch, pottered indoors, and came back with two mugs of coffee.

"I belief in my Lor' Jesus Christ," he announced, lowering himself back on to the bedstead. "It'sa one man I belief an' that's it. I got every theen to eat. I got every theen to chew. I got house, four goats, I got fifteen chickens an' I don't hurt no body." The voice was like an old hubble-bubble, gurgling away in the sunshine. "If I need it a whiskey, or I need it a wine I jus' buy my leedle boddles an' I promise it my Lor' I help everybody. Jes, my fren'. Every body he need it a help."

George stuffed a little tobacco under his lip. I'd assumed he must be Mexican but this wasn't the case.

"I born there in Colorado," he said. "Beside Pagosa Springs. I work in gol' mine all my life. Damn right." He nodded towards the distant mountains. "Three jears ago I take my son-in-law. Now he got riches. Got a nice car, but he don't give me nothing. Yup. Jes my fren'."

George lent forward and spat over the railing.

"You know Plata? Silver? I got one mine over there, see? – way up there. Just question one horse he kick to my leg, so I don't work my hole no more. But I got alfalfa. I got a leedle corns. This week some guy gonna bring machine to cut my corns. Jesterday I wait for him but I guess he busy."

George's canyon led onto a road, and the road led to a place called Chama. I was halfway there, head lost in the looming mountains, when a soil conservation vehicle stopped and the driver offered me a lift. Her name was Eileen.

"I'm walking," I said, "but my rucksack doesn't have to."

"Pick it up at the office."

I felt almost giddy without the pack. The first few miles were like walking on the moon. I bounced into the first store I came to, downed a couple of Cokes, and bought peanut butter, broccoli and oranges.

"Show me the broccoli," said Eileen. She didn't think a lot of it. "Don't get enough fresh stuff here," she said. I mentioned that George Carillo's alfalfa patch was the only cultivation I'd seen in the whole state.

"Right," said Eileen. "It's wetter here under the mountains. That's why the Spanish stayed. But if you stick to the Divide you won't see any farms. In fact right now you won't see anything. You ski cross-country?"

"No," I said.

"May have to," said Eileen. "Record snowfall in the San Juans last winter and most of it's still up there."

Flowers, wet earth, mosquitoes, snow peaks, the changes had been slowly coming, and on midsummer's day, June 21st, I crossed the Colorado state line. The young Chama river was roaring beside me, a ravenous storm of green water. I threw off the pack, undid my boots and lay flat on my back in the larkspur. Bees droned against a backdrop of pines. The valley was drowsy and coniferously green. I felt physically strong, my skin was tight, my muscles ready for the mountains. I'd come a long way since Antelope Wells. I remembered how stupid I'd felt telling Señor Casillas the customs official that I was walking to Canada. And he'd offered me a tin of sardines – son sardines to help you, he'd said. In a way, they already had.

Statistical note:

New Mexico – May 5th to June 21st less 2 complete rest days and 11 days doing the food boxes with Connie. 594 miles, 33 nights on the trail. Used the tent 4 times; ate 4½ boxes of food; averaged 18 miles a day. Rained once, drizzled once, hailed once. Hit 10,000 feet altitude once.

Colorado – June 21st to August 5th less 4 complete rest days. 562 miles. 41 nights on the trail. In tent or some other shelter every night except 2. Ate 5 food boxes and bought supplements; averaged 13 miles a day. Rained over half the time. Walked at over 10,000 feet for about 500 miles altogether.

PART III

Colorado

1 Altitude

I woke up, still in the larkspur though the bees had surely changed. I wanted to improve their lives, to put little labels on the already visited flowers – Done, Done, Done – but why should I spoil their adventures? I picked at my teeth with a sharp pine needle instead. I was . . . unsettled.

For the past two or three days I had been, as it were, perusing the Colorado brochure: blue sky, white snow, dark forested slopes; meltwater cascading down distant headwalls. It had all looked so lovely on the approach, so spectacular, but I was no longer a spectator. I was about to clamber on stage. Looking up, I remembered that pit of the stomach feeling as I'd stepped off the bus between Lordsberg and Deming. But I'd got over it, built mental levees as I'd meandered north which the millrace beside me now calamitously threatened. I doubt the Chama was ten yards across at this point, but the volume of water, the sheer power of the torrent, was sobering.

I was out of the larkspur by now, veering through tight dandelions, the clonk of tumbling boulders growing fainter as I drew away from the river. A light cavalry of aspen was nodding at the edge of the meadow, a screen thrown forward of not just an army but of a whole nation of spruce. I felt conspicuously lonely. The trees were all right – they had each other, the few dead ones prominent as bone-white standards, reserve units of fir posted high in the gullies to counter the swooping talus. I should have ordered them all to turn round, to face the looming peaks, but I wasn't a Joshua. I was a shit-scared David, heel-dragging at the back, about to be pushed through the ranks. I began to climb.

Leaving the meadow, I ploughed uphill through the aspen. After so long on the open range, the sensation of branches closing overhead was novel. Small burns roared down through the trees. Where the slope eased were bogs with skunk cabbage and globe flowers, and, in deep shade, a primrose called Shooting Star, its bright, rose-red petals flared back like the tail of a comet. Navigation was easy – uphill all the way, left and right didn't matter that much. I poured sweat, nothing new, but I was panting like a dog. My whole body was changing rhythm. Back on the flats I'd been Homo erectus, striding along, brain in contemplative trance. There was none of that ectomorphic nonsense up here. It was sweat and saliva and biceps and lungs and kneecaps and sinews and thighs – the muscular commitment of the sprinter, except this was a 600–mile event. The next flat bit wasn't till Wyoming.

Fat candles of spruce had replaced the aspen, though with engines on full burn I'd been scarcely aware of the change. I felt crumbling lichen under my palms and looked up – a jumbled scree fall, angles and faces, warm in the afternoon sun. I played hopscotch for another hundred yards, finding sanctuary on dun-coloured grass, the dishevelled clumps just free of their nine-month duvet of snow. The bare patch ran steeply uphill, curling over the crest between shattered outcrops of stone. I stopped to look back, the river which I'd been unable to cross now no more than a silvery hair.

I'd been climbing for nearly four hours, but despite the diversion of physical effort I was getting jittery again. What would it be like at the top? I was now right under the crestline, groping for a way up when, stopping for a breather, I discovered I was no longer alone. A furry creature, its back to the wind, was sitting hunched against the sky.

I whipped out the camera: "Mountain Lion!" I thought, making a frenzied lens change, though the animal could as well have been a ginger cat. It wasn't all that far away, but the vertical distance between us made it oddly remote, like a statue up on its plinth and unless you can stand right next to them, statues are impossible to size. So are mountains. I was in wonderland. The rocks above and below me could have been smaller than footballs, they could have been larger than desks. And the view across the valley – the map said the gap was six miles but what did that actually mean? I was having to learn a completely new language. The very idea that a mile could vary according to which end you set out from seemed preposterous. In New Mexico a mile had been a mile – twenty minutes there and twenty minutes back, if, for some reason, you had to go back. In Colorado a mile was irrelevant. Actual distance was about the last thing to be considered. In fact it hardly existed – exposed for miserable artifice by the realities of rock and deep snow, of inclination and outcrop; blown to shreds by the wind and the rain. Colorado wasn't just a new state, it was a new way to think.

But the Euclidian world of uniform sage was hard to shake off. I'd been climbing the side of a finger-shaped trough, roughly three thousand feet deep. Thirty cubic miles had been summarily removed, ground out by the long-vanished ice, and my mind was trying to put it all back, to refill the valley, to bring order to these new dimensions. To a certain extent I succeeded. The Mountain Lion was a marmot.

The snow as I climbed had been patchy and thin, the steep upper slopes almost bare, but gaining the ridge I was faced with a continuous drift. I gave it not a thought. Here was I and there, not fifty yards away, was the still oblivious marmot. I was going to get a great picture. How much closer could I get?

My screech came on the third step. It was as if I'd never seen snow before, as if it were simply white ground. I'd gone in to the waist and was gasping, shrivelled, for mercy. I was shocked at my naïvety. This, I realized, was what the hurtling river had been getting at. Wake up, it had been telling me, realize where you are.

I floundered back to solid ground, the history of the past few seconds imprinted on the dirty snow. I just stood there chewing my lips, a half-hearted coxswain putting off a second wintery launch. I had been expecting – what? Zigzaggy lines for mountains, little upside down w's in the sky for birds? But this was horrible. No relief in any direction. I was 12,000 feet above sea level, desolate tundra rolling white to a cold horizon.

I shuddered. I didn't have to be up here. There were roads round these mountains, snow-free valleys below the Divide. A detour would have been simple. But was I really considering the ejector seat after only two legfuls of snow? I hadn't thought of myself as a quitter, but, for the record, my first impulse in these novel circumstances was to turn back. I squashed it and strapped on my gaiters, feeling slightly more confident now I at least looked like a climber.

The snowdrift ahead appeared to straddle the whole ridge, but at the very edge I found a corridor blown free by the wind. Twenty yards of bare rock through a snow drift – a gift exactly timed. It led on to the next patch of bare ground, and suddenly I was free of the jitters. The plateau lay open before me. From that moment on, barring acts of God, I had not the slightest doubt that I'd eventually finish the walk.

The sun had just disappeared. From now on the days would be dying, though not noticeably for a few weeks yet. I wondered what my friends would be doing tonight – on Midsummer's eve back in England. Lying wrecked on some hillside no doubt. I blew them a grin and looked for somewhere to camp.

Yes! I looked for somewhere to camp. Not to doss, not to crash, not to unroll my mat, but to properly camp. I hate camping. Tents are a suburban hassle. But it was cold and I needed somewhere to put mine up, the problem being that there wasn't any actual ground – not what you'd call real terra firma. You had either snow – of which there was plenty – or quarry-like residues of stone. Ecologically speaking I was parked on alpine tundra, in which a few windproof plants do take root, but in which little tent pegs do not. I ended up stringing the guy ropes to low shrubs and weighing down the flysheet with rocks: at this altitude the trees survived only as prostrate dwarves, taking as much as a century to reach knee-height. This stunted habit, called krumholtz, is what I'd pitched the tent in.

My lifestyle was obviously changing. Whereas in the deserts I'd undressed for dinner, here I did the complete opposite, slipping into knee breeches, long socks and a fibre pile jacket. Quite the little mountaineer. The meal itself was the usual stew with a stick of beef jerky to follow. I felt not one whit less hungry, lit a cigarette, and watched the stars pickle the darkness.

The brightest were actually planets – Venus and Jupiter, low in the southern sky. They'd been in roughly the same position since May, but some of the constellations had changed. The stick men of Gemini had gone, leaving Leo to head the march west; behind him came the heavies – Boötes the waggoner and the giant Hercules, the unmistakable torque of Corona Borealis between them. At that hour Cygnus was just gliding up from the east. I imagined her lonely trumpeting as she stretched her neck through the sparkling night, though what I actually heard through the sleeping bag hood were the myriad sounds of trickling water – snowmelt, which I hoped would freeze hard by dawn.

2 The Southern San Juans

It was still dark when I got up. Nothing moved. I dropped my aluminium spoon and there was a sharp clink as it hit a rock. Sounds up here had such hard, clean edges that the silences were clarified too. You heard them, especially at night. I swung sixty-five pounds on to my back and shrugged into the straps.

I ground to a halt twelve hours later. The terrain hadn't been particularly rugged – a few ups and downs, no more than sharp hillocks really – but the ground itself was a wearisome nougat of rock, mud and snow. I'd covered just eight miles.

For the first two hours the crust remained firm and I was able to link up long drifts, crunching forward for several hundred yards at a time before the surface gave way, sometimes to dump me into a stream, most often into buried krumholtz. It was slapstick stuff, though I gradually began to anticipate the laughs. In New Mexico I'd Scanned The Flats; here I Read The Snow, looking for tell-tale signs of a cave-in. I was glad I was alone. I got stuck on telltale sign jokes for hours and would have driven a companion to distraction. Stopping for a mid-morning brew I veered into a tight circle, following my tracks round and round in the snow and going "thought so, thought so – Telltale Signs!" I fell over, weak with laughter. Soon everything was a telltale sign. My hands were cold: telltale sign – my hands must be cold. The water on the stove was boiling: telltale sign – the water on the stove must be boiling.

But by noon the snow had softened and my new-found knowledge was useless. No matter where I stopped I was breaking through to my thighs. I took off the rucksack and tried dragging it behind me to spread the weight. When I found a firm stretch I'd footle along, making the most of my reprieve. I was into naughty legionnaire jokes by now, pretending, each time I fell into a pit, that I'd just been decimated. I've no coherent Latin and would shout, as the snow gave way, whatever came into my head – "Hon y soit qui mal y pense!" or "Pourquoi moi, oh Caesar?" – grunting my way out with little translation exercises: it would have gone ill for us had this hole not been less shallow; I wish to send forward Caius Centenius, the praetor, for the purpose of seizing the defile.

The crestline dropped into a belt of spruce at a place called Dipping Lake. I found a way down, picking up a loose stone as I went to break a hole in the ice for my pot. The warm tea lulled my stomach for a while. My work-rate had increased dramatically, and what had been at best an indifference to food in New Mexico had become a constant rat-like hunger.

The trees round the lake were drooping, soundproofed and white. Flat plates of snow fell – thoof – from the upper branches. Coniferous dandruff littered the snow – gnawed cones, shed needles, stiff branch-lets, bits of bark. A squirrel chattered its disapproval as I kicked my way uphill again, each foothold dug with the toe of a sodden boot. The map showed a trail right on the Divide, and I did see a few marker cairns, but most of them were indistinguishable from a thousand other white pimples.

Having smothered the last patch of blue-sky, serge-suited clouds were now bickering among themselves about an acceptable level of gloom. Those against any form of daylight whatever were holding a rally with what sounded like tambourine and drum – a squall was twirling down from the north.

Thud – bag off. Bzzt – release cord. And – dive, dive, dive, groping for . . . ah! up it comes, my wetproof jacket, dripping creases as it breaks the surface. I was distracted by a sharp detonation. A whiff of black smoke curled off the rock just ahead. Pink zigzags were ripping the sky. But I'd got the jacket zip crooked, damnit, and was missing it all. In the excitement of my first storm I'd forgotten that lightning is bad for you. There were more strikes, then a ping-pong bombardment of hail, the white pellets twitching like seabirds in the creases and folds of my clothes. Hail always looks such useful stuff – a sort of free gift. It makes me feel guilty to see it melt.

The storm passed and I moved on, splashing across a mile of waterlogged hillside, snowmelt streaming in sheets through a morass of gravel and mud. Clumps of dwarf willow made occasional stepping stones, but by late afternoon my boots were so wet that I just sloshed indiscriminately forward. Marmots whistled like suspicious pimps, warning each other of my progress. The ptarmigan were more subtle, and just before sunset I nearly trod on a female. Her mate, still pure white, took off with a whirr but her own summer plumage was complete, her camouflage against the mushy tundra near-perfect.

When I opened my diary that evening I couldn't think of anything to put. The hail and the ptarmigan were the only things I could recall. The rest of the day was a blur. The previous entry contained a lot of drivel about apprehension which now, a day later, I could hardly believe that I'd written.

I woke at five to the sound of rain on the tent. The snow would be softer than ever, and I lay in the bag wondering if I could make snowshoes out of the krumholtz. But I was going to need real ones. Illogically, I was less concerned about where I'd actually find a pair in this uninhabited country than about how much they would cost. Money was one of my fall-back worries, an old bone to chew on when nothing else filled my thoughts. Distance was another. Could I gain this point or that by nightfall? Where would I be in a week? It was just adult thumb-sucking.

I shook out the tent and night rain drops spangled the air. The clouds had dispersed and the sky was zingingly blue, though despite the wax I'd globbed on my boots the mush underfoot soaked through straightaway. My toes looked more and more like white stuff in drains everytime I stopped to wring out my socks.

This second full day on the plateau was turning out even worse than the first. The initial three miles took five hours, but this was greased lightning compared to what lay ahead. Conditions (conditions! – there'd been so few conditions in New Mexico) conditions deteriorated rapidly. Traversing the headwall of the Conejos valley the snow was continuous, everything white, the Divide swooping round precipitous corries containing, far below, the blue-green veins of ice-covered lakes.

These little tarns had stultifyingly unimaginative names, and those of the rivers they spawned were duller – North Fork East Creek, Middle Fork South Creek and so on. Despite the evocative few, American place names never felt right to me – a whole continent still wet from the font. The secret of a good name lies in not knowing exactly what it means, so the Spanish ones were far more convincing – Laguna Ruybal, Trujillo Meadows and, below me now, El Rito Azul, so much more exotic than plain old Blue Creek. How blue El Rito actually was I couldn't say because it lay under six feet of snow, though with the spring thaw underway it was probably black with peat.

I trudged on towards more trees, a lonely brother, late for a union meeting. When I got there I found myself wading through a nightmare of drifts piled high against the closely packed trunks. The gross physical effort of clambering forward and the constant necessity of removing the pack made the next mile one of the most arduous of the whole trip. It took me over three hours. The six days of rations I had left on my back weren't going to get me far at this rate.

The map showed a forest hut about eight miles ahead and it seemed the best place to head for, though I'd have to drop off the Divide and into a valley to reach it. It had a name – Platoro – and if it were manned I might perhaps get a lift out to somewhere for snowshoes. If not, I'd have to find an alternative, low-level route to the next food box at Creede. I'd got over my must-hold-out-at-all-costs phase and was no longer taunting myself with accusations of retreat. This was a tactical withdrawal, though I almost killed myself twice getting down – first when I slipped on ice and tobogganed two hundred yards down a gully; then getting swept off my freezing cold feet as I tried to ford the Conejos river. I crawled out and sat on the bank, feeling cold, sick and grateful. I ought to have made some sort of thank offering – what was the opposite of a funeral? – but in the event I just got dressed and walked away.

3 Platoro

I was alone in a long, grey valley. It was sure to lead somewhere, all valleys do, though the Divide of course leads nowhere at all. It has no upstream or downstream, doesn't get bigger or smaller, does not, as valleys do, generate expectation. But this soggy trail would, sooner or later, become a road; the burnt tent I'd found at the edge of the trees would, perhaps, become a town.

Meanwhile there was the forest hut. I'd picked up vehicle tracks, the stream had widened, and there, in green waders, his hat full of lures, was a Texan. At least, the jeep plates said Texas. The cigar and the accent confirmed it.

"Platoro?" he said. "Ain't but an old mhaanin' kayamp."

Not just a hut then! But did anyone live there? And what could you buy? Coffee? Snowshoes? Food? But I was so nearly there it could wait. I hit town, a scattering of cabins in the cold June drizzle, at nine the following morning.

Platoro, Colorado: 10,400 feet above sea level; population – it varied. Fishing June through September, hunting in fall, snowed out November through May. So much I learnt at the first four doors I'd tried, but, as yet, no snowshoes.

The fifth place was El Ranchero Lodge. I walked into reception, smelt coffee and warmth and saw a line of elk antlers mounted on the wall. Directly beneath them sat Fred Blair.

"Snowshoes?" he said. "My wife Debbie and I stayed up here all last winter – only ones that did – and we slept in our goddamned snowshoes. Beats rubber panties hands down."

I stayed two days. It rained nearly all the time. When it didn't we went fishing (Fred seven, me nil), saw the first elk of the season, and paid a visit to Fred's gold mine. It looked like a large badger holt. With his partner Chuck, Fred had just blown a hole through to the old shaft.

"She's not been worked in fifty years," he said. "Gonna suck her dry then blast her right out. Chuck's going down to Alamosa tomorrow for a pump."

"No problem getting explosive?"

"No, no. This is America."

Fred's real passion was aeroplanes. He was a freelance pilot. The Second World War had started without him, but he'd cut his teeth in Korea. He mentioned Biafra and the Congo. There had, I gathered, been Certain Deals – small packages, jeep headlights, rushing night air; not a lot of paperwork involved. I asked how he'd discovered Platoro.

"Union Minière outa Brussels," he said. "They do a lot of prospecting in this area. Me and Debbie managed a drilling camp. Then along comes Chuck and Leslie and we set up the hunting outfit."

We had steaks grilled over hickory that night, pecan pie, ice-cream, and Scotch. It was still raining outside. A log spat in the hearth and a thin curl of smoke rose from Sarah, the Newfoundland asleep on the carpet. I patted her out and lay sprawled with my head on her back. The ceiling was leaking a bit, dripping into a washing-up bowl.

"What d'you do in the winter?" I asked.

"What do we do in the winter? You have in this room one helluva cross-section of talent. I'm a bush pilot. Debbie, Debbie's an exotic dancer. Yeah, she's twenty years younger than me but the doctor says it's good for my breathing. Chuck's an electronics specialist, and Leslie's a bookkeeper in a bank."

"I worked as a meatpacker last winter," said Leslie. "Was it ever great to get back here in May! I like to stand on the porch nude and stretch and say hi! to the mountains. Back in Texas they'd lock me away."

"Seen that bear skin in the hall?" asked Fred.

It covered half the floor.

"I was stark naked when I shot that bear. Where could you do that in a city? Heard a noise in the night and the bear was right there by the door. Shot it literally from the hip. Weighed 320 pounds. It's living out your fantasies up here. Like our clients. They don't primarily want a trophy. They want the campfire, the guitar, the images they remember from the movies as kids. And that's what we give them. We got creamer and sugar on the table right now, but when a client flies in the coffee round here's served vicious."

It was low cloud, wipers and headlights on full for the two-hour journey down to Alamosa. Leslie drove me round to the K-Mart, Tru-Value, the Sporting Goods Store and finally to the Pink Elephant junk shop, but there were no snowshoes I could afford. Eventually we went out to Taylor's Machine Tool and Rental for the pump and there on the top shelf was a pair of what looked like red milk crates.

"Not the best you can buy," said Mr Taylor. "Had them five years and I haven't rented them out once. I'd be glad of the shelf space. Ten dollars do you?"

"Sure," I said, "sure."

It was Fred's turn that Sunday to give the sermon at Platoro's informal church. The congregation wouldn't be more than a couple of dozen, all of whom he knew, but he was nervous, especially when we asked him what he was going to say. But after supper that night and a couple whiskies he scraped back his chair and stood up. Instant silence.

"Evenin'," he rapped. "Rev'rend Freddy heah, at the Church of What's Happenin' Now!"

"A-men," yelled Chuck. "A-fuckin'-men."

Freddy smiled acknowledgment. "Now meneah of you've been listenin' to Rev'rend Freddy's broadcasts drivin' the highways an' byways of our Great Countreah, an' ah wanna thank you fo'wa all those do-nay-shuns, all those donayshuns you've been sendin' to help with his GOOD WORKS!" He raised a hand. "An' ah wanna tell all mah fren's out theah in radio an' TV land that tomorrow Sunday ahm gonna be preachin' up in Platoro, Colorado – that's P-L-A-T-O-R-O, Platoro, Colorado, zip Eight One One Seven Naahn – an' ah wancha all to be theah."

"We will be theah!" we shouted.

Freddy beamed. "Mah testimoneah tomorrow will concern the hazards, the hazards of deeemaaahn RUM! Now ah know you've all done it. Ah know you've all smoked them crazy cigarettes, an' ah know how you call that yo'wa crutch! An' ah know you call that crutch SCAATCH – yea verily – an' you call that crutch BURRBHAAN an' you call it Beer an' you call it waahn.

"Well whatever you call it – whatever you call it, GAARD don't wancha drinkin' it! Rev'rend Freddy don't wancha drinkin' it! An' ah don't care what them boys in Louisville, Kentucky want – ah wancha to give it up, to give it up now! because it's bad, bad, BA'YAD, FO'WA YOU!

"Now ah think we should take all of the waahn, yeah, all the waahn an' throw it in the ri-vah! An' all of the whiskey, the whiskey should be thrown, where? – in the Ri-vah! An' all of the drugs an' the nar-co-tics should be thrown, Yeah! – in the Ri-VAH!

"An' now, if you'll turn to page two two three in yo'wa hymnals,
we're gonna join in the old song" – Freddy raised both arms wide –
"LET'S ALL GATHER AT THE . . . "
"RI-VAAAAHH!!!!" we all yelled. "Yea, verily!"

4 The Northern San Juans

Rain in Platoro became sleet as I approached the Divide, the snow at
11,000 feet sodden, granulated stuff and again arduously hummocked.
It was a lousy afternoon, the surrounding peaks looming jampacked
and wet through flying carriage windows of sky. Most were coniferously
hatted and scarved, but there! – a flash of unbuttoned spruce pressed
up against a murky pane. I blinked. The mountain was completely
naked, a spotty white bum leering at me out of the gloom. The volcanic
debris of these bare slopes, common in the southern Rockies, form
unstable gashes, often yellow or red, in which almost nothing takes
root but pimples of bristlecone pine.

The trees opened out and I was squadging across an open flat –
miserable, but at least I was here. I was slipping into my Virgin
Territory fantasy again – the old "Have-these-forests-ever-known-the-
imprint-of-a-human-boot" gambit which I often played as a defence
against the hose-down-king's-pawn attack favoured by Colorado's
afternoon skies. But what if the forests *had* known a human boot print?
What did it matter? Wasn't it enough just to be here, at one with
nature – wait a minute, what was that? I'd passed a small yellow tag
fixed to a spike. There was another, way down through the trees –
some sort of fire break perhaps? Rain dripping from my face, I bent
down to read the words. "Pipeline", it said. "In case of emergency,
call collect". I felt completely upstaged. If I'd been an actor I'd have
stormed off, demanding a phone and my agent. "Mickey," I'd have
said, "Mickey, these people are *ruining* my show."

Actually, the pipeline had been very skilfully buried. The trees
would all grow back in time. I was back under them again, floundering
over more snow, a wet vest of sweat freezing under my jacket as I
stopped to strap on the milk crates. There'd been no snow to practise
on down in Platoro, so this was for the very first time. The trees rustled
politely. What had Debbie Blair advised? Glide, shuffle, glide, she'd

said. A waltz then, folks – Les Ponts de Paris . . . and, two three, la
da dee whoops – get up; dee dee damn – that hurt; bom bom bugger
– I've got stuck again; grunt grunt grunt grunt, grunt grunt.

The snowshoes were much like joke door mats – the kind that stick
to the soles of your feet and send you crashing straight into the hat
stand. I'd get the hang of them soon, I thought, a Nanook of the not
so far north, but I never really did. Though they got me over the
southern San Juans and down to Creede, the snowshoes were never
an integral part of the journey. They were just a bit of fun really –
props which seemed to amplify the sometimes rather faint call of the
wild.

Including my two nights in Platoro, this was the sixth since crossing
into Colorado. I spent it in the attic of a forestry hut, smashing my
forehead on a beam when I sat up in the darkness to shoo off a mouse.
I'd only done forty-five miles that week. Climbing out of the valley of
the Chama, I'd crossed the high plateau of the southern San Juans,
dipped down to Platoro, regained the watershed and was now about
to swing west into the Weminuche wilderness above Creede.

The wretched mouse was still scrabbling under the eaves and I
couldn't get to sleep. I reached for the torch and spread out the map.
It was a bit like reading a comic – a strip cartoon of mountains which
I'd savour instalment by instalment. Following the Divide, the torch
beam cruised west, jinked north, travelled slowly back east, the watershed folding back on itself to enclose the Rio Grande. Coming up next
– in theory at least – was the longest hairpin of the journey, a traverse
of roughly a hundred miles, mostly above 12,000 feet. Even on the
forestry map it looked stupendous.

It was snowing next morning and took three hours of heavy effort to
reach the saddle of Bonito Pass. From there I bailed out, cutting off
the next six miles of the Divide by describing another wide curve
through the rest of a long afternoon; but by noon next day – the third
from Platoro – I was back above 12,000 feet again, on a summit called
Table Mountain.

Strange to say, I began to cry; sometimes the sheer scale of America
overwhelmed me.

I sniffed, frowned, and wiped a sleeve across my cheek. I suppose
that an American coming to England would do the complete opposite
and burst out laughing. I wouldn't blame him – our diddy little fields
and tinky-winky hills must look a bit like a model. Scotland is
grander, but even there a valley twelve miles long is impressive. Here

valleys twelve miles long were sideshows. It wasn't just the size of things continental that hit you, but their extent. You saw whole geographical features from up here – complete mountain ranges, entire drainage systems. You began to see how massive the scale of things really is. You saw weather sweeping in, cloud shadows racing over sage miles below, dappling whole forests, sweeping unhindered across snowbound tundra, the clouds themselves torn on the jagged peaks. And you saw all this in a single glance. No craning your neck or driving on to the next lay-by. All you had to do was stand there and look.

A bandsaw of peaks, dazzlingly white, enclosed the entire horizon, forest of the darkest, silkiest green rippling down the muscled flanks of the valley. Somewhere, miles below me, was the infant Rio Grande. This immense, blind valley was its home, the high trail round it one of the most spectacular sections of the Divide. At this time of year it was also one of the most dangerous. The snow was in a highly unstable condition, huge cornices curling off ridges, smashed trees below marking fresh avalanche trails: it would be weeks before a full traverse of the Weminuche was possible. Months later I had a letter from Nolan J. Doeskin, assistant state climatologist for Colorado. "You may be interested in knowing," he wrote, "that you hiked the Colorado Continental Divide in the year of greatest late-season snowpack on record . . . "

It is a letter I have kept, impassability being easier to live with when it's official. I turned away and headed for Creede, a day's walk away down in the valley.

5 Creede

My food box was at the forestry office and Mrs Rogers was behind the desk. A camper had pulled up outside and the driver clacked in, an old man in virulent shorts.

"Where can I go that's lower than here?" he demanded. "I cain't breathe." He obviously could.

"Just drive right on down the valley, sir," said Mrs Rogers, "then head south for New Mexico."

The shorts clacked out again. There was a grumpy sort of conference in the camper. I could see a blue rinse yakking away in the passenger seat as the vehicle pulled away.

I spread myself out on the lawn. My stuff looked like filthy wet football kit. But the sun shone, and by noon it looked like filthy dry football kit.

"Had your troubles, right?" said a guy in the parking lot. His vehicle had "District Wildlife Officer" on the door. His name was Glen Hinshaw and he had good news for me. Though higher by a thousand feet, the mountains north of Creede would be less snowy than the San Juans, which was exactly what another wildlife service employee had told me below Bonito Pass. He'd been driving a bowser full of young trout.

"You seen old Louis then?" said Glen.

"Yes," I said. "He gave me a peach."

"That's nice. Old Louis is doin' all right. Fish parachute programme's been cut back this year so he's kept his job restocking by truck."

The material wealth of America was something I was used to by now – fat people, fat fridges, fat cars – but the opulence of a fish parachute programme quite shocked me. I mean half the world is starving to death . . .

But I liked it. I liked the idea of chucking fish into lakes from the air. America was good fun. Unhealthy old men in ridiculous shorts and fish raining out of the sky.

Wildlife had a dandy programme with Bighorn Sheep too, said Glen. "We hook 'em on fermented apple juice. They get so smashed we can drop-net six at a time. We've reintroduced herds all over the state."

Glen obviously loved his job. He'd been in Creede nineteen years. "Pretty tight little place," he said. "Miners mostly. You seen our firehouse yet?"

I wasn't sure what a firehouse was.

We drove up mainstreet and stopped just past the last buildings, in the cold shadow of the volcanic crags which dominate the town. If Creede had been in France there'd have been statues to the Virgin perched up there. Instead, abandoned mine shafts were terraced one above the other into the cliffs like rock climbers waiting for rescue.

Glen pushed a button and a steel door in the cliff whirred open.

"Couldn't get the money for a regular building, so we done this here," he said. Neon strip-lights fluttered. "Goes back 150 feet – just a buncha fellas getting together after work and some free explosives from the mine."

Red firetrucks gleamed in embayments which had been blasted into the rock. A side door led to an office, and through it stepped county judge Robert Wardell – ex-marine corps, six foot three, call me Bob. He crushed my hand.

"Hello, Steve. You're from where? Ireland, Germany or England? You've got a bicycle somewhere I bet."

"He's walking the Divide," said Glen.

"I envy you," said Bob. "How d'you like our firehouse?" His voice echoed in the huge chamber. "You're talking a half-million-dollar engineering job here, homebuilt for sixty thousand."

We strolled down the line of trucks.

"Look at that," said Bob. "Our old twenty-niner."

Frog-eyed lamps gleamed. "Does it start?" I asked.

"She's a Chevvy, partner." The engine chortled, then roared. Siren wailing, Bob shot out of the cavern and did a boyish circuit of the forecourt. "Heads the Fourth of July parade through town," he yelled. "You be here for the Fourth of July?"

Glen grinned. "Steve's English," he said. "He might not appreciate that."

We drove back down mainstreet. It was pretty quiet, though things hadn't always been so. N. C. Creede, with pickaxe and mule, made the first strike here in 1889, and by 1893 a million dollars in silver was leaving by rail per month, with a courtesy sidecar provided for dead bodies and bankrupts. Mayhem had been the town's strong suit. The man who shot Jesse James, for example, was himself shot down in Creede – two barrels right in the head.

"Creede is unfortunate in getting more of the flotsam of the state than usually falls to the lot of mining camps," moaned the *Creede Candle*. "Some of her citizens would take sweepstake prizes at a hogshow."

The old obituaries were superb:

> Lulu Slain, a frail daughter, laid aside the camelia for the poppy early Wednesday morning. She and the Mormon Queen had been living in a small cabin, but the times grew hard and the means of life came not. They sought relief from life with morphine, the inevitable end of their unfortunate kind . . .

Of which Rosy "Timberline" Vastine had been another:

> Weary of the trials and tribulations of this wicked world she

decided to take a trip over the range and to this end brought
into play a forty-one calibre pistol. With the muzzle at her
lily white breast and her index finger on the trigger she waited
not to contemplate the sad result . . .

Even Nicholas Creede himself met a sad end. "He left," so the town
history records, "and went to live in California to enjoy his wealth.
However it was short lived because he killed himself when his wife,
whom he had divorced, insisted on living with him."

"There's a lot of drinking still goes on here though," said Larry
Robinson, who kindly put me up for the night. He had rather pinched
lips. "Sunday's nothing particular to most of them either."

A humming bird feeder hung outside the kitchen window, a column
of clear sugar water dangling across my horizon, the top half pink in
the sunset. Larry went out to give the lawn a trim. The dishwasher
was broken so I was doing the supper things. Larry's wife and daughter
were at Bible study class, and he was due at a prayer meeting shortly
himself. He came back in for his prayerbook and car keys and paused.
Revelations, Ephesians – books I couldn't even pronounce – he knew
them chapter and verse. He had quotes of every calibre, quotes to fill
any breech, quotes he could fire off in tremendous salvoes or target
one at a time. But he was more of a medic than a gunner – one of the
Lord's stretcher-bearers, stumbling in with the morally wounded, body-
swerving the damned, hankie up against the foul reek of sin. By this
time the washing-up water was cold and he had missed his meeting. I
hoped his absence wouldn't matter – Larry's God sounded pretty strict,
though at least you knew where you stood with him, which in Larry's
case was in trepidation. "Revelation 20:15," he said, handing me the
liquid soap. "For whosoever is not written in the Book of Life shall
be cast into a lake of fire."

"Ow!" The tap water was scalding hot.

"Yeah," said Larry. "Be careful. We just had a new furnace."

And that was the closest I got to him. I wanted to know what he
liked, to see what he saw, to feel a little of his spirit, but I couldn't.
His belief was like a shield I couldn't get round. And now it was dark,
so the humming bird feeder was just a black tube of plastic.

Larry dropped me at the post office next morning. A man in an
apron had just finished sweeping the step. He unlocked the door.

"Lessee," he said. "Pern. That's P for Peter. P for . . . P,P,P . . .
looks like you got three."

I read them in the sunshine: a wedding invitation – I'd be in

Wyoming; a letter from my mother – someone had died and I felt sad for his wife; and a letter from Connie which made me laugh. A black pick-up hooted from across the road.

"Wanna coffee, partner?"

My hand was braced this time, but it got mangled anyway. Bob Wardell's repair shop and garage was decorated with Old Glory wallpaper – red, white and blue – with a dozen comfy old chairs pulled up round the stove. Bob had been county judge for some time.

"Twenty-one years, partner, and I never had a single appeal. Bet you thought that wasn't possible in America, but in a place like this if people respect you they respect your judgements. If they don't you're out the next election. I got ninety-one percent last time."

6 The La Garitas and the Cochetopa Hills

I paid a slow and gluttonous farewell to Creede, zigzagging up mainstreet from french fries to doughnuts to a Coke. The last eats place had cheesecake in the window and "Dear Prudence", a lovely old Beatles' song, floating out through the door. I was still humming it back up at 11,000 feet.

I hadn't forgotten the cheesecake either. My guts were tight as a drum. A stopover in town always blew me out and I'd reach the first secluded squat with relief. Sometimes I'd linger, down on my haunches, especially if the view was good, examining mountains ahead and stools underfoot with just about equal curiosity. It was a good opportunity to look at the ground – to watch beetles and spiders and flick at dead twigs and wonder how long it takes for pine needles to rot away – though what you gained in immediacy from defecating outdoors you definitely lost in comfort. Cramp usually forced me to change positions within a couple of minutes. I never used paper – it is a hassle to bury and alternatives were always to hand, of which by far the best were rocks. A lichen covered stone is the equal to any tissue on the market; dry twigs are no worse than old-fashioned hard paper; but foliage, which might seem to be the most suitable, is often the least good of all, and especially bad from this point of view is spruce.

Probably because I didn't much like them, one conifer looked much like another to me. What I like are trees with huge, spreading crowns

– Oak, Lime, Beech – and I felt ill at ease with the anorexic evergreens of the Rockies. My initial reaction had been to ignore them, but on Inspiration Point, way above Creede, my interest was stirred.

There had been no loose stones within reach and, having broken off an intrusive frond, I now steeled myself for the application which hygiene demanded. Englemann spruce is about as soothing as a stiff wire brush, but the expected scourging did not come. I even experienced slight pleasure. I looked sharply down at the frond in my hand and then glanced up at the tree. It looked no different from the rest, but my backside had insisted otherwise. It was actually a fir, one of the seventeen sorts of conifer I eventually encountered. By the end of the journey I could tell them apart with my eyes shut.

Glen Hinshaw had been right about the snow. Half thawed, the La Garitas ahead looked almost vulgar. Like Russians in their smalls, I thought, as I chugged up to Half Moon Pass, the tufted grass raised like gooseflesh in the cold wind. I'd seen the pass from Table Mountain three days before, lost it on the descent to Creede, but now, ten miles north of town, it was directly above me, an unmistakable notch in the skyline.

With three-quarters of the state still to contend with, unmistakability was just what I wanted. A quick tug north and south to straighten the Divide would have saved three hundred miles in bends, but it wasn't the Divide's meanderings that muddled me so much as the ordering of its parts. I wanted coherence, succeeding ranges colour-coded perhaps, or sporting team T-shirts, for swift recognition. Why, looking up from my clearly marked maps, did my eyes see just jumbles of peaks? For the first few weeks in Colorado I was like a harassed bus conductor, barging down a packed aisle, trying to get everyone to sit down.

I felt very isolated that evening, the fifty-seventh since Antelope Wells, the wind hurrying clouds through an indifferent sky and blowing spume off a cold, grey tarn. The north face of the La Garitas was as forbidding as the southern aspect had been smooth, huge aprons of talus spilling from elevated boneyards of rock. I'd stopped in a jagged corrie for the night, snagging tent pegs into peat which peeled back off the rock with almost embarrassing ease. There was nothing chummy about life above timberline, no gradation from stone to soil but abrupt, sharply drawn boundaries, even the marmots denied overnight passes. Movement here was in homage to the wind, in deference to the stark rock. I felt small, unforgiven, like a spider in an empty bath. The

looming amphitheatres seemed to invite a performance, as if, by
inducing a storm of applause, I could pull the loneliness in like a
blanket around me.

The next sixty miles, round the headwaters of the Saquache river,
looked easy, a gentle romp through high parkland dappled with forest.
From my elevated position the woods looked like model armies, the
far northern horizon flecked by the peaks of the Sawatch.

A stream dribbled out of the corrie, and I followed it down through
the grey dawn, pushing across acres of waist-high bog willow as I went.
The water was damned into a series of ponds by neat banks of mud-
plastered twigs, each sliced through so cleanly that the cuts didn't look
natural. But what was the point of building ponds so far up a mountain?

My knowledge of beavers had till then been strictly Walt Disney:
they were always busy and they chopped down trees. This sub-alpine
bog didn't look like beaver country to me – no forested lakes, no birch-
bank canoes, no perfectly chiselled tree stumps; no trees at all till the
timberline still way below. But beavers don't actually eat wood. What
they like is soft inner bark, especially of aspen which grows quite a bit
taller than they do. So they chop it down.

Later I was to see how pig-like beavers can be, turning wide areas
of forest into sodden, muddy bogs, though they were, till roughly 1840,
the North American equivalent of gold. In fact they were the Russian
equivalent of gold too. Both Siberia and the American west were first
penetrated in search of their pelts, with sable, foxes, sea otters and
ermine thrown in for good measure. But why, I wondered, with so
much real gold under their feet, had those early trappers not become
miners? The first major strikes, in the American west at least, weren't
made till the late 1840s, more than a century after the first Europeans
– Frenchmen from the east, Spaniards from the south – penetrated the
Rockies. Had the rush for pelts (turned into felt they hatted half of
Europe) blinded the fur trappers to anything else, or was trapping such
fun, in this then pristine land, that prospecting hadn't entered their
heads?

As the La Garitas rolled into the Cochetopa Hills I discovered a
misprint on the map. I was absolutely delighted. A stream – it was
called Lake Fork Saquache Creek – was shown crossing the Divide,
something water cannot naturally do. I stood at the point of the
misprint in boyish triumph.

Shortlived triumph. The woods, which had been model armies from above, were, at close quarters, like riots. They were dense and next to impossible to get through. I became completely lost and ended up on a road well off my map. A car overtook me and stopped. Two men got out, obviously father and son. Both had glasses, both had paunches, both peered at the adjacent hillside where two or three dozen bighorn sheep were grazing in the afternoon sun. I hadn't noticed them. What else must I have missed? I wondered how different the trip would have been if I'd had a companion. Or would I have got sick of being constantly told to look at this or give an opinion on that? The beauty of being alone is that if you don't want to react you don't have to, though in this case I did want to, and, camera in hand, crept stealthily through the roadside willows. Prattish mosquitoes kept swarming in front of the lens. I ignored them aloofly, got my pictures and, hearing a car door slam, squelched back to the road. I wanted to know where I was.

The two women in the back seat had handbags on their knees and looked nervous. I don't blame them. The road was deserted, and I don't suppose I came into their category of a nice young man. The menfolk weren't sure if to wind up the windows or what. They came from Philadelphia and didn't really know where we were either. The son, who was driving, said he thought they had passed a forest guard place two miles back down the road.

"Nearer three," said the father. The mother and daughter-in-law patted their hair as they drove away.

It was actually eight and a half miles – I counted the mile posts – and when I got there it wasn't a proper guard station at all but a locked storage hut. Perhaps there'd be a map up inside. I clambered on to a bucket and, cupping my hands, peered through the dirty windows. I nearly fell off my perch. Pin-ups were so unexpected. Photographs of naked women! I felt like an innocent with his first row of beads, tinsel still in my eyes when, passing a ranch house, I turned off the road and was knocked flat by a friendly St Bernard. It let me up and I was invited in for a drink.

I left at six-thirty next morning.

"Turn off the road in eight miles," the owner of the St Bernard had said, "and head straight for Antora Peak."

Traffic was light. I could see for miles – dry grassland rising to a dark band of forest, with nipples of snow on the skyline. A pick-up zipped past down the empty road, dithered, and came back. The passenger leaned across the driver. He looked exactly like Charles Manson.

"Hey, man, you wanna beer?"

"Bit early, thanks," I said.

"S'a fourthajuly, man!" He ducked under the dashboard. "Aw shit!"

The can he'd opened had sprayed the cab. He thrust it out of the window and a slug of foam crawled through his fingers, leaving a bright trail down the door. The can wiggled insistently.

"C'mon man, s'open. Hey, you English?"

"Yes." I'm allergic to drunks and wasn't handling this well.

"My wife's from England."

At this point the driver shoved Charles Manson aside – his name was actually Flaco – and said, "She ain't no fuckin' English. She just don't look Mexican is all."

This, Flaco ignored.

"You gotta, you gotta climb right in here," he said. "You gotta c'mon down to Salida to meet her."

Salida was seventy miles away.

"Putcha bag in the back an' climb in. Whatcha carryin' anyway? Cameras? Whyncha take a photo? Have a beer an' take a photo. Here" – I was nudged by the can – "Here, man, take it."

Drunks, like dog turds, are hard to shake off. A certain tension had developed, but the driver eventually said something I didn't catch, Flaco withdrew his arm and they roared off.

But not for long. I saw them stop – the vehicle a pinprick three miles down the road – turn round, and cruise back for a second time.

Alarm bells rang. There were two of these guys, both drunk, and the road was completely deserted. I slipped the knife from the camera bag into my pocket.

"Hey, man!" Flaco was leaning out of the window again.

I shed the pack. The knife was in my hand as the vehicle drew level and Flaco got out. I wondered if they had knives too. He took off his hat.

"Wancha to have this, man. It'll keep the sun off your face. An' if you ever do get to Salida you'll find us easy. Wife's the only woman in town with a buggy for twins."

And with that they sped away, leaving me standing in the middle of the road with a white hat in my hand and egg all over my face.

The hat was just excess baggage – my burnt nose was well healed by now and the rest of me was nut brown – but I carried that useless pound and a half for something over one hundred miles: past box number six at Garfield; right along the crest of the Sawatch Range; up and over the second highest peak in America; and down to food box number seven at Leadville, where, crushed and broken as it was, I posted it home in apology to Flaco.

I turned off the road, these last sixteen miles the only long stretch of tarmac I walked in the state, and slowly drew out of the sage. Aspens closed over my head, became spruce, fir, stunted bristlecones, nothing. For the next four hundred miles I dropped below timberline only to escape storms or for food boxes until, a month later, the Divide itself delivered me into the deserts of southern Wyoming.

7 The Southern Sawatch

One of the beauties of Colorado in general, and of the Sawatch range in particular, was that the Divide is so blatantly obvious. You were either on it or you were not, the knife-edge I'd only imagined in New Mexico a frequent reality up here. Off the crestline, even by a few feet, and you were a mule, blinkered by the rising hillside; but on the Divide, on the tightrope itself, you became a condor. You dreamed condor dreams, you spread condor wings, you filled to bursting your great condor lungs. You lifted your head and you breathed in the peaks and you laughed at the dizzy blue sky, the whole state a gigantic funfair – zigzags, gaps, precipitous drops, each ride better than the last. The next one, a meringue of bright snow round the hillside ahead, looked tricky, but a detour would have taken hours, so picking up a bleached root to use as a deadman if I slipped I ploughed up-hill to the cornice. It was cold in the shadow of the overhanging snow, but I hesitated, the overhead curve beyond words, the denominator, perhaps, of a truth buried deep in the soul. I lifted the root and began to dig, a silly thing really because the whole drift could have collapsed on my head, but it was a gorgeous morning and I felt like some chancey action. Boring through the cornice was good fun though, more a nice calculation of risk than an act of blind faith.

The plants up here were gamblers too. Back in the deserts one sage bush had grown much like the next but here every square yard seemed to have a different climate – snow cover for ten months of the year in this hollow, the next dip constantly blown free; a minute desert under this little rock, damp cavelike conditions under that one; roots here penetrating the thin soil, there dangling over a cliff. The first bloom I saw above the timberline in the Sawatch was the crocus-like Pasque flower. Pasque is the Spanish for Easter, but at this altitude they flowered three months late. If you don't have much time, and six-week summers is all that tundra plants get, you either react as saxifrage does in a carnival frenzy, costuming, parading, and dispersing pollen in no more than a long weekend, or, like alpine phlox, take decades to reach the size of a pincushion. I hated to tread on these tiny plants. What a paradox, in this huge, rugged land, to feel so unwittingly clumsy.

Clouds had gathered with unusual fervour and, anticipating a storm, I weighed the tent down with stones, but next morning the ground was still dry and I went on under clear skies, the Uncompaghre Peaks glistening white on the western horizon. Pine-dark foothills rose from the sage of the Gunnison Basin. I could see the raw scar of route # 50 slashing up through the timber, the dinky-toy traffic grinding its way up to Monarch Pass. The growl of traffic grew louder as I dropped to the head of a ski lift, following the silvery pylons down to a large car park on the saddle. Brightly coloured bubbles, full of people, were popping out of the station and swaying back up the hill.

"Gondola to the sky", said the notice by the door. "Take a never-to-be-forgotten ride . . . see 150 miles . . . photograph five major ranges . . . " View this, see that, experience the other – why did Americans express themselves in this roll up, roll up way? Most of the high passes read like the *Guinness Book of Records* – an alliterative mass of statistics and facts for easy readin' at the roadside. Coming away you knew everything about a place except what it was actually like. You judged it by its signs. This was America's trick: to lure everything, even emotions, into gaily painted bubble-cars, and with encouraging whoops of "The sky's the limit!", set you off to see the signs. I sometimes wished, in the interests of my own education, that I were illiterate.

Creede to Garfield had been a short stage – just over a hundred miles in six days. The food box was at a hotel below the pass, and I wound down the road to collect it against a stream of motorized campers – Winnebagos, Renegades, Braves, Jamborees – hauling up from the Arkansas valley. By the time they'd climbed this far the excitement of hairpin bends had worn off, and a guy backpacking the kerb became the star distraction. Vehicle after vehicle crawled by: Walkman headphones were pushed back, picnic chicken legs were raised, all the kids waved and smiled. And I waved and smiled back – real waves and genuine smiles at first, but six miles of them was too far.

The hotel was large, a tight squeeze in a valley already in shadow by mid-afternoon, and though I was grateful to the staff for looking after my box, there was no one person in particular to thank. This made me feel like a representative of myself, and I took a few minutes to relax. I picked up a pamphlet in the hall: "Fifty manicured ski trails," it said, "On 700 sub-alpine acres. Horseback riding . . . white water rafting . . . sauna . . . jacuzzi, pro shop, gift shop, heated pool, nautilus and bar . . . " Outside, spruce trees ran up the steep slopes. Inside, thick carpet lined the walls. The personnel were nearly all still in their twenties and most of them lived in, though the lady in the health centre did not. This was just as well. Her breasts, even through two glass doors, put me back at least three incarnations. The receptionist told to me to regard myself as a guest, to use whatever I wanted, and led me down through the basement to an outbuilding which was mine for the night. It was like being on a corporate account. My laundry (I'd slammed the machine door on two T-shirts and two pairs of socks) looked like refugees in the back of a Bentley. I picked up a crisp white towel and, extending just the tips of my fingers, adjusted the shower to hot.

"See you in the bar," Carla, the receptionist, had said, and, glowingly clean, I climbed the stairs to meet her. She was already slotting back lagers, but being-indoors-on-a-nice-day-like-this is a sin I've never managed to shake off, and I fidgeted on my stool. Carla ordered another round, the barman hovering with a spatula to deal with the froth. It was odd how the land of fast food had produced such time-wasting beer. You could practically shave in the stuff. The barman caught my eye in mid-sip and I nodded into the froth. Yes, I'd have another – a tell-tale-sign joke was coming – another small one, shaven not . . . I sent a mouthful of beer over the barman and reeled howling into the gents. I wanted to belch, I wanted to breathe, I wanted to hiccup and fart. I leaned heavily against the urinal. I love dropping quips into people's soup bowls – ten points if you spray the hostess – but this time I'd scored an own goal. I took a deep breath, reconquered my stool, and apologized to the splattered barman. He thought a bit of crisp had got stuck in my throat. I said I was OK now and asked for a glass of water. One of the cooks – his name was Jim – had come in from the kitchen, and hearing I was English stayed for a game of darts. He and Carla invited me to go rafting the next day.

They called for me early, we drove downhill for an hour, and turned left. It was hot. We were in the Arkansas valley, the snow-capped peaks of the Sawatch rising sharply to the west, the gentler slopes of the Mosquitoes to the east. Following the crest of the Sawatch, the eighty miles north to Leadville and food box number seven would take me another six days, but today was a holiday, and with the river in full flood the raft trip was really good fun. We were laughing and sparkling all the way back up to Garfield, where Jim returned to the kitchen, Carla to reception, and I, after a good night's sleep, to the mountains.

To the wrong mountains. So much for a good night's sleep.

8 The Northern Sawatch

I was way above timberline before I realized my mistake. There were peaks all over the place – fleets of them – but no amount of shouting and stamping my feet would get a launch sent across to collect me, and it took the rest of the morning to tack back into convoy.

The San Juans – now a full week behind me – had had their rugged moments, but tended, especially in the south, to plateau-like horizons. The Sawatch, by contrast, bit greedily at the sky – an upthrust core of ancient granite with residual scraps of this and that still on its back. I like to know where I am geologically but tend to get muddled, taking the age of the rock for the age of the formation, or mistaking later conversions and adaptations for original constructions.

There is nothing inherently complicated about the process of mountain-building itself. The San Juans, two weeks south, had been an example of the poured-concrete method, the molten ingredients having flooded about until they found their own level. The Sawatch, however, had been jacked up en bloc from below, though what I actually saw – the summits and the valleys – weren't so much erections as demolitions, a coverless merry-go-round, huge and scrumptiously looming. There! – a stone had bounced down the talus ahead, the hurdy-gurdy advancing in a series of infinitesimal chinks. Some of the peaks around me weren't far off three miles high. Supposing they lost a quarter of an inch a year, how long would it be till they were flat? The answer trickled out a mile later. Three-quarters of a million years. Was that all? Mountains were almost butterflies.

Somewhere next morning – it was July 9th – I passed my eight-hundredth mile. I threw off the pack and was rolling nose-down in an alpine meadow. It was spattered with sunflowers and gentian. I stuck a flower in each ear, let out a yodel, and ran all the way down to a nickle-sized lake way below. The yodelling was cut short about a hundred yards before I got there. I'd seen people sitting on the rocks, and I wasn't ready.

Above the road passes Colorado was unmarked territory, the high tundra a kind of free state: I'd descended to America when I'd felt like it, otherwise I'd been in a world of my own. Not that I regarded the people ahead as intrusive. Far from it. Approaching the family fishing from the rocks, I felt just as if I had guests.

I knew I was going to like them. They'd already scored straight A's in their hundred-metre test – the rule being that voices be inaudible over that distance – and having chatted to them for a couple of minutes, they flew through the clack test as well. Clack is the conversational equivalent of hill fog, a meaningless drizzle which obscures just about everything it touches. But the Mitchells had the blessed knack of beholding, of being able to look without smothering, lassoing, hogtying and branding whatever it was that they saw. When Mrs Mitchell said that they'd lived outside the States for ten years I wasn't surprised.

"Thing with America," she said, "is facts. Everything is facts. The flag, the constitution, it's all facts you can't argue with, the result being that we don't think about things so much as react to them. See, the rest of the world, especially Europe and Asia, has tradition between it and reality, a grey area, a kinda flexible cushion. What we Americans have between us and reality is the goddamned NBC, and you ever see a television so much as blink you be sure and let us Mitchells know."

I had lunch with them and moved on, bees with red bums droning over the Divide, the air thick with the scent of dwarf clover. Deserted though the tundra was, it was here that I felt most at home, almost every square foot a new hideout into which I could snuggle with my tea and cigarette. I felt psychologically at ease up here, no longer in the least bit eccentric: given a suitable vehicle and a winch I could have driven at least half of my route through New Mexico, but there was no possibility of that in Colorado. With the snow as it was you couldn't even have ridden a mule along the route that I'd taken.

The Divide pitched through the Sawatch at between twelve and thirteen thousand feet above sea level. The summits varied, but, rough or smooth, the same ridgeline rolled forward, the same personal discomforts persisted. The little events that broke through these continuities were, therefore, the more memorable – the vivid lichens of

Sawatch (rough); a lone bumble bee hitching a ride on my pack; a fox
– what was a fox doing up here? – and, in the loose granite of Sawatch
(smooth), my discovery of the pika.

The stove was roaring under a potful of snow when I saw my first
one. I was on a peak called Emma Burr Mountain, leaning out for a
second scoop at a drift, when I saw what looked like a very small RAF
officer flicking about in the rocks. It vanished. I reloaded the pot – the
meltdown ratio was about three of snow to one of water – and the
pika reappeared, minus its ridiculous moustache. It was evidently
stocking up with dry grass for the winter. It brought back a vivid
memory.

As a Wildlife Officer in West Africa, I'd had a pet Rock Hyrax, a
young one, which could jump – boing! – straight from the floor to your
shoulder in one go. It generally did this at meal times, and, being a
little unco-ordinated, would invariably overbalance as it landed. For
which it generally received a round of applause and helping hand out
of the soup, ink or gravy into which it had unerringly toppled. Its first
performance, and so its name, had been into a bowl of custard. The
pika on Emma Burr Mountain, and all subsequent pikas, reminded
me so much of young Custard that I sometimes had to sniff and move
on.

The pika wasn't the only sign of life on the mountain. I'd seen a
couple of ptarmigan and a few white-crowned sparrows, and could
now hear rocks below displaced by something a good deal larger.
Something which spoke English. Grunts of "Motherfuckin' hill!" and,
"If Emma Burr made it, we can," were getting louder by the second.
Finally a head popped over the ridge and said, "Shit, some guy's
already up here."

The three of them – teenage boys – were on holiday in Tincup, an
old mining camp turned summer resort in the valley three thousand
feet below. Emma Burr must have been quite a slog for them. They
assumed I'd come up from the east, and when I told them I was
actually walking the ridge-top – that I'd been up here for the past fifty
miles – they weren't particularly impressed.

"So you haven't climbed this mother from the bottom then, huh?"

I admitted that I hadn't.

"And you're not American, right?"

I admitted that I wasn't.

"D'you always stop for tea at four?"

I admitted that I generally didn't.

"You really English?"

We scrambled together for a few hundred yards before they peeled off the crest and headed back down the scree. The last I saw of them were three multi-coloured dots having a rock-hurling contest off an arrette. High on the skyline, I laughed with the idiotic joy this walk so often brought.

9 The Collegiate Peaks

Route # 50 had tacked inexorably up to Monarch Pass, but – two days and twenty-five miles further north – the ribbon of dirt draped over Cottonwood Pass had a pleasing innocence, like a wriggle of spaghetti against the jagged cutlery of the mountains ahead. At just over 12,000 feet Cottonwood is the highest vehicular crossing in the Rockies, which makes it, therefore, the highest point from which things can be chucked from car windows. Nappies, for example, half a dozen of which were lolling about in the breeze.

I moved upwind. Despite the altitude a sort of press corps of mosquitoes came with me. The pass was only a few hundred feet above timberline, the few individual spruces above the main mass of trees patient figures in dark green cloaks, or, where tall ones and short ones stood close together, like adults and kids holding hands. It was as if the whole forest had come streaming down from the Divide, a hurrying crowd which had packed the lower slopes tight and was backing up the gullies as the tail-enders came scuttling in. There was plenty of flattish ground up here but the 11,800-foot contour seemed to be the upper limit of tree growth. Six miles further north I could see other limits too, where descending rock glaciers had pushed the treeline another 400 feet downhill.

For the next seventy miles the Divide arched through a great sickle of peaks enclosing the upper Arkansas valley. Directly ahead, the spines of Mount Harvard and the Three Apostles were off-handedly shredding the clouds. I could almost feel myself saying "whoops" as huge chunks of space swam into view. But I wasn't equipped for a technical mountain climb, so, slapping irritably at the pursuing mosquitoes, I turned down through a steep mile of timber to a bog drained by Texas Creek. The water was freezing, it didn't flow towards Texas, but it was nice to feel clean.

I stayed west of the Divide for the next fifteen miles, drumming though the Collegiate Peaks Wilderness along a clear path called the Timberline Trail. There was no one on it – Colorado remained as empty as ever – but, empty or full, a trail is a trail and I felt its constrictions keenly. In gastronomic terms the high, trackless ridges were meals of organic simplicity; foot trails were heat-n-serve dinners; roads were fried take-aways.

The path wound on through the trees, my boots thumping over the roots. The sound made me think of buried treasure. Juvenile gangs of grey squirrels were playing peek-a-boo through the branches above, reckless infants who – one knew – weren't supposed to be wearing those tails. They would roar up the thin trunks then stop to make sure you were watching, the sort of I-don't-know-what-your-father's-going-to-say behaviour to which new babysitters are generally subjected. Below them sparkled bilberries wet from the rain.

The rain. Impossible, when you're dry, to imagine. Rain that doubles the weight of your clothes, that turns innocent dust into mud. Rain that blends, that spatters, that spreads, that glues, diffuses, clumps and combines; that changes coefficients of this, alters factors of that: miserable, godawful rain. It poured every day bar three for the following month.

I survived by following a simple rule, learned on playing fields far from Eton. In fact they weren't playing fields at all but bleak meadows, and through them ran a ditch into which I and my rucksack had slipped. I was small for my age, and so, luckily, was the ditch. Covered in slime, I had stood in a dung pat and cried – no towel, no dry clothes (I'd thought that rucksacks were waterproof – at that age you believe anything) and no friends: they were half a mile back down the tow-path, sensibly sheltering from the downpour which I, a ten-year-old blimp, had stiffly refused to acknowledge. They dried me out and said nothing, the lesson being that heroes, even small ones, get wet if they push their luck. The rule was never to do so; to be, in fact, a complete cissy; to pre-empt the slightest hint of a dousing with as much wetproofing as possible.

Luckily, the Rockies left you in little doubt as to whether it was raining or not, the typical weather pattern being clear skies till mid-morning, gathering clouds, and a downpour by mid-afternoon. There was little of the on-off-on business that so bedevils a day in the Scottish Highlands, and so far my theory that the Rockies would prove no worse than Scotland had been right. The ground was, in general, dry underfoot, the wind neither misty nor damp, and, despite all the snow, it was much warmer than I'd expect upland Britain to be. I wore shorts most mornings and didn't need my gloves till September. If you're happy above 2000 feet in Britain, you'll be happy, in summer, in the Rockies.

In the contiguous states – mainland USA excluding Alaska – there are about sixty peaks over 14,000 feet. I could see a third of them from where I was sitting. Huron Peak, twelve miles to the south, made the height by the skin of its teeth, but Grizzly Peak, 13,988 feet, did not. One hundredth of one per cent short. I could have played the height game all day. There was Mount Princeton, 14,195 feet; and there Mount Yale, 14,194 feet. How could a mountain over two miles high be just one foot taller than its neighbour? And why were these abstractions so gratifying? Slicing off the qualifying 14,000 feet I was left with theoretical nipples: Holy Cross and Huron, both five feet tall; Snowmass, a white whale on the western horizon, 92 feet; and, tough luck there Harvard, Mount Massive beats you by a foot to third place as the all-American mountain. First is Mount Whitney in California, and here I was on top of number two. So let's hear it now! A round of applause. It's your own your very own – Mount ELBERT!

To give it its due it did at least look like an Elbert, swelling dumpy and fat straight from the Arkansas valley. Mount Elbert isn't actually on the Divide – only one fourteener is – but it lies directly between Lake Pass, where I'd crossed the spine of the Collegiate Peaks, and Leadville, for which I was heading. I could see the town spread out in the haze, ten miles away and four thousand feet below. From the summit I had a bird's eye view of the entire Sawatch sickle, roughly 500 square miles in each eye. I could see absolutely everything.

When Yuri Gagarin, the first man in space, undid his seat belt and looked down, his first words, no doubt, were "Stone me!", but the ensuing silence must have had misson control rattled. It was surely a lovely day. Yuri must have seen the whole chain of the Urals. Here came the Baltic, Denmark a rampant sore throat. And that patch of cloud must be Britain. Everything was fitting into place. Everything was coming to be. Yuri in his rocket, atlas on his knees, and me on Mount Elbert, map on mine, were happy men. For us the world was confirmed.

Meanwhile, I had company. Mount Elbert is a tourist attraction, and a summer camp group – bobble hats and crisps – had arrived panting at the top. They were all kids from the east coast, except one whose name was Hans. He said, "The mountains are good, I like they," – at which a kid from New York said that Hans liked girls as well.

"Ja, but only on Saturdays do we see they for our activities."

Everyone giggled.

"For activities is best the infirmary."

"Anyone in it now?"

"Yeah," said the kid from New York. "The nurse is."

Everyone giggled again and looked at Ron, who was in charge. He was picking up scraps of orange peel. He said it wouldn't be bio-degradeable up here and in any case it was time to get back down to the truck.

"'Kay, you guys, listen now. Gonna teach you how to glissade. You sorta run down the snow kinda jumpin' an' slippin' . . . " but the bobbles were already flying, anoraks unzipped and yelling for joy till they ran out of snow. They looked back to hoot as Ron set off himself. I lumbered after him, nose-diving half way to a fusilade of raised Instamatics. Then on we went – lots of questions, like could they try on the pack and did I take baths and how did I like America? No why-are-you-doing-this questions though – no requests for a motive. That was obvious. Glissading is a good laugh.

10 Leadville

At dawn the moraines of the Arkansas basin were wreathed in a drenching mist. I'd come off the mountain through aspen-choked bogs, guessing my way round disruptive dredgings, and had camped by an evil-looking pond. I compressed the tent into a horrid wet ball and marched briskly down route # 24.

From the air – and Mount Elbert had been the air – the townsite of Leadville appeared as a threadbare patch in a dark rug of pine. I could have guessed at, but not seen, the usual sign outside the bank winking time and temperature down mainstreet – 10 a.m. and 70 degrees when I got there – though I could not have known that mainstreet was in fact called Harrison Avenue; nor that lace curtains and old-maidish blinds would hang tasseled in all the windows – sash windows, set back into four-storied brick running all the way down both sides of the street. There was even an opera house.

My excitement at Leadville's Victorian façade was a worrying sign.
I was already calling petrol "gasoline", and saying things like "Hi"
and "Sure" and "I guess", and now my sense of historical perspective
was going native too. The worn flagstone pavements, the brickwork,
the cast-iron lamps – things that wouldn't have even registered back
home – here seemed tremendously significant. In nine hundred miles
I'd seen nothing bar a Navajo *hogon* to seriously suggest other times,
but here was proof that today really did have yesterday behind it.
Some of these buildings were as much as ninety years old.

Eleven different minerals had once been mined in Lake County (it
said so in the museum), principally gold in the 1860s, silver in the 70s
and 80s, lead, copper, tin, zirconium, and today, molybdenum – for
which the market had collapsed. The local cinema (called the Cine-
moly) was shut. So was the big mine up on Freemont Pass, and so
were a lot of the shops. One house in six was for sale. When I asked
a guy in the post office if there was a cobbler in town, I got a lecture
on Japanese imports.

Village Outfitters had a good smell of leather about it. Denis Wakeen
gave me his card, told me to sit, and fixed the rucksack while I waited,
a pre-emptive replacement of a partly frayed strap and a couple of
suspect rivets. I liked Denis. He got on with the job. In America you
bought services in much the same spirit as groceries; you didn't have
to perform minuets round intrusive sensibilities.

My bootsoles, new on the Mexican border, were significantly worn,
and I asked Denis if he could replace them.

"Could do," he said, "but they don't really need it yet."

"Will they last another fifteen hundred miles?"

"Might do," he said. "Only one way to find out."

I put Denis on my postcard list and walked north out of town, past
Ron Sweet – Dentistry, Safeway, Best Western and the speed limits.
Pine needles and ring-pulls littered the verge. I thought of coconut
matting in summer marquees as I hauled in under the pines. I unrolled
the mat, put too much salt in my stew, and slept. Despite broken toys
here, the odd lump of brick there, the midden of my days seemed to
be decomposing nicely, building up to that not-quite homogenous
mulch that is the lasting treasure of a journey.

11 Leadville to Hoosier Pass

While my past was maturing, and the present entertaining, the future was, as ever, a blank, my ideas about what might be lying ahead as loose as my bundle of maps. In the mountains I took each mile more or less as it came, though the next 135 were to be especially trying, the Divide wriggling in all directions but directly south. I was on it most mornings, driven off it by storms most afternoons. It rained a great deal, I was fog-bound at one point, and though I hadn't planned to, I ended up at a place called Grand Lake. It took me two weeks to get there from Leadville, averaging about ten miles a day. It was the slowest section of the whole trip.

I turned off the highway next morning twelve miles north of town, cutting across part of the molybdenum complex to approach the Divide through a sunless defile. Huge metal castings were stacked in the open on pallets. Windowless structures, linked by conveyors, cluttered the valley floor. The place was deserted, not even a cat among the weeds. I walked a little bit faster. I was nearly free of the complex, less than a minute from the first boulders, when I heard a vehicle behind me. Oh God. I'd never make it to the mountainside in time. They'd have dark glasses (they always did); and polo-necked jumpers; and dogs. On leashes. Hot, meaty breath; pitiless, guttural accents.

But this wasn't a security patrol. I turned to see a battered old jeep being driven by a man with one thumb. The rest of his right hand was missing. A mining accident, he said. He asked how I'd got into the milling area, and I said I'd come in off the road. It had seemed the best place to start climbing.

"Ha!" said the man. "Ha! You didn't see the main access then?"

I'd ducked under the chain.

"All-right!" The thumb jabbed at the map, at the mine straddling the pass directly above us. "You ducked in! Well I broke in. I gotta legal claim up this valley and Climax's blocking me out. So I finally got me a journalist!" – he nudged his fat passenger – "and I bust them chains right off. Small man gets trod flat too fuckin' easy these days."

The maimed hand dropped to the wheel. "Where you from yourself?
England? Exchange rates must be hitting you hard."

Exchange rates? Did he say exchange rates? How very exotic. Verbal
sash windows almost. Just as I'd grown used to flat time – to the
constant present of American buildings (hence my reaction to Leadville) – so I'd grown used to flat culture, to conversation, for example,
in which the slighest acknowledgement that a world existed outside
America was intriguing.

"I deal with a guy in Lancashire county," the man in the jeep was
saying. "That anywhere near you? Your pound's kinda diving and his
stuff's getting cheaper all the time. Nazi insignia mostly. Stuff over
here's always fake."

History, culture, and lately geography – a third subconscious change
I noticed in myself was in the way I now handled mountains. From a
distance they seemed so honest. They looked you straight in the eye
– no ravines, no foothills, no demoralizing false summits. But a mountain is your basic con man, your man-in-a-suit with that sharp little
hankie of snow up there in the breast pocket. You have to get right
up close to see how dirty that snow generally is. You have to jam your
boots right into the small print of the slope before the hereinafters of
dead ground and the wheretofors of false summits become apparent.
But that cardboard cut-out skyline didn't fool me anymore. When I
began a climb now it was in anticipation of hitches – of loose, cruddy
rock; of suddenly doubled distances; of straining kneecaps (what a
curiously liquid, grinding sound they made); and of storms. The main
thing was to keep going, no matter how slowly, so as not break the
upward rhythm. By this time I was looking down on the mine, having
climbed fifteen hundred feet in exactly the time I'd anticipated –
nothing short of miraculous expertise three months ago was now just
another ascent; the mine just another mine, though from up here to
down there wasn't far short of a half-mile drop – an entire hillside
removed for something I could hardly pronounce.

Molybdenum is a silver-grey metal, about as heavy as lead. It melts
at 4730 degrees Farenheit (iron is almost a gas at this temperature)
and it was first used by the French to toughen armour plate. Economic
recession had currently halted operations at Climax, but at full rip the
conveyor belts process 48,000 tons of ore a day. There were vehicles
down there with tyres ten feet high; machines under the mountain
which could grind immense boulders to sand. They were silent. Many
of the miners had found jobs in nearby ski resorts – the guy in the

Leadville post office had mentioned Aspen and Vail, but, "Ain't the same, though," he'd muttered.

I could see what he meant. Manning a ski tow might be fun, but blowing up an entire mountainside is power. So is a thunderstorm. Two miles to the south, Mount Democrat had taken a direct hit. It was time to drop off the Divide. By doing so I stepped from the Arkansas basin to the drainage of the South Platte.

"Scarcely any person but a madman," wrote Zebulon M. Pike, lieutenant, 1st US Infantry, "would attempt to trace [the Arkansas and the Platte] further than the entrance of these mountains . . . " – the mountains I was now in. Pike had been in difficulties though – the winter of 1807 being one, the fact that he was completely lost another. "A great mortification," he recorded, but he managed to sort himself out and struggle south to further adventures in Chihuahua. I, however, straggled east – the Divide was being perverse – and dropped off McNamee Peak to avoid the storm. I regained the watershed by early evening at a place called Hoosier Pass.

The tent virtually erected itself these days. I was hardly conscious of doing it, nor, generally, of the other mundane chores about camp: I continued to cook by numbers; I walked from dawn to dusk; I slept the rest of the time. It must have been all the fresh air.

I usually got up at six – albeit reluctantly, the earth which had punched and kicked me all night now being perversely seductive. My first thought on waking was always the same: "Must," I would insist to myself, "must fix up a better pillow." But I'm a what-goes-up-won't-come-down-for-ages sort of person, and, fifteen hours later – tent up, gear stowed – I'd have a last swig of tea, a slash in the bushes, and crawl into the bag. And goddamn it, I've forgotten to fix a good pillow yet again. But it's not worth disrupting everything now, so I reach for whatever is closest – almost always the camera bag. I stuff a wet sock under my cheek, feel a lens hood digging into my temple. I shove another sock under my cheek. I toss; I turn; I tell myself not to be so soft – tonight is, after all, The Very Last Night of All This. Tomorrow I'll definitely remember. And, with a zip in my ear, I do eventually fall asleep. So far, I have had ten weeks of Very Last Nights.

It may seem that my traverse of the high Rockies was an interminable round of packing and unpacking, of putting up and taking off – and with an inconstant mixture of sweat, rain and sleet to contend with this is just about the truth. I spent most of the time in a sort of long-distance limbo – truck drivers will know what I mean – thumb up bum, mind very much in neutral. But at least truck drivers have truck stops. They have hash browns to order; eggs over easy and the waitress' love bites to ponder. I had none of these things.

It had been the emptiness, the nothing-to-do-ness, that had most hit me when I first went hiking. Frog-filled ditches were nothing compared to the awfulness of unfilled time. Then I went to Africa. I spent two years with very few books in a very great deal of bush. My accustomed input disrupted, I was faced with large gaps on my plate, gaps where the meat – the social intercourse, the radio, the TV, the books – should have been. Africa's gift was the revelation that this meat wasn't as vital as I'd previously supposed. Africa leavened the guilt of not-doing. It helped me to face up to being.

Meanwhile the drumming on the flysheet had stopped. The last half hour of daylight was getting grimier by the minute and I wanted at least some tea. But even the tundra – subdued and dwarfed – keeps rain in play long enough for a jolly, post-downpour game. It's called "Wet the Camper", a contest of subtlety and skill in which size isn't always an advantage. The heavily drenched spruces of Hoosier Pass, for example, were too obviously laden to play. It was spiders' webs I had to look out for, and the near leafless bilberries under my knees as I crawled from the tent. The flysheet played a blinder right down my back; a guy rope flicked me in the eye – but the whistle for half-time had already gone. I'd caught sight of a flimsy bivouac rigged under the trees straight ahead. Beside it was a blue trail bike. In the ten weeks since the Mexican border this was the first night's pitch I had shared. I called out a hallo and strolled over.

A short, damp youth was eating dried bananas and raisins.

"Trail Mix," he said. "All I need."

This was just as well since it seemed to be all he had. I reckoned I was in for a classic "nice blade" conversation. His name, by the way, was Steve.

"Climbed any fourteeners?" he asked.

"Only Mount Elbert," I said. "There were lots of day-trippers at the top."

"Waste products," said Steve.

I said nothing. His moustache was pathetic. So was the bivouac. I gave him one out of ten, not for the camp, but for having a motorbike on which he could escape down the valley. He looked the sort of guy who might need it. I continued to say nothing, and in ten minutes had produced a potful of supper. What the hell for? Steve didn't thank me, he wolfed the lot, and said he hoped the noodles weren't made with lard. He didn't eat animal fats. Then he lay in the tent – my dry tent – drivelling on about rock groups and making free with my sugar. This was food I'd carried for miles, scarce, rationed food which no one would expect me to part with. But I was playing the "nice blade" game too. This barrage of apparent generosity was a potlatch, a tribal feast, an exchange of wealth for status. I hadn't cooked supper for Steve because he was hungry, though he was – very – but to shame him. My motives should have been better, but they weren't.

Having got up I could crack down a campsite and be gone in about twenty minutes – half an hour if I breakfasted, though I'd gone off breakfast recently. It only led to a craving for lunch, so my tendency was to sneak in as many miles as possible before my stomach woke up. On Hoosier Pass, though, I ate before I set off – tea, porridge and peanut butter. Peanut butter! Tincture of honeydew, acme of all desire, and certainly not to be wasted on the still sleeping Steve. To consume ten days' supply at a gulp was the greatest temptation I knew. The second greatest was to eat all the jam.

I had alternating flavours. Leadville to Winter Park happened to be a strawberry stretch. Winter Park to Rabbit Ears Pass would therefore be apricot. I kept the jam in a plastic tube. When it was finished I'd pour in hot water and swill it round to get the last smears, but I could trowel a whole biscuit through the peanut butter container. The level went down by an exact quarter inch per day: any man caught taking more than his share to be keelhauled, shot, tortured and burned, then flogged to a jelly at the masthead. Luckily I knew the captain, a daft old sod who let me off time without number.

My third favourite goodie was sugar which I didn't ration because half sweetness is so frustrating – like only having a half-stick of chewing gum. Half hunger, however, was something I just had to put up with. This was day two from Leadville, the euphoric effects of hot dogs and milk shakes fast fading. Hunger, exiled at the edge of town, was back, a bad fairy I had to placate. My tactic was to eat as often as possible – on average every two hours – but in such minute quantities that stocks were always preserved. This called for good timing. If I left it too late I'd get the dreaded colleywobbles, feel faint, and have to sit down. Too early and I'd just waste the effect. It was a bit like having your fuel gauge permanently on red because of a hole low down in your tank.

12 Montezuma

I'd set out from Mexico on May 5th – today was July 15th – and in all that time I'd not seen a single backpacker. Encounters with anyone actually en route had been such rarities I remembered them all: Peggy, the drunk li'll cowgirl; Dolores, the Navajo with whom I'd walked a mile or so; Dee and Bonny, the couple following the Divide on horseback; and, rumour only, the Canadian sisters who were supposed to be walking the Divide like me.

The outside world, then, had impinged largely on my terms. But Denver was only an hour's drive away now, and a number of small mining-turned-vacation towns – Breckenridge, Fairplay, Dillon – were tucked into the valleys below, though up here there were no signs of them yet. I picked up my gear, and, already dreaming my way up the opposite hillside, stepped across Hoosier Pass. I was sent flying by a guy on a bicycle.

Fortunately no damage was done. I apologized for not looking and tried very hard not to stare – glistening spokes, designer tracksuit, and here came his girlfriend, also bronzed, though a bit wobbly as she turns on the crest. How marvellous! Denver was close – I knew that from the map – and hey presto, up pop a couple of yuppies, expectation, confirmation and realization all suddenly flashing together. I love this delicious congruency. Put the milk out for the cat in the morning and boink! – there he is. The mind somehow manufactures him from the saucer, the milk, the noise of the back door opening. His actual presence isn't necessarily required, but when he does turn up he fits perfectly into the headspace provided.

George and Suszu, who I met at midday, also lived in Denver, but they had separate flats. They were out for a day's hike with George's wife's dog. Despite the altitude – over 13,000 feet – it was warm, and Suszu asked what I usually wore. Shorts, I said, and a T-shirt. A pile jacket in the wind, knee breeches in bad weather.

"D'you ever, I mean, take your clothes off?"

I was astounded. What an excellent question. Easily the best of the trip. Bang! – right to the heart of the thing. No hovering round for poundage or mileage – she didn't want the rules or the score but a direct feel for the quality of play. Unfortunately, the answer to her question was no, except sometimes in camp. I knew what she was getting at – walking in the nude is a fabulous feeling – but on this trip I needed something between the pack straps and my skin.

I made my usual detour that afternoon, swinging down to the timber to avoid the approaching storm. George and Suszu had given me a carrier bag full of food – chicken, sausage, peaches, a wedge of cheese and some grapes – which had lasted roughly twenty minutes, but spitting out the last of the grape pips I decided to keep the chicken for supper. This was a mistake.

A torrent pouring down through the boulder-strewn peat had induced me to take a leak – the sound of running water often seemed to have this effect – and I was in full flow when I heard a scuffle round the carrier bag and looked up. A ferret-sized creature had the chicken leg right in its mouth. Its black eyes were entirely unflustered, a pair of beady computers calmly assessing distance and speed. Ping! The answer arrived, the chicken leg was dropped, and the animal slithered into the trees. I let out a pent-up breath and water-cannoned a pine cone. Could I hose it into the stream before my main tank ran dry? I'd just got it rolling when I heard the scuffle again. This time I was too late. I got a brief glimpse of abducted flesh, and the raider, a pine marten, was gone.

The following morning I reached a saddle called Boreas Pass, and the glee I had felt – two weeks before – at discovering a misprint on the map, evaporated. Teacher was right after all. A yard-wide conduit, obviously man-made, was flowing purposefully over the watershed. I realized that Lake Fork, Saquache Creek, must have been an irrigation channel too. There is no absolute shortage of water in Colorado, in fact water is the major export, but the Colorado river, down which most of it goes, flows completely the wrong way – towards Arizona and Southern California instead of across the prairies where all the good farmland and most of the people are waiting. A series of reservoirs in the upper Colorado basin supplies the urban sprawl below the Front Range via tunnels driven straight through the mountains. It seemed somehow stupendous that cities as large and as far apart as San Diego and Denver should depend for their existence – via pipeline and tunnel – on a river in whose basin neither lie.

The maps I'd bought in Leadville – thirty-five miles back by now – were delightfully contoured. The Sawatch were shown as swirling green djinns, the headwalls almost solid blocks of colour, while the contours beyond Boreas Pass swayed north-east in a sensuous flamenco. The change was quite abrupt. On the map a swarm of giggling green lines had become a few amiable chuckles; on the ground the Divide now wound ahead across hills much like Scottish moorland, lolloping over convex tweedy slopes, treeless, soothing, and dotted with what looked like fresh burrows.

The symbol for a mine on the maps I had bought was a tiny cross. Kiss kiss kiss kiss – there were hundreds of them, passionately thick along some deep valleys, isolated pecks on the summits, some so high up, and on such steep slopes, that log platforms had been built to terrace the entrance shafts. I could see where mule trains had stitched their way up to these long-abandoned hermitages, the pale splash of the spoil visible for miles. There was something strangely impelling about the scattered diggings – tiny windows of hope set into the rolling hillsides.

The hump-backed country had put a spring in my heels. I was dreaming on the wind, no longer having to look down at each step but flying for miles, the only boy on the roof of the world. Then suddenly I wasn't. It was "Hi!" and "How are ya?" and click click click click as a posse marked Breckenridge Jeep Tours gunned past. I stepped smartly out of the way. This was one of the few places in the high Rockies where in a suitable vehicle you could not just drive across the Divide but along it.

A second safari cart went past, then a third. I felt like a lion in a game park. Should I lie in the trail and give the folks a thrill by gnawing a Snicker? The sound of the jeeps died away, to be followed by an unhealthy splutter. A private car was being nursed over the brow of the hill. There was a burst of rock music, laughter, and a jolting of heads as the tyres lurched over a rock.

"Hi," said the driver. "Trying to get away from it all?"

The car, impressively inadequate for rough hill-driving, was cheerfully crowded – three Americans, two New Zealanders, and a guy from Blackpool, Lancashire. Eric, the owner of the car, was in the back.

"Come on down to Montezuma," he said.

"That's Montezuma, Colorado," said Corrie, on Eric's lap.

"Bloody hell," said Dominic. I had dumped the rucksack on his knees.

"Where is it?"

"Just . . . " Lindsay pointed into the valley ". . . just down there. It's a very small place."

"Average age twenty-seven years and four months." This was Brad. "We got two pensioners only, but they both like Pink Floyd. They'll be at the pig roast tonight. Ask for the Tiltin' Hilton."

"The what?"

"The bloody Tiltin' Hilton," said Dominic, who was almost too thin to be true. "It's their house. It was designed by a psychiatrist. This bag's bloody killing me."

Everything about Dominic was thin, as I discovered over the next couple of days, especially his voice, which was devoid of any expression whatsoever. To meet a fellow-countryman on top of a mountain so far from home, one who, far from being a climber, had run a fishing tackle shop on Blackpool sea front for the past six years, should have been a riot. But that voice rinsed everything to death. Crisp adventure, and Dominic seemed to have had plenty, came out worse than school cabbage. If he had suddenly stood up and screamed "Fire!" there would have been no exclamation-mark, no capital letter, and no one would have taken the slightest notice. The consequence was that nothing he said sank in till hours after he'd said it, and I was still picking bits of him out of my brain a month later.

Brad, on the other hand, picked bits of me out of my brain almost straightaway. He took a couple of pictures the next afternoon and I was in the *Summit Sentinel* the following week – "thin and well muscled, Pern stands five feet ten inches . . . as he heads towards Canada his one wish is . . . he sees America as . . . bla, bla, bla, he says. Behind the heavily bearded face is . . . a man who has . . . and will continue to . . . on a journey few people take." But I liked Brad. He is the only journalist I've ever met who wanted to own and run his own paper.

Eric wasn't sure what he wanted to do – law back home in South Dakota or history somewhere else. Meanwhile he had a summer job at a hotel down the valley. So had Corrie, who knew exactly what she wanted to do but Eric hadn't quite got the message. Lindsay worked at the hotel too. She was the reason that Gerry, the other New Zealander, had turned up in Montezuma. Gerry didn't really look at you when he spoke but more or less interviewed his beer glass, wondering perhaps what had happened to the Lindsay he was used to from back home. Things weren't working out. He and Dominic left next day for Denver and I headed for Loveland Pass, an eleven-mile haul through thick drizzle.

I could hear the traffic swishing up Interstate # 70, in top gear for the past hour now since leaving Denver and no need to change down for at least another fifty miles. I # 70 doesn't bother with hairpins. It bangs straight up Clear Creek valley, smacks through the Divide via a two-mile tunnel, and sails calmly down the far side. I'd be looking down on the tunnel entrance in the morning. Meanwhile I snuggled down for a torchlight inspection of the map.

A torchlight inspection of the map – how dry that sounds, how frightfully British. But this was no deadpan perusal, no cool peck on the cheek before lights out. I didn't just look at the map: I raped the bugger, every night of the walk without fail, gave it the most thorough scrooging any map could possibly receive. This was the moment I counted up the day's gold; slavered over the ledgers; worried – about food, about fuel, about time, about anything I could think of; the moment when, licking my lips, I would put that pink dot – it was always pink – on the map. The one, two, three, four . . . the twenty-fifth dot in Colorado. And my eyes would snake after them, dot after dot, one for every past campsite. I wrote "arr. 1930, 18 Jul" beside the latest and switched off the torch. I even got pleasure in that. Torch on – I could drool over the books; torch off – I was saving the batteries.

It had not, however, been as gratifying a map session as usual. I # 70 marked – near enough – the latitudinal half-way point of the journey, but I wasn't quite as pleased as I might have been. I'd taken a closer look at the peaks by-passed by my diversion down to Monte-zuma – a line of rheumy old colonels drawn up round Horseshoe basin. I'd not missed much by the look of it – nice, open ascents, nothing like the last-of-the-Mohicans knife edge I'd had to traverse that morning. So just out of interest, which peaks had I actually missed? I shone the torch. Argentine Peak, Mount Edwards, Grays Peak . . . I'd regained the Divide a couple of miles north of Grays Peak. Looking back I'd noticed nothing unusual about it. A light scramble would have got me to the top. But the name rang a bell. Where had I heard it before? I looked through some long-congealed notes at the back of my diary – addresses, shopping lists . . . and there it was, GRAYS PEAK, followed by an oriental-looking bodyguard of asterisks. I closed the diary. Well? What were the asterisks for?

What are any asterisks for? To stress. To enhance. To draw attention to. Grays Peak, 14,270 feet, is the highest point on the Divide, and I had missed it.

13 Loveland Pass to Berthoud Pass

Two easy miles along the crestline brought me next morning directly above I # 70, a strip of old dental floss draped through the tunnel 1200 feet below. Up here on the ridge alpine sunflowers were in bloom, hundreds of small Harpo Marxes, grinning inanely at the sky. I sat on one by mistake. They take years to mature, flower only once, and die. And I had destroyed one. The green juice on my hands was real; the broken stem, the sun, my feet in dry socks, the packstraps, the breeze – all real. But I # 70 down there was not real. I # 70 was like a film. If below me now a car had spun out of control, if black smoke had poured upward, if ant people had scurried, I would have yawned no less deeply than I was yawning now. "A crash," I'd have thought, and moved on.

By making a fist and resting it palm down on a table your fingers form a steep slope. Reduce yourself now to the size of a nit, set off over your knuckles with a large rucksack, and you have some idea of what the Divide had been like for the past few days; and of how relatively small the tops of most mountains really are. The dramatic stretches – the impassable crags – are generally even smaller.

Now uncurl your fingers. They form a series of parallel valleys running at right angles to the main ridge – exactly the country ahead of me as I pushed north that morning. The heads of the valleys formed immense, grassy basins, cut off from each other but open to the commanding height of the Divide, the treeless slopes below spattered with hundreds of elk, drowsy and brown in the sun. They had no idea that they were being overlooked, but then neither had I. The ridge had grown stonier, bare outcrops becoming small cliffs, swooping talus smothering the grass, and, on the ramparts above me, I'd caught sight of a pure white dot.

There was nothing between it and the feathery moon. It was the bobble on the cap, the fairy on the tree. It was Tenzing and Hillary, up on the topmost tip. It was just where a Rocky Mountain Goat ought to be. I shot off a half dozen frames, the goat a mere pinprick against the blue sky but sure to leap away soon. I crept forward (why I crept is a mystery – the goat could see my every move) and raised the camera again. I got closer and closer and still the goat hadn't moved. The white speck was the size of a tennis ball now, definitely not just dust on the lens, though not yet large enough to convince Aunt Mabel – good old Aunt Mabel, the bane of family slide shows – that it was a goat. I was determined to silence her this Christmas, and the goat, it seemed, wished to help. It was certainly coming down towards me. It would soon fill the whole viewfinder. I was snapping away like a demon, had almost forestalled old A. M., but not quite. I had run out of film.

This was perhaps no bad thing. I lowered the camera, and in place of mere image was experience. The goat was incredibly tame – hardly a wild creature at all. I saw the wind carding its moulting fleece, heard the click of its black hooves. I could even see the texture of its pointy little horns. It was a very deliberate animal – it reminded me rather of a snowman – very grave, very slightly old-fashioned. I tossed it a piece of chocolate and regretted it instantly, a brash young passerby handing out sweets to a monk.

The plod uphill became a scramble and in places an actual climb, though Mount Hagar wasn't exactly the Eiger. It was more of a Hadrian's Wall, a precarious ruin, but this was the sort of walking I loved, high-altitude tag – agility, judgement, momentum, risk; both hands involved; no stopping, and definitely no tripping up. A careless body would have dropped sheer to the talus then – bouncey bounce bounce – go spinning – wheee! – off a buttress. I was really enjoying myself, the prisoner of Zenda, parrying blows, taking that! and that! on the skyline. Suddenly I came to a gap, a breach in the castle walls. Errol Flynn would have dived straight over. Errol Flynn would have broken both legs.

I lowered myself gingerly over the edge and into a new role. Goodbye Brylcreem, goodbye puffed sleeves, hallo green slime and rags – it was instant demotion from Swordsman and Hero to bit part as Scrabbling Wretch. Finger-nails full of unsightly lichen, beard pressed against the wet rock, I had inched myself into an impasse. I looked down. Only a fifty-foot drop to go then on along the ridge top in a twelve-mile arc towards Berthoud Pass – fabulous walking, a mass of snowy antimacassers from one horizon to the next. And fifty feet such a piffling detail. I sent a foot off on a dangling recce. I sent a hand after the foot. It was raining again, I had sixty pounds on my back, and the cliff face was bulging beside me. Edging my backside out into space was an act of pure faith. Misplaced faith. Beyond the bulge the cliff had crumbled clean away. Emergency substances flew round my body – lead, sand, pneumatic drills; I felt as if I'd swallowed a blender. With a rope I could have easily abseiled to the talus, but I had no rope. I had no climbing gear of any description. What I did have was a fucking problem. I was stuck on a cliff face, miles from anywhere but sickeningly close to oblivion. If anyone ever stumbled over my body they'd be all day collecting the bits.

I had, on the other hand, paid off a mounting debt. To leave the Divide, for whatever reason, was to leave the front line. There were usually good tactical reasons for withdrawal, even strategic imperatives, but time spent down among the timber always slightly rankled. One felt, or imagined one felt, the lightest touch of a white feather. Guilt in the valleys, expiation in the hills: getting stuck on Mount Hagar had made up for missing Grays Peak. It put me about even with myself. Getting unstuck put me well ahead. To get back up the cliff I had to re-negotiate the appalling bulge. I was petrified. For the first time in years I was really and truly afraid.

Which is probably why I fell off. As the swing of the pack pulled me outwards I saw myself back above I # 70; as I felt my hands slipping off the dark rock I seemed to hear traffic approaching the tunnel. The blood was roaring in my ears. White fingers twiddling with wet stone up here, busy with car radios down there. In the tunnel, yawning indifference; up here, a scream as I fell. I smashed into a ledge about four feet below the bulge. A biro had fallen from the camera bag and I saw it wedged in the rocks way below. It looked about the size of a needle. I felt oddly calm and reached up for the first handhold. It didn't take long to get back to the top, where the shock waves struck with a vengeance. I sat and shook without stopping for fifteen minutes. I was in credit now all right.

There was more drama to come – light entertainment by that afternoon's standards – as I set off on a flanking traverse. Black bones of rock were disgorging sodden marrow into the cirque far below, a saturated glop of gravel and mud and a terrific strain on the ankles to cross. But I made it and in two hours had dropped 3000 feet to the bottom of Berthoud Pass, a prudent diversion as it turned out.

Trouble had been brewing all afternoon, the sound of drunken gaming, increasingly slurred, coming down through the dark ceiling of cloud. Looking up now from the bottom of the pass there was an ominous pause. Then – crash! – the saloon I'd imagined directly overhead was being utterly demolished, six-guns and rifles blasting through the ceiling, venomous knife-play through the floor, Zeus and the boys still tricked out as cowpokes, the crazed Otto flipping the switches: Frankenstein was somehow in on the act, brilliant discharges lacing ski pylon to pylon as the prankster shrieked in the storm. The ground under the front section of the tent was battered to a soup and by morning my gear was mud brown. Luckily I'd not far to go. Winter Park and food box number eight were just over the hill.

I wound up to the pass through misty shoals of hail, the frothy grass beaten flat at the roadside. A few early tourists came gliding downhill, cautious tyres on the steaming tarmac. Brown water roared through the culverts; small stones which had rolled down through the forest lay in the road like fresh heads. An empty dump truck growled past. It stopped up ahead where a mudslip half blocked the road and, plodding past the cab, I waved. The driver ignored me and looked at his watch – the time was just after eight-thirty. He looked very pissed off for such a lovely morning and, waiting for a ride on the crest of the pass I discovered why.

At some time after nine a convoy of highway department vehicles came up from the Winter Park side. Orange lights flashing, a mechanical digger pulled in and the driver joined the road crew for a coffee at the ski tow café. I could see them through the window, munching doughnuts and smoking cigarettes. Not far short of ten – I still hadn't got a lift – they cruised slowly downhill, evidently to rendezvous with the waiting truck-driver. Being a private contractor it was obvious why he was so fed up.

Constant movement, day after day, has deleterious effects, one of them being that sequence is exchanged for consequence. You really have no idea of how things come to be, you just witness them as they are. The little cameo played out over Berthoud Pass was, therefore, quite a treat.

14 Winter Park

I was looking forward to Winter Park because of a girl called Naomi. She worked at the ski shop where I'd left the food box. It was her exuberant grin on the resort brochure, but I'd only just got there in time – next month she was going home to Wisconsin. She said six years in the fast lane was enough.

Colorado: molybdenum, aerospace, skiing. Wisconsin: zinc, dairying, church. I couldn't understand it. But Naomi's father was a Lutheran minister, an ex-marine, she said.

"It was yessir, nosir, and I guess I was a bit rebellious. If you love to ski you don't really worry about how rich you'll be someday. But I got into a stream of life up here that I guess I don't agree with in my heart. I need the law and the gospel. At least once a week. I need to know what Jesus demands of us."

The minister's prodigal daughter, I wondered? "No!" she said. "I've done OK. My father can see that's not it. He wrote me last week. He said to look up Ecclesiastes – to everything there is a season, you know? I'm going back because it's time."

Much later I was dimly aware of Naomi choosing a tape. A headset muffled my ears. "Goodnight," she said and shut the door. She'd put on a track by the Doors: "Riders on the Storm".

I woke up at five, washed up the supper things, and left. I hitched for an hour, got nowhere, and when at seven the smell of fresh bread drifted down the road I followed it to Carver Bros. Bakery. A guy with floury hands was loading the newspaper dispenser.

"Here," he said. "It's yesterday's. You can take it."

I went in for a coffee, caught up with the – almost – latest news, and saw Naomi cycle past the window. Winter Park seemed the most desirable place in the world, a paradise of good bread and hot running water. What was I doing, a month short of thirty-three, still boy scouting around in the hills? It wasn't as if long distance walks are much fun. Anything less like a holiday would be difficult to imagine. Most of my friends had jobs and children by now. Few of them still worried about how many doughnuts they could afford. Even fewer could be found still waving their thumbs down the road. I was, as you see, discontented. But not fundamentally. Each moment still either stood or fell on its own. Not having an extra doughnut was, in the final analysis, no worse than having one.

15 The Front Range

I eventually got a lift back to Berthoud Pass and was dropped off just after ten. Next stop was Rabbit Ears Pass – two mountain ranges and 120 miles to go. So far I'd done just under 1000 miles altogether.

Looking back down the Fraser valley I could see that the ice had been kind. The foothills were rounded, softened by blankets of spruce. Ski trails had been scrawled through the trees, crude strokes which I felt might be greatly improved. Here was a rare opportunity. Why not hurtle down, say, the words "Coca Cola", cut through the far conifers? Sell as you ski! I would patent this idea. I would buy the advertising rights to every forest in the United States. All I needed was a chainsaw and a guy with a loudhailer to keep me on track. I'd climbed way above Berthoud Pass by now and could see the whole thing. I'd go public. I'd lobby Congress to build roads through inaccessible mountains just so my stuff would be read. Not only that, I'd post speed limits past the most important accounts – 5 m.p.h. for City Girl Pantyhose spread right along the Front Range. The only drawback would be fog . . .

The two-day traverse from Berthoud Pass to Rollins Pass was fraught, visibility nil. For the first time the Rockies really were like Scotland – howling wind, driving rain; for the first time I was thoroughly cold, and for the first time I advanced solely by compass.

I had, of course, used compasses in the army, where, like other pawnable kit, they are classified as "attractive items". I hadn't found mine attractive. I'd have thrown it away if I'd been allowed to. But I wasn't allowed to. Compasses (plus lanyard, ID discs, Very pistol, binoculars and cravat) are part of the army's handicap system – second lieutenants hobbled as above; majors conceding a pound or two in the form of a shooting stick; brigadiers and above carrying nothing more strenuous than canes. You can't strangle yourself with a cane. You can look cool, keep one hand in your pocket, point out relevant targets – that shower over there, for example, obviously begging: Fire!

They're ours, sir.

Why're they holding their hands out like that? Expecting rain?

They're reading their compasses, sir.

No we weren't. The compasses were pure artifice – crystal balls in which we tried to discern our instructor's intentions. Never mind the map and the bearings – which hills hadn't we done?

But there were no instructors between Berthoud Pass and Rollins Pass. Nor were there any trees. There was fog, nothing but fog for two days, my progress metered by step count and time. In those forty-eight hours I covered just fourteen miles and saw a sum total of nothing. Then, just beyond Rollins Pass, a figure loomed out of the mist. It looked a bit like a heron. The wet poncho formed wings as the guy cupped his mouth with his hands.

"Do . . . you . . . have . . . any . . . bug . . . dope?"

I had plenty. The mist and the wind hadn't deterred the mosquitoes.

Glen took off his glasses (it was more like undressing his face), and dabbed repellant on his cheeks – clean-shaven, possibly once-acned cheeks, electrically razored that morning.

It was the weekend, otherwise Glen wouldn't have been here. His wife usually dropped him early on a Saturday, he told me, and would pick him up somewhere on the Sunday. She wasn't a hiker, he said. Also, she was expecting a baby – their first – which made me feel rather more uncomfortable about not liking Glen than would otherwise have been the case. I didn't like him because he was a snob. When I asked him where he was from he told me where he lived; when I asked what he did he gave me his rank – executive vice-something or other. I said he looked too young for that. He said yes, so far he'd done pretty well.

Being the first actual backpacker I'd met on the trip I wasn't quite sure of the form. Did one casually move on, an embarrassing few yards ahead, pretending to be a total stranger? Or was there some sort of wrist-scratching ceremony of eternal brotherhood to perform? Thank goodness this hadn't happened before. My herding instinct is weak, though as occasional phenomena other hikers were welcome, and I suggested that we might step forward together. Glen said, "Sure, why not?" and set off at a ridiculous pace.

It's no good asking guys like Glen to slow down – they think it's a sign of weakness. You have to train them, so being a good deal fitter than he was I galloped into overdrive for a while. He responded beautifully. I reckoned he'd last about another mile at this rate before the set of his body changed – a millimetre here, a degree or two there – and the suffering would begin. I didn't want to ruin him though, just to stretch him a bit, to bring him to the point of wishing he could give up the undeclared race. He'd almost certainly find some excuse – boot laces perhaps, or a halt to check the map – but I'd forestall him by a split second, slackening the pace little by little until we were back to a comfortable speed. No points scored, no loss of face, nothing said. It worked a treat.

By mid-afternoon we had struck a trail called the High Lonesome Trail. It turned out to be neither, delivering us from the fog at 12,000 feet to evening sunshine at 10,000. Kids were yelling, dogs were barking, dads were fishing a lake. We had reached a trail head. I asked at one campfire if I could dry out my socks. Glen said he'd have to go on or he'd miss his wife next day. I'd just finished a large piece of cake as I waved him goodbye.

"You want another?"

"Er . . . thanks very much."

Jennifer was in her mid-twenties. The short, fat man staggering out of the pines was her brother-in-law. His name was Alex. He dumped an armful of dead wood by the fire and smoothed down a wisp of black hair.

"Where's Scott?" he asked. Alex was from St Louis. He, Gloria and young Scott drove out every summer for a week's vacation with Terry and Jennifer, who lived in Commercial City, Denver.

"Commercial City ain't that nice a place though," said Terry. "That's why on the weekend we bring them out here. Gloria, you seen Scott?"

Gloria was doing something in the car. She wound down the window. "Ain't he with you?"

"Scaat!" yelled Alex.

"Scaa-aaat!" echoed Gloria.

"Yeah?" said Scott. He was in the small tent with a comic.

"Got a guy here from England."

"Yeah?"

"He's hiking the Divide."

"Yeah?"

"You want some cake?"

Scott had a large sheath knife and spots. He was sent for more wood while Jennifer opened another tin. I hoped my socks would take a long time to dry.

"You really English?" asked Gloria. She wanted the low-down on Charles and Diana. Were they – you know – OK? Not splitting up?

"How should Steve know?" said Alex. "See," he added, "Gloria ain't used to camping."

At that moment (I had not yet worked out the connection between Gloria's camping experience and the British Royal Family) – at that moment there was a yell from the trees. It was Scott. He'd found bear tracks.

"Bear tracks!" said Gloria.

"She ain't used to camping," said Alex.

They were not bear tracks. The mongrel which had made them could still be seen wagging its tail on the far side of the lake. But Scott didn't care, and his subsequent forays were made with exaggerated stealth.

We didn't do much that evening. I pitched my tent near theirs; it got dark, the fire glowed; Scott saw a UFO; the rest of us missed it. Jennifer said it was waffles for breakfast, Terry just looked at the stars. It was all pretty quiet except for the car radio. Alex didn't give St Louis a prayer in that year's World Series.

"No baseball in England, right?"

"No baseball," I said. "Our summer game's cricket."

"So you have what, like a European championship? Italy, Germany, France?"

I explained that cricket was confined to places like Australia and India.

"They play cricket in India?"

I liked these people. They knew virtually nothing about other countries (one Californian I'd met had even asked if New Mexico was part of the States) but they didn't wallow in their ignorance. It wasn't a badge. They handled knowledge as a kind of frontier zone in which they wandered freely, bagging the odd fact here and there but remaining refreshingly untrammeled. Facts didn't bother Americans. What shook them was ideas. You can't really lasso an idea, so what Americans do is shoot them down and stuff them: free-range facts, exhibit philosophy. It was one of the things about America that bugged me.

The sun had risen. Terry was throwing bits of wood for the dog; Alex was yawning; Gloria was still asleep in the car. Scott said the tent had been spooky. He had kept the torch on all night – a police department model, big and heavy, not easy to obtain. What kind of torch did I have? Oh, just a small one. Not very powerful.

I'd already set off and had drawn out of sight of the tents when Scott, torch in hand, caught me up.

"Here," he said. "I want you to have it."

I felt like a football star.

16 FOG

The waffles and ham I'd gorged for breakfast were blowing my insides back to front. I sought relief in the first clump of spruce. Rocky Mountain National Park was close by, and, screened from the path, I was able to watch a stream of hikers bob past, day-trippers mostly who wouldn't be straying far off the main trails. I began to compare my gear with theirs, to mock the bright new colours, the dangling tin cups, the vacuous chatter. I crouched tighter behind my tree. It was so easy to be alone, to raid humanity for company then leave with the spoils – the goodwill, the waffles, the torches. I didn't like myself much that day.

I liked my stomach even less. As the afternoon wore on I felt iller and iller and I stopped walking early at a place aptly named Thunderbolt Creek. It wasn't raining and I had my first night under the stars for several weeks. Something disturbed me at about midnight, a sort of snuffling sound. I opened one eye and almost threw up in panic, rolling left into a tight ball. Luckily the porcupine rolled right, rattling nervously as it retreated through the moonlight.

Fresh, white cloud was billowing over the Divide next morning. A solitary elk watched me from the skyline. I could see why the bulls tend to keep themselves to themselves till the breeding season. This one had what looked like candelabra stuck to its head – stumpy, half-grown antlers still in velvet. The bulls wouldn't start shoving each other around for another six weeks yet, by which time I hoped to be through Wyoming and well into Montana. But when, at midday, the sun went in, I wasn't so sure.

The crestline ahead was enveloped in thick fog once again, rain spitting through soiled bundles of nimbo-stratus. The range of colours was anything in grey, the scenery almost Chinese. Looking down I could see the debris-strewn snouts of the St Vrain glaciers nosing out of the dark cirques below. There were hints of immense crags around me. I hated the mist. It boxed my spirit. It was doleful. Even the pipits looked depressed, flitting from boulder to boulder with an occasional dispossessed tweet.

I'd reached the flanks of a mountain called Isolation Peak, and could see from the map that the next twenty miles would be rugged. If the weather didn't improve I'd have to bypass the lot, but I couldn't even do that till the cloud lifted and I could see down into the valleys. I was stuck.

I retreated to 12,000 feet, found a flat patch and put up the tent. I was still feeling queasy and went to sleep for five hours. It should have been getting dark when I woke up but the mist had hardly changed colour. It was colder though, and raining hard, the thunder which had rolled all afternoon now booming closer.

You can do almost anything with statistics, especially climatic statistics, and a statement like "it rained every day for a week" can be very misleading. The question is – when did it rain? Was it at night, with you tucked up dry in your tent? Was it at midday, when you simply broke out your wetproofs and carried on walking? Or, and this is the real misery, did the heavens open just as you'd strewn everything out to dry, to cook a meal, to make camp? These were the moments of greatest vulnerability, when "it rained for a week" really meant something. This is why my meal times and halts were so varied. In Colorado I stitched day to day life onto a tough backing of storms, and so far I'd avoided pricking myself too badly. This was the first time I'd been involuntarily stranded on a high ridge for the night.

By now it is dark. Heavy rain slants down in the torchlight, but in here, in my two pounds, ten ounce house, I am dry as a maggot. I flash the torch upward, water shadows trickling down the stretched fabric. How thin it is, how close to my face. Sitting up in bed with the sheets over your head gives an exact idea of its size. The flysheet overlaps the inner tent by a couple of feet and in that front section are my boots, the rucksack and the stove. Here, between the sleeping bag and the inner wall, are the maps, the camera bag and a bundle of damp, smelly clothes. If I lift my head and shine the torch I can see the end of the bag in the darkness. My most distant possession, the furthest outpost of my empire, is the single tent peg, eight feet from my head, which secures the longest guy rope. Everything else is within reach.

The first lightning cracks into the mountain. The tent flashes blue then orange as the storm intensifies. The noise is something I can almost crawl into. I latch on to a particular roll and it takes me miles away into the black night. But the lightning is now directly overhead cracking down all round the tent. I smoke two or three cigarettes and try to relax; the storm goes on for hours. When I finally doze off it is with the tent pole gripped in my hands.

I wake up lying in what feels like wet bread. The bottom end of the bag is soaked in condensation. I kick off the bag, unzip the tent and stand up. The fog is thicker than ever.

From what little I could see I was camped on an alpine fell field, the coarse grass spattered with granite. You could tell from the way that the boulders lay that the turf had built up slowly round them. They were deep seated; the swirling mist gave them a strange potency. I wouldn't have been surprised to see chaps drifting about with mistletoe stuck in their ears. A druid or two would certainly have helped pass the time.

The fabric I'd salvaged from the burnt-out tent above Plataro was still in the pack and, confined for the duration, I threaded a needle. Till then I'd been using plastic bin liners to protect the camera bag in wet weather, but I thought a customized rain cover would be easier to slip on and off. I cut, glued and stitched all morning and the result was a pretty good fit. It was also a complete waste of effort – the fire must have damaged the shellac lining and the material leaked like a sieve. I went back to using bin liners.

Hands stiff-armed into pockets I stared morosely at the fog. I felt like a frustrated goldfish. Some bastard kept steaming up my bowl. As soon as it looked like demisting itself there'd be another great hurrrr and I'd be fogged up all over again. I stared morosely at the tent instead. It was beginning to look well used. My boots had obviously kicked about a bit too, the laces frayed, the soles deeply cut and scarred. They'd lost a lot of traction – crossing wet rock had been hard work lately. The stove wasn't roaring like it used to either. The jet probably needed a de-coke. Perhaps I should record something of this deterioration on the tape machine? A few on-the-spot-thoughts about what it's like being stuck in thick fog with nothing but a second skin of old gear for company. But I couldn't be bothered. I wanted to get going again. I needed exertion. I was fed up with bloody Colorado, with crawling along at zilch miles an hour in the pissing rain for day after day. What was the use of a high traverse if all you could see were your feet? Talking of which, where was the goddamned tent? Oh, over there, about fifty yards off to the left. The mist seemed to be lifting slightly. Rocky Mountain tease: it dropped again until midafternoon.

At three there was a hole in the cloud. I was patrolling forward and had caught a glimpse of the valley below, of a possible route down, and I roared back for the tent. Three minutes later, gear stowed on my back, I was swinging off the lip of the cliff, jamming my way down a rock chimney. I felt the sweat beginning to trickle under my jacket as I worked, a cap of cold mist in my hair. I sucked happily at my dew-drenched moustache. I was humming – How many bom bom, boddle boddle bee in an English country gar-ar-ar-stretch for a hand-hold diddle diddle dum . . . Ha! I was flowing again.

I kicked across loose scree and on to the first clumps of wet grass, dropping one hundred, two hundred, three hundred feet, under the clouds and into the pelting rain. Marigolds and globeflowers spotted the basin and out of the stodge came a stream – Paradise Creek – flowing down towards the treeline. The sun came out and for a while the whole world steamed bronze. The stream flattened into a meadow; trout swirled in a deep pool. I unzipped my wetproofs, sat on a rock, and watched. A nose was carving through the water, nostrils pumping like fleshy valves. I must have inadvertently moved – there was a sudden swirl, a pancake-like "Splat!", and the first wild beaver I'd ever seen was gone.

I squadged past a chain of small ponds, black forest reflected in grey water. The sun had vanished and the smell of damp trees closed in. I knew what was coming and gritted my teeth – swish, swash, an eight-mile gauntlet of closely packed spruce until I hit the first trail. I'd follow that out to the township of Grand Lake, dry out, and hit the Divide again in a couple of days. Meanwhile the creek had dived into a gorge, the outcropping rock a map drawn in vividly primitive plants of the water coursing down from above. Fledgling spruce grew erect from the ledges and cracks, quills tipped with the emerald green tufts of that year's growth, though the growing season was all but over. I'd been walking for eighty-two days.

17 Grand Lake

Grand Lake was blue, the sailboats white, the breeze a pine-laden green. I'd walked until dark, been dripped on all night, but ahead of me now was the township, a string of folksy shops and chalet-style motels basking in the sunshine.

The tourists on mainstreet were scoffing french fries, and within a few minutes of getting there so was I. I say "mainstreet", but like most of the mains on my route through America, this one had no competition. I wasn't exactly taking the pulse of the nation on this journey, but I did what I could to keep abreast of current issues. Which is why, having hung my soggy belongings over railings outside the sheriff's office, I was sitting on the grass with a quart of milk and a copy of *Weekly World News*, headline: IS YOUR NEIGHBOR A SPACE ALIEN?

I had to know but, seeing my stuff all hanging out to dry, a fat guy in a headband had just wobbled up to say how much he loved the woods, didn't I? Yeah, yeah, love 'em. I turned the page.

"SHORTAGE OF MALES DROVE BLUE-EYED YETI TO MATE WITH A HUMAN!"

I didn't believe it! The fat guy was saying he'd come out here from New York and was just living off the land. I didn't believe that either.

"I saw a huge shadow," said 34–year-old farmer, Shosan Fong. "A woman beast with great breasts . . . "

". . . fishin', pickin' berries . . . " said the fat guy.

". . . scientists in Peking," I read. "Irrefutable evidence . . . "

". . . packin' out to the back country," said the fat guy.

". . . legendary beast of the wilds . . . "

". . . just gettin' back in touch . . . " I looked up.

"Here," I said. "Have this torch. I've got two."

The sunshine over Grand Lake didn't last long. By three that afternoon the postcard racks were being taken in, car headlights were on, and people were running into doorways with magazines over their heads. There was nothing to do but get back into wetproofs and leave, but as I sloshed past the last motels I heard a shout and turned around. A slight, puckish figure was streaming barefoot towards me, fingers fumbling at the zip of his jeans as he splashed across the parking lot. Perhaps he meant someone else?

"Hey, Steve! Englishman! Hey, man, stop!"

It was Dee Fogelquist, 800 miles on from the Black Mountains of New Mexico.

"We're in the motel right there," he gasped. "I'm taking a shower and I think shit – is that raining again? So I stick my head out of the window – it's a million to one, I mean bathrooms have real small windows – and I go, 'Bonny! There he is!' She goes, 'Who?' but I'm out the door. She yells, 'Put on some pants,' I grab hers and I'm holding them up all the way across the lot . . . "

He held them up all the way back as well, finished his shower, came with me to buy steaks and a quart of ice-cream and still hadn't stopped

talking. Dead beer cans were nudging each other off the table by the time we fell asleep, Dee and Bonny in the bed, me in a mound of gear on the floor. I woke up sweating with fright just before dawn, scrabbling for a handhold on the grey rockface beside me. It was the wall. Dee and Bonny were still asleep, so I shook their feet a gentle goodbye and left. I didn't see them again, but that Christmas they sent me a card.

"Reached Canada on 27th October," it said. "Hope you got home safely too. This is the first letter we've ever sent overseas. What an amazing thing that mail can be sent anywhere in the world. Dee has now almost recovered from being kicked by the mule. He practically lived at the dentist's for a month and now has a mouthful of gold teeth (and the dentist has all our savings!), Your friends, Dee and Bonny."

18 The Rabbit Ears Range

The detour to Grand Lake had been unscheduled and I still had sixty disheartening miles through the Rabbit Ears Range to pick up food box number nine – disheartening because when I got there I'd be no nearer Canada than I already was. The Divide ran west all the way. With the Wyoming line only a few days' walk directly north this seemed like deliberate malice.

A housing tract confused me on the edge of town but with no one up yet the curtains were still drawn and I took a compass course straight through the gardens. I disturbed a few deer, crossed a wet meadow, and reached a dishwater river where it slithered over a collapsed bridge. It was the Colorado, not yet ten miles old and washing out girders already. But the main span of a replacement was in position and by eight the next morning I had rejoined the Divide on a hill called Park View Mountain.

For the past 500 miles I'd been clambering across what amounted to a box-room full of junk – desks, tables, chairs just chucked in any old how. I'd hardly touched the floor once, but now to the north the furniture had been moved back. Though I had another week of jumble to traverse, I could see clear floor space at last. Somewhere out there in the haze was the Wyoming line and deliverance, and suddenly the strain of the past five weeks came flooding out. I hadn't realized how much pent-up effort had gone into crossing Colorado, but to judge from the tears streaming down my cheeks it must have been considerable.

I romped west through the Rabbit Ears Range for two more days, the approaching right turn into the Park Range always in sight. The sky was deep blue, the afternoon storm clouds preoccupied with the Front Range now forty miles behind me. Forty miles seemed about the closest anything was that day. My lungs were bursting with the champagne of distance. I could see a week's walk ahead, I could see peaks behind me I'd traversed ten days ago. I imagined great "our hotel" biro marks pointing down from the sky – there's where I met Glen in the fog; there's Isolation Peak; the Never Summer Mountains and the bits of Rocky Mountain Park I'd missed out. It was like looking at the slides of the journey already.

I was whamming along – after the rock and fog of the Front Range the Rabbit Ears were a doddle, the grassy hilltops free of timber and swarming with herds of elk. An odd word, "Elk". Stumpy, but with that slinky glide in – a contrast which exactly suits its owners. Cinnamon brown hides, glistening and fat, would ripple across the green hillsides, but there was something ungainly, almost muleish about the way they held their heads. On the whole I liked them. Other than the elk and one golden eagle there were no further distractions until, on the third day west of Grand Lake, I reached a place called Troublesome Pass where a rough logging road crossed the Divide. There was a small hut back in the trees. It was hardly midafternoon, the weather was fine and huts were invariably locked, but for some reason I strolled over. Just to check, I suppose. Check what? I dunno – it's just one of those things you do when you're on your own. And the door happened to be open.

I looked around – dried mouse shit on the floor, old jam jars on a shelf, candle wax congealed round a spent match. I was just leaving when a piece of paper caught my eye. It was stuck on a nail by the door.

"A warm welcome to our fellow Continental Divide hikers!" it said. What fellow Continental Divide hikers?

Dee and Bonny were the only ones I'd met, and they'd been riding horses. I read on: "We started from Columbus, New Mexico, in late February and despite the heavy, heavy snowpack we hope to be home in early November."

Home was British Columbia. Ding! McGee's Canadian sisters! The ones Mr Gonzales had mentioned. They were real! The message was dated July 13th. Today was the 29th – a sixteen-day lead, equivalent to roughly 200 miles. I did some complicated sums on the dirty window pane, ran out of spit and went outside for a biro and some paper. The result was 600 miles: I should overhaul them somewhere in southern Montana, though the chances of an actual meeting were remote.

The Continental Divide is a geographical feature, not a set trail. (I'd had a bit of a shock when I got to New York and discovered that moves are afoot to create one, but I needn't have worried because nothing yet had been done on the ground.) It wasn't like the Pennine Way or the Appalachian Trail, not an established route-way pulling you forward but your own individual idea. You just made it up as you went along. Dee and Bonny had taken a route so different from mine that Grand Lake was about the only place we could have met and that we actually had was, as Dee had so breathlessly pointed out, a monumental coincidence. But coincidences do happen. Approaching Rabbit Ears Pass next day a motorcycle overtook me and screeched to a halt. A blue motorcycle.

How many people did I know in Colorado with a blue motorbike? Answer: one. It was Trail-Mix Steve, the guy from Hoosier Pass.

"I thought you were following the Divide," he said.

"I am."

"How come you're on a road then?"

In the entire state of Colorado the Divide follows a tarmac road for less than a mile. This just happened to be it. I walked on, grinning. Steve, I saw with some satisfaction, was about to drive into a cloudburst.

19 The Park Range

The establishment at which I'd left the final Colorado foodbox was under new management and there had been some confusion over my mail. If I had any it would be in a nearby small town, but the post office there was now shut until Monday. Since the next leg of the journey was a long one – seventy-five miles up to the state line; thirty more as the Park Range overlapped into Wyoming; the last seventy through blinding sage once again to food box number ten at a place called Wamsutter – I decided to forget the mail and press on, spending a hot, irritated Sunday blundering through the recently logged foothills of the Park Range. It was party time – plaza after plaza of liberated undergrowth yelling "Viva!" and thrusting its jubilant arms up my shorts. I eventually stumbled across a dirt road, breathed a sigh of relief, and stuck out my thumb.

I'd changed my mind and was going back down to the town for my mail – I'd return here in the morning – but the loggers churning past, a hard-hatted lot, didn't stop. They probably thought I was a communist. I slept by the side of the road and next morning had descended right through the forest and was three miles out on the range before deciding that hitching wasn't going to work. I had a few letters to post, though, and turned down a ranch road to ask if someone could drop them for me on their next trip to town. Through the binoculars I'd seen a guy in the barn doorway. He was feeding a dog – nothing unusual in that – but I'd kept the binoculars on him: yellow blob of T-shirt, blue blob of jeans, black and white blob of dog – like puppets, I thought, against the dark frame of the doorway. I walked on down.

The man was very friendly. "England?" he said, taking my letters. "Had an English couple doing the bookkeeping here in my grand-father's day." It sounded a real family ranch. I asked if his kids were going to carry it on.

"That would be kinda difficult," he said. "I've only been married three months. I was sixty-two on my wedding day and my wife's five years older'n I am."

"No kids by a previous marriage?" I asked.

"I didn't have a previous marriage."

"You got married for the first time at sixty-two?"

"Yeah," said the rancher, pulling up a chair. "I'm gay. I hope that don't offend you."

Sparrows were chirping dispassionately up in the rafters. The dog trotted in from its bowl. I'd only been here five minutes.

"Why did you get married then?" I eventually blurted out.

"Companionship, I guess," said the rancher, "though if she hadn't been so damned persistent I probably wouldn't have done it."

"But why didn't you, I mean, just live with a boyfriend?"

Boyfriend! I was getting the hang of it.

"Never found the right guy, I guess," he said. "Some stayed two days, some of them a week then usually I couldn't hardly stand them. One guy years back I figured I was very much in love with, but he didn't want to leave the city and I guess I just felt too strongly for the ranch.

"Occasionally I have, I guess you'd say, more or less regretted that I've settled down, but something that's helped real well is my in-laws, who no matter where you meet them they hug you. It don't give me a surge of pleasure or somesuch just because it's a guy hugging me, but I kinda feel that if there was more just touching and hugging among all people we'd be happier. Maybe better adjusted. The French and the Russians – don't they kiss on the cheek?"

I was back on the Divide by noon the next day, squelching through meadows red with a species of figwort, and on August 3rd hauled up and over Mount Zirkel, the last 12,000–foot peak of the journey. The alpine flowers were nearly all finished, though as I lost altitude I noticed young fungi bubble-gumming out of the ground, the freshly disturbed earth clinging endearingly to their heads. Something about them made me want to get down on the forest floor and establish some sort of contact, perhaps to give them a pat before I ate them. There were squirrels and small birds too; one, the Western Tanager, a startling daub of red, yellow and black against the dark spruce. It looked like a bit of parrot.

The higher ground was dotted with ponds – cold but not absolutely freezing – and so I was cleaner in the Park Range than I had been for weeks. Most of the ponds had a resident population of frogs whose choir practice was abruptly terminated the moment my toes touched the water. Not that I cared. The weather was dreadful and I didn't care about that either. I didn't care about anything at all that week except crossing the Wyoming line. I got there at eight on the morning of August 5th, though my satisfaction was a bit artificial because the badly drained bog of the Park Range ran on for another thirty miles: it wasn't till I got to Bridger Peak next day that I saw the Red Desert waiting.

PART IV

Wyoming

1 Bridger Peak to Wamsutter

Unbroken forest rolled, smooth as a stocking, off the last ridge of the
Park Range, the foothills, down to the 8000–foot contour, a satin of
closely packed trees. But beyond the dark 'foreground there was
nothing, the bleached sky an inversion of the brittle wastes below. It
was a landscape of mirage and death; a landscape I tried not to believe.
Only by shading my eyes did a horizon materialize, a vague thickness
– not a cloud, I decided, but the southern tip of the Wind River Range,
135 miles to the north. Between here and there lay the next week of
my life. I picked up the rucksack and descended through the forest
towards it.

The air grew warmer, the trail at the sudden edge of the trees
dustier. Sage closed round my knees. After the high Rockies this was
Antelope Wells all over again. I aimed in the approximate direction of
Wamsutter, seventy miles over the horizon, and walked all afternoon.

At about five I saw a ranch house off to the west. I'd had contact with
no one for two days, and though I didn't need water, I changed course.
By six I was swigging Coca Cola on the porch. A friend of the ranch
family – she was about my own age – happened to be there for the
summer, and supper turned out to be an irritating delay for both of
us. She had a great sense of humour – nearly woke the whole house
up laughing when I mentioned the gay rancher.

"He was the last person you met in Colorado?" she whispered,
stifling a giggle.

"Just about," I whispered back.

"And I'm the first in Wyoming?"

"Yeah," I said, tugging at the blanket.

"Shoulda been the other way round. You know what they say about
this state?"

"What?"

"They say Wyoming's the state where the men are real men, and
the sheep, why the sheep are real nervous."

Sunrise caught me heading west for Ketchum Buttes. I went down

Bird Creek, up Cow Gulch and stopped for lunch in Cottonwood Draw. I lowered myself gingerly into the creek and lay back feeling completely knackered. In forty-eight hours I'd lost nearly a mile in altitude, from 11,000 feet up on Bridge Peak to 6500 feet down here. I'd also not had any sleep. A fly bit me on the penis. Little fucker. I let it get as far as my knee and squashed it flat in a shadowless ambush. The body drifted slowly downstream.

The surrounding country was dry as a bone, not quite flat but utterly bare, my twenty-two miles to the inch yours-to-cherish-with-every-ten-gallons-of-four-star map of the entire western states all I needed. Indeed, I was to cross the northern half of the desert with only a "Historic Wyoming" beer mat to steer by. I swiped it from a bar in the town of Wamsutter the next day. Getting there had been a close thing. I'd been down to my last three cigarettes with forty-five miles still to go, and worse, had only one tea-bag. I used it three times, knocked off the final thirty-seven miles overnight, and flicked my last butt at an alsatian dog as I walked into town.

2 Wamsutter

Unless you count Interstate # 80, Wamsutter doesn't really have streets. It has a lot of tired looking telegraph poles and wonky strip-lights and bunches of dry grass in the cracked paving outside the post office, but no streets. It doesn't actually need them: rainfall – five inches a year (though not this year by the look of the hard-baked ruts); population – around 200; main attraction – Black Cat Fireworks, a bright orange trailer parked just off the freeway. In fact the whole place was parked just off the freeway, the one civic amenity being light – great pools of it flooding the oil installations and soldierly lines overhanging I # 80 – so that at night the town resembled a cruise liner at sea. But by day it was just a bunch of old tyres and large dogs on smoothly worn chains.

The first guy I met lived in a bus. His name was Smiley and he had Harley Davidson tattoos on his biceps. He was the manager of the firework stand. His girlfriend's name was Kathy. She was wearing hot pants and dark glasses.

"I'll take you over to the Sagebrush," she said. "Then we'll have breakfast."

The Sagebrush was a motel about 200 yards away. We drove. It was eight in the morning and already hot.

"Room won't be clean," said Kathy. "We pay a couple of dollars to take a shower after someone's checked out."

Though I'd forego the pleasure of ripping open a fresh soap, a second-hand room for two dollars was fine and I attacked the pink sliver left in the shower unit with gusto. Then I sat on the bed and watched TV until Kathy came back. The day had started well for one lady – hardly nine in the morning yet here was a TV game show host presenting her with a cheque for $10,000. She was in the middle of jumping up and down when the adverts came on – Hooray! I've won ten thousand dolla – flick – Things Go Better With Coke.

Smiley made french toast for breakfast. The bus had a curtained divan at one end and a small galley at the other. Dumbells and pulp novels lay on the floor. Kathy read more or less all day, but Smiley and I got a little stoned after breakfast and the dumbells stayed where they were. He'd been working in Utah – pipefitting and welding – for the past year.

"Sage hens used to come right to the door," he said. "Used to knock them off with a blow-pipe. Wanna see it?"

We spat darts at an old tyre for about half an hour, had coffee, and opened for business. I unbolted the flaps of the trailer, absorbed in the labels pinned to the shelves while Smiley set the "OPEN" sign alongside the highway. I'd spent a month that winter in a village in India where whatever you bought – sugar, rice, tea – was weighed out loose and deftly twisted into little paper cones tied with string. The fireworks were like that. The packaging revolution had passed them by – no blister packs or plastic containers, but rough, brightly painted cardboard: Happy Lamps, News Transmitter, Chirping Birds, Artist's Dream. How lovely. I'd never thought of fireworks as Happy Lamps or Chirping Birds; but here were items more familiar to a western mind – 3-Shot Comets, Aerial Barrage, Smoke Grenades, Crackers, perhaps fifty or eighty different kinds altogether. A car pulled in for gas.

"You got any Blackcaps?"

"Fifteen cents apiece, my man."

"My Man" looked about eleven and was breathless. He'd been halfway across the garage forecourt before his parents were out of their seat belts. I could see the father still fiddling with the petrol cap.

Smiley had left a few old fruit crates out front so his customers could see over the counter.

"What do you have that blows up?"

"We have several things that blow up."

"For a dollar?"

"For a dollar? For one dollar you get an Aerial Barrage. You get a Thunder and Rainbow. You get four crackers."

Small lips chewed furiously.

"Four crackers."

A car with Delaware plates disgorged an earnest looking boy whose elbows joined My Man's on the counter. "They outlawed crackers back home," he observed, a shrill voice in a baseball cap. My Man looked up.

"Are crackers outlawed, mister?"

"No, honey, these are all legal."

"We've been staying with my cousin in California," said Ernest, "and they're not allowed there either."

"Well, sweetheart, this is different states. Fireworks are legal here."

There are Grizzly Bears in northern Wyoming, and a few crackers, I thought, might be just the thing for emergencies, but the Delaware kid said, stiffly, that pyrotechnics were illegal in National Forests. In any case, he said, a rocket would be better.

"Yeah!" said My Man. "You can strike it and shoot it right at them."

But Smiley had found some old flares. "Should do the trick," he said, "but if I get a letter back with blood all over it, means they weren't no good – right? I'll give you two for the price of nothing, how's that?"

He gave me a pair of woollen socks as well. I slept in a vacant caravan and left at four the next morning, planning to sleep through the heat of the day.

3 The Red Desert

The Red Desert isn't red, and isn't strictly speaking a desert, though it's dry enough to make no difference. Even the Divide avoids it, splitting just south of Wamsutter to enclose a basin of roughly 4000 square miles. The two arms meet up again at South Pass before rising along the spine of the Wind River Range. I'd decided to cut straight across the basin from Wamsutter to the northern rim, a distance of fifty-five miles. The local sheriff thought there was a windpump somewhere in the middle but he couldn't say if it worked. The beer mat showed a dirt road, route 4–23, heading north for Jeffrey City. "Lotta new dirt out there lately," said the sheriff, "oil and gas drilling and such. Could confuse ya. Best stick to route 4–23."

So I did. I stuck to 4–23. Bored hot and largely fed up – yes; confused – definitely not, except I couldn't remember if it was three cars that passed me on the first day and two on the second or the other way round. Otherwise, this is what I saw.

One white road in the darkness.

Roadside trash – surprisingly little. The sun, incidentally, had been up for three hours and the road was now biscuit coloured. So was everything else, including a torn page of *Erotic Encounters*, flapping in the roadside breeze. Absurdly, I looked round before picking it up. There wasn't a cat in hell's chance of being caught unawares out here – not a scrap of cover in any direction.

Item three was a red and blue sign with BLAIROIL 1/3 25 stencilled on both sides. Why did all the oilfield workers wear hard hats? The only ones I saw were cruising pick-ups over the unobstructed landscape, heading from one natural gas installation to the next. Most of them were nice guys. They'd stop, offer beer, talk economic recession. The land drew no comment at all. The Navajos, back in New Mexico, hadn't said much about the San Juan basin either, but you could tell from the way they drove that they were at home. Out here, no one was at home.

Item four: the windpump. It was working. I rigged up the tent for shade, dozed, and the cattle I'd disturbed came back. So did the Pronghorn Antelopes. I'd seen dozens of them in the past few days.

Item five: a sign which said "Wamsutter 26, Jeffrey City 33".

Item six (100 yards north of item five): a sign which said "Wamsutter 22, Jeffrey City 37".

Item seven: shorebirds. This amazed me, but item eight was a lake, grey under an uncertain sky. Long streamers of rain sailed west, descending thousands of feet through the air though evaporating far short of the ground. Some of the squalls had made it though. The lake I'd passed was only six inches deep but it covered several acres. Lightning splashed the horizon, the sky massively bruised. The road seemed to go on for ever, hour after hour of it, straight as a runway, or, where the landscape rolled, like glimpses of white flesh when fat ladies bend over. My unvaried pace, mile after mile, awoke old irritations. The belt chafed my hips; my neck muscles ached; I stuck my thumbs under the pack straps to ease the weight. Where did I normally put my hands? In my pockets, behind my back, on my head, or what? I walked for hours through the desert with my head cast down, lost in the details of the road surface. I tried to stop them with my eyeballs as they flowed by, like trying to read the words on a turning record.

Item nine, an assortment: dust devils, horned larks, a half dozen wild horses, their manes and tails flying in the wind. It took them five minutes to vanish over the horizon, rising now to the rim of the basin.

Ahead of me was Crooks Gap where, for the first time on the journey, I opened a guidebook. It was a good guidebook, one of a series, describing section by section a route north to south along the Divide from Canada. I'd seen the Wyoming volume in a shop window in Grand Lake, though the author's route and my own had not coincided until now. Reading it backwards – I was travelling south to north – was awkward, but the style was commendably clear: "Pass the gully at mile 7.4 and angle left. Note the mining operation ahead." Yes, I'd passed the mining operation – Western Nuclear Golden Goose Mine – and I'd angled left. This was great!

"Pass the storage tanks at 7.8 – despite the human activity mule deer may be observed."

Oh. No mule deer. Never mind – there were the storage tanks, what next? Camp! "A camp can be made at Sheep Creek. The water is turbid but presumably all right to drink. Another possibility is to fill canteens and water bottles at the mine."

Good idea – fill canteens and water bottles at the mine, and yes, a camp could be made at Sheep Creek. But the mule deer still weren't observed. In fact almost nothing was – not the wind in the sage, not the fragrant new moon, not the dark oil stains in the dirt. I'd walked 0.4 miles, seen everything but the deer, and observed sweet bugger all. But it was a very good guidebook. I got out my knife and I dug a small hole in the ground – a small grave at 7.4 – and I walked on a few ounces lighter.

4 South Pass

The Wind River Range was now well above the horizon, though dwarfed, like me, by the massive sweep of the prairie. Grasshoppers flared ahead of me, insect dolphins under my prow. Even the sky looked left open, as if too much of something had got out. I could easily have switched to automatic. Taken time out for a cabin announcement: "This is your captain speaking. We are cruising at 6500 feet, our forward airspeed three miles an hour. Ground conditions are reported dry and sunny and we will be landing at South Pass in approximately two days. Thank you."

But why, with so much space so freely available, was I still stumbling along the crown of the trail? Why not, at least, walk in the ruts? They weren't particularly deep ruts, no more than pale grooves in the sage, though this is to say the Last Post is just notes in the air. I was on the Oregon Trail.

Oregon. The very word rolls away like a wagon wheel. Never mind that half the migrants were actually headed for California – whatever their final destination they all had to come through here. This twenty-five mile gap between the Red Desert and the Wind River Range was the natural wagon route west. The trail followed the North Platte, winding upstream for weeks to turn off along the Sweetwater and so through South Pass to the Pacific slope.

I could see the Sweetwater ahead of me now, looking much like a wagon train itself, a meandering trail of cottonwoods and willows winding over the lemony plain. Swallows were screaming downstream, slicing the air ham-thin above the placid water. I shrank myself to the size of an insect and shivered.

A fringe of green grass, pleasantly fresh, overhung the low banks. I waded out, blew bubbles, and sank, my body swinging round like a weed. It was good to use a river like this, to welcome a stream as more than just picturesque scenery. I like the way ends follow means on a walk – a river suggests a bath, fuel a fire, dry rocks a time to sit down. What a stupendous leap our ancestors made from opportunism to determinism, and how satisfying it was to leap back.

My dip in the Sweetwater was, then, a kind of present. I normally washed in my two-pint cooking pot, which was far too small and made a very bad basin. It made an even poorer clothes tub, two woollen socks being just about a full load, and whatever satisfactions I could extract from handwashing were constantly subverted by the image of a large white machine.

I felt the same way about brew-ups. Making tea back home was a shoosh of water into the kettle, a flick of the switch, and the soft phlooph of the fridge door for milk. Tea by the Sweetwater was: get out the stove, pump up the fuel, put up the windshield, squirt in the petrol, etcetera, etcetera, etcetera. Waiting for an electric kettle to boil meant reaching for a bit of cake and scanning the morning's headlines. Out here it was eating one third of a Snicker and a battle royal with my conscience not to unwrap the rest.

Though things were a great deal more convenient at home, they weren't necessarily more valuable. At home, for example, it was *a* spoon, never *the* spoon as it was out here. I once went through my kitchen cupboards and discovered the quite staggering total of fifty-three spoons, half of which I didn't even know that I owned. If they'd vanished down the sink I'd never have noticed. But if the faithful old codger I had with me now had fallen into the Sweetwater, I'd have dived straight in after it. I really loved that spoon. It had been all over the world with me and though I mislaid it four or five times a day, I never moved on till I found it.

The trail flickered on through thin cottonwood shade, past calf-yellow willows, under an old wire gate. The churnings of cattle were clear in the dust, scribbled over by the scratchy hoppings of birds. I must have been walking for several hours that day – it was August 13th – before I realized that I was following consecutive human prints too, not the wavy-sole pattern of training shoes, but the imprint of real hiking boots, a set in each rut, and both of them extremely small.

The Sisters! Yes, yes, yes!

I'd walked 1300 miles; I'd found two sets of bootprints; and I knew, without anyone telling me, exactly who had made them. It was very satisfying.

So was the prospect of pursuit. Blind to the transition from prairie to gorge I roared into the canyon of the Sweetwater – open sky one minute, wild disorder the next. I felt ridiculously cheated. I liked to savour the first tree for two hundred miles, to touch the first outcrop of rock. But I'd missed them, and was awash with new sensations – at sunset the Sweetwater laughing; wild currant bushes up to my waist; a shrub sprouting a screw-top bottle. It had been hung there deliberately. Inside the bottle was a typewritten sheet, dated six months before.

"Know all men by these presents . . . " it began.

Hmm. Not another "Warm Welcome to Fellow Continental Divide Hikers" then. I read on: "Know all men by these presents that the undersigned, having discovered within the boundaries of the following described claim a valuable gold-bearing deposit, to whit and hereinafter described . . . "

A valuable gold-bearing deposit! It was minutely described, from here to here to over there, but there was, in fact, nothing to see. The language grew denser as my eyes slipped down the page, and my lips gradually stopped moving. Groucho Marx's ghost slipped by in longjohns, mumbling legal small print through a cigar. I followed him into the twilight.

The sound of the river filled the canyon, drowning my initial greeting. I had come on another couple of miles to see a tent pitched among the junipers ahead. It had to be them.

As children, my twin brother and I had been invariably addressed as "You Boys" – as in "You Boys are a disruptive influence" (school), or "Have You Boys written to Granny?" (home) – and so I tried hard not to collectivize Mugs and Jo. I hardly succeeded. They were, after all, walking as a unit together. Amazingly together. They not only shared the same book – sensible, saves weight – but they shared the same page in the book. They took it in turns to read aloud to each other at night.

"It's neat," said Mugs. "We'll be walking along and one of us'll say, 'Hey, what d'you think Zane Grey thought about this?' And we'll know what we're talking about because we're both at the same place in the book."

Jo said they sometimes held hands as they walked.

"Even in towns?"

"Well, no. But back home we do. We have these T-shirts which say 'WE ARE . . .' on mine, and 'SISTERS!' on hers."

They got up appallingly early. They'd mentioned that they generally walked for two hours before breakfast, but I forgot and was halfway through making tea as they finished dismantling their tent. I surreptitiously threw the water away and we set off in single file. I saw a mule deer, and, being in front, also saw her twin fawns. I wondered if I should point them out. Or would that be an intrusion? Walking in company was tricky. I was constantly leaning over my bows or staring back at my own wake. I turned up a ravine without consultation and we emerged onto open prairie, three little specks to the eagle high overhead. At midday the specks halted. Ate. Shook hands. Laughed. Then one speck pulled ahead. We still write. They reached Canada on November 9th that year.

I passed one more plaque on the Oregon Trail, a tombstone in bronze, all on its own, with a bunch of plastic roses beside it. This is what it said:

WILLIE'S HANDCART COMPANY

CAPTAIN JAMES G. WILLIE'S HANDCART COMPANY OF MORMON EMIGRANTS ON THE WAY TO UTAH, GREATLY EXHAUSTED BY THE DEEP SNOWS OF AN EARLY WINTER AND SUFFERING FROM LACK OF FOOD AND CLOTHING HAD ASSEMBLED HERE FOR REORGANIZATION BY RELIEF PARTIES FROM UTAH, ABOUT THE END OF OCTOBER 1856. THIRTEEN PERSONS WERE FROZEN TO DEATH DURING A SINGLE NIGHT AND WERE BURIED IN ONE GRAVE. TWO OTHERS DIED THE NEXT DAY AND WERE BURIED NEARBY. OF THE COMPANY OF 404 PERSONS, 77 PERISHED BEFORE HELP ARRIVED. THE SURVIVORS REACHED SALT LAKE CITY NOVEMBER 9TH, 1856.

Ten miles later I turned north, the residual snows on the Wind River peaks now clear white tusks in the sun, the mountains themselves like great grey elephants, jostling north through the haze.

A jeep track led me out on to route # 28. I turned right, and in a mile or so reached an isolated bar and food box number eleven. The lady answered the door in a housecoat, yawned and said, "Oh yeah, it's you."

Mice had ravaged the peanut butter – why couldn't they have gone for the rice? – but otherwise the box was intact. The lady in the housecoat, dressed by now, couldn't help with the peanut butter problem but she did sell me a quart of milk. I sat at a table in the empty bar and drank it very slowly. The pink neon of the Coors beer sign fluttered palely in the window, and the lady threw a log on the stove. I remembered that Mormons had frozen to death as early as October around here.

A quart of milk was more than I could comfortably handle, but I drank it all down because there are people in the world less fortunate than myself, material evidence of which was mounted in a glass case over the bar. The actual jackrabbit – stuffed – stirred my conscience not a whit. It was already dead. Nor did the antelope horns – their original owner being dead too I supposed. But the macabre combination of the two – known as Jackaloupes and available in souvenir shops statewide – excited the missionary in me. I wanted to ban them, to make due respect for all living things compulsory in the state of Wyoming, but instead I finished the milk.

5 The Wind River Range

I'd walked 200 miles in the past eight days, from Bridger Peak to Wamsutter and on through the desert to South Pass. The next 170 miles, through the Wind River Range and the breccia country south of Yellowstone, took ten days, and in that time I passed not one permanently inhabited building.

To keep me company I had a book called *Wind River Trails* by Finis Mitchell, 422 M Street, Rock Springs. The address, on the title page, was the friendliest thing I encountered for days, of which it rained for the next seven in a row; not just the afternoon storms I'd experienced in Colorado, but plain, all-day rain for a week. By the time I reached Green Lake, where the Wind Rivers peter out, I was definitely going daft. I very nearly hit a guy who made fun of my pack – I'd already killed a grouse – and I almost burned down a shed. With so much rain and so little peanut butter it was only the Finis Mitchell book that saved me from cracking up altogether. Mr Mitchell – no poet – was, I felt, your basic good bloke:

> I came to Wyoming [he writes] with my parents, a span of mules, a wagon and a cow. We arrived April 26th, 1906.
> My father started me climbing mountains. In 1920 I began taking pictures as a hobby with my climbing so I could show people where I'd been and what there was in our National Forests. Since then I've taken 105,345 pictures.
> I went to Rock Springs and began working for the Union Pacific Rail Road June 4th, 1923, but was laid off March 4th, 1930 due to the big depression. I had gotten married June

4th, 1925. When they laid me off I went back to the mountains to trap because there were no jobs, not even for beggars.

At that time the great Wind Rivers Range had been used only for sheep and cattle grazing and because there was no way to earn a living, in June 1930 my wife and I bought a tent, borrowed horses and saddles and started our Mitchell's Fishing Camp in the Big Sandy openings.

When we set up our fishing camp there were only about five lakes that had fish in them, all Cutthroat trout, native to the Rocky mountains. Most of the hundreds of lakes in the Wind Rivers were in glacial cirques with steep waterfalls that prevented fish from ever getting upstream.

The hatchery brought fish to us in five-gallon milk cans. In the seven years we were there we packed out two and a half million little trout. They could be Rainbow, Cutthroat, California Golden, Brook or German Brown. We stocked 314 lakes during the time we ran our fishing camp, free for the public.

We charged a dollar and a half a day for the horses. We also served meals in the tent for fifty cents a meal. Believe it or not, that first summer we made three hundred dollars and fifteen cents.

These waters were all virgin and were just full of water lice, leeches, fresh water shrimp and that kind of stuff, so these fish just gorged themselves. Some of the Brook trout weighed three pounds the third year. Even the hatchery superintendent was amazed at the fast growth.

Later on we were trying to find fish to plant that would get bigger than the kinds supplied by the hatchery. We went over the Continental Divide to Grave Lake. This was the only lake in the area that had Mackinaw trout in it. We caught five. We had selected a beautiful lake to put them in and named it May's Lake as we had to name and record all the lakes we planted fish in. That was in 1933 and to this day I have never caught a fish in that lake. Other people are catching them though and the biggest I knew of was caught by my foreman on the railroad and it weighed ten and a half pounds. They all came from those five and are there to this day.

Finis Mitchell had made the Winds sound wet, and they were. For the next hundred miles it rained from morning till night. Wet cloud, wet rock, wet trees, wet grass, wet absolutely everything. Sodden colours stuck to the ground. Sodden hair stuck to my head. Sodden sounds bunged up my ears. There was no dry place under the trees with spiders webs still stretched across them, no light-coloured patches when you lifted a stone. Even the woodlice looked depressed. My boots felt like cold rice puddings; my fingers and toes looked as if I'd fallen asleep in the bath. The wart on my left hand went soft as a bean, though it was too near the knuckle to get at properly with my teeth so I sucked the rain from my moustache instead, the flavour varying according to circumstance. On August 19th, for example, it tasted of peppermint and blood. Cleaning my teeth in the pre-dawn drizzle I'd snapped my toothbrush off at the neck, the sudden loss of resistance inside my mouth matched by an uncontrolled uppercut and a prodigious nose bleed. My nostrils were rusty all day.

Toothbrush failure was not an eventuality I'd foreseen, though scouring London for the best gear I could afford I'd not been entirely naïve. I'd tried to project whatever I bought into just this Wind River weather. How then could the down sleeping bag, so fluffy in that warm London shop, be this selfsame bundle of soaking wet crud in which I'd just spent the night?

"Three Seasons", the label had said.

Was that all? I told the assistant I was looking for something far tougher – something to last five or six seasons at least, I'd demanded. The youth looked at me strangely. Then a smirk had spread over his face. A blush was spreading over mine.

"It's seasons as in autumn or winter," he said. "Four is the heaviest you can get."

"I see," I said crisply.

I bought the tent in the same shop, seduced, in the end, by the pamphlet. "Hydrostatic Head", it claimed. "UV resistant inner, high performance PU".

"What's PU?" I asked the salesman, but he hadn't known, and I'd left the shop with my ego happily reflated.

Perhaps it stood for Put Up. In the Winds that's all I seemed to do: put up the tent; put up the stove; put up my anorak hood (which I hated because it was like having eardrums on the outside of my head). I snatched meals between showers, stopping when I could to shake out my damp gear, my wetproofs off and on sometimes twelve times a day; but the discipline exacted by constant rain began gradually to wear me down. There was no spontaneity in this. No joy. When one morning I disturbed a sandpiper chick at my feet I caught it and ran my nose through its down just to feel something soft.

Life became a numbing drill, every movement prescribed by the weather. First ceasing to think, I ceased even to imagine. I was just a wet carthorse, head down in my traces. But I was a good carthorse. I handled the weather, and despite the foul conditions I put in some heavy mileage. I'd developed a kind of lope and could keep it going for hours, though when I stopped I'd have no idea where I'd been, the trail still just the same brown crease across the rock-spattered moorland. Somewhere at the back of my head must have been a link between my eyes and my feet, but I was largely unaware of it. In fact I was unaware of just about everything. I lived from one brew-up to the next – tea, cigarettes and sleep were just about all I thought of. My whole existence was suspended between tiny points of physical comfort.

Other than a few mushrooms and perhaps the odd cupful of berries, I had no expectation of supplementary food anywhere between South Pass and Moran (there wasn't anywhere between South Pass and Moran) so this time my stuff really would have to last the full ten days as planned. Oppressed by the incessant rain, I drew a perverse morality from my enforced self-sufficiency. I don't really subscribe to the myth of totin' your own victuals – I'd much rather have enormous meals parachuted in on request – but I fell into a sort of "Come, let us give thanks and subdivide this humble Snicker yet again" mentality, and if, somehow, an ice-cream van had come trundling through the drizzle I think I would have ignored it.

Four days went by in a blur. I was walking through some of the most spectacular mountains in North America, but they were bandaged in filthy tatters. The grey dressings slipped only once, on the evening of my thirty-third birthday. I was just north of a place called Temple Peak Pass when I got a brief glimpse of what I had been missing – rock heaped on rock, greasy remnants of snow, dark steeples of ice-bitten granite. Then the mist closed in. It was like being shown the bones of the earth.

Although I missed most of the mountains, I saw enough lakes to last me the rest of the walk. I passed hundreds of them and crossed dozens of streams, the sound of running water so familiar that in the tent at night I'd imagine it was human voices. By day I tried to see beauty in the swarming lakes, and in the distraught-looking streams trying vainly to pull them together, but the reality was as grey as the sky.

I'd just forded the East Fork River when dismal boulders in the grass ahead began to bleat. They were sheep. They hardly seemed to notice the rain. The lambs had reached the podgy stage when their frenzied attempts to still suckle their mothers looked frankly perverted. It was the best laugh I'd had for days.

Sometime that afternoon I reached latitude 43° north, which is the sort of thing that sounds great in a diary but means absolutely nothing at the time. In degrees and minutes this journey was the equivalent of a walk from southern Morocco to northern France, and here in central Wyoming I'd just about reached the Pyrenees. The timberline ran about a thousand feet lower than in Colorado, though the trees were the familiar mixture of spruce, fir and limber pine, thickening to lodge pole pine at lower altitudes, which is where I got most of my mushrooms. The self-sufficiency craze was eroding fast. Never mind one ice-cream van, I could have slurped my way through a whole fleet. Anything edible would have been welcome as long as it wasn't more of what I already had, and when, on August 20th, I saw a troupe of Blue Grouse by the trail, my pack was off and a hail of rocks flying a clear length ahead of my conscience. The birds were stupidly tame – made absolutely no attempt to fly away – and on about the twentieth shot I got one. They'd scattered at last, but with a bang of adrenalin I saw something still twitching in the bilberries. I was on to it in a flash, a moment of utter abandon, no rules, no anything, and there I was with its head in my hands. It was a small bird, not much bigger than a pigeon, and didn't take long to pluck. I ate it that night, boiled with curry powder, and left the bones on a rock for the crows. I was neither happy nor sad about what I had done, although I was very surprised. I'd never caught and killed a wild creature with my bare hands before, and I have to admit I enjoyed it.

I also enjoyed my tin whistle. I'd had it since mid-Colorado, the perfect backpacking instrument – small, light, and unbreakable – except that I couldn't actually play it. But the Winds provided ideal conditions in which to learn – long, mangled evenings, longer and even more mangled days, and the mournful weet weet of marsh birds inspiring me to produce something better. I had hoped, in these mountains, to climb Gannet Peak, the highest point in Wyoming, but thanks to the weather my sole achievement was a painful limp through "Clemantine". By the time I reached Green Lake at the northern end of the range, I could pipe out the "Skye Boat Song" too.

That last day in the Winds was – predictably – perfect. Way below me lay the lake itself, jade under harlequined crags. The sun had at last got his hat on. I gave it two fingers and pushed on. It hardly rained again for a month.

6 Green Lake to Moran

I slid down through the timber, mossy and wet, and hit a trail alongside the lake. Shrivelled iris were scattered like *pot pourri* in the long grass. The clouded peg of Square Top Mountain receded, petalled limestone enfolding the crags. The valley widened, the Green River now a drowsy slither through the trees. Morning heat broke through the steam. Ahead in the mist something thin loomed up on stilts. I heard the whoof, whoof, whoof of rising wing beats and the rattling gar-oo-oo of a crane, invisible over the fog-bound lake.

Next day I reached a nick in the skyline called Gunsight Pass. For the first time in months there was hardly a mountain in sight, though the respite lasted only two days. I spent most of that time on logging trails, linking them largely by instinct, an instinct which, at the beginning of the walk, I hardly knew I had. To simply trust myself to the valleys around me, to climb when I wanted a view and adjust course accordingly, was an inexpressible freedom. I was still using the map, of course, but I was not longer an addict.

Wild geraniums, streaked with red, were racing yellowed willows into autumn. Was there a faint tang in the air? The weird descant of Coyotes howling at noon suggested that there was.

That night was the ninth from South Pass – just one more day and my food would have lasted exactly as long as I'd planned. I got quartermasterly pleasure in this neat unfolding of my plans (plans which, for nine-tenths of the time, I completely forgot I had made), and when, at about four that afternoon, I saw a hutted camp through the trees, I very nearly walked straight past it. I had only one day to go to complete a virtually self-sufficient stage and I didn't want to spoil it. But smoke hung over one of the cabins. A lorry was being unloaded beside it. A six-tonner. Containing nothing but food.

Boxes and boxes and boxes of it. Honey by the gallon, bread by the yard, eggs by the tens of dozen. Forest and Mike even had hot water. Mike got the generator going when we'd finished unloading and I stood under the shower for an hour. Teton Country Outfitters were establishing themselves for the hunting season. The first clients were due in about three weeks' time, and it looked as if they were to be fed until Doomsday.

We spent the entire evening in the cookhouse – the hot plate was the size of a carpet. Empty bread wrappers mounted in the bin, eggshells rolled on the floor, and about halfway through supper – theirs, mine lasted hours – I became aware of something unusual about my hosts, both of them still in their teens. It took me a little while to pin it down, though it was quite a simple thing really. They listened.

Most conversations are more of a firework display than actual communication. You send up a verbal rocket and the other person goes, "Ooh!" Then they shoot off a quick display of their own and you go, "Aah!" in reply. Somehow Forest and Mike avoided all this. They didn't get listening muddled up with reacting.

When I mentioned my impression, Forest said they were aware of it too.

"We're Mormons," he said.

"What, the guys with short hair and raincoats?"

"Yeah."

How did being a Mormon affect whether you listened or not?

"You ever read the *Book of Mormon?*"

I hadn't. "We believe some real weird things," said Forest. "Boring things half of them. Things that as kids we don't really understand. But the average kid, in the States at least, mostly gets input it can handle. All chopped up, presented just so, all on the appropriate level. Stuff just gets sort of glued on. Kids over here have lost what you might call the ability to incorporate things."

I left bootmarks in the frost at dawn and climbed with the sun through meadows of dying lupins. Young elk were wading wet-bellied into the trees, not bambis anymore, their white-spotted flanks now a cinnamon brown. And I saw, as I had for several days now, the rocky wigwams of the Tetons thirty miles to the west, pitched six thousand feet over the Snake River valley. Teton means "tit" in French, though they looked more like broken bottles to me. I sang hymns to myself all day – "Jerusalem" mostly, and "Hills of the North, Rejoice!" – and eventually stumbled out of the forest to strike route # 28 at sunset.

A forest service layby just down the road had hard standing for two dozen vehicles. There was a picnic table at each bay. I'd begun to quite miss furniture and it was good to feel something flat under my elbows. The Pattersons from Michigan had the table next to mine. Their son lived in Australia. Mr Patterson was strolling about with nothing to do; Mrs P. was making popcorn.

"He likes popcorn," she said. "I make it every night."

Mr Patterson came over, jingling loose change. He nodded towards his wife. "She likes Wyoming," he said. "Bring her out every fall."

Before they folded their camp chairs for the night, Mrs P. gave me six pecan tarts. They were just out of date and she hoped I wouldn't be offended. I gave her a big hug and a kiss on both cheeks and crawled into the tent.

I did nothing the following day but swill milk on a motel lawn. I was forced to move a few times because of the sprinklers and the letter I was writing got wet. The manager, who had food box number twelve in his cellar, kindly fed me, and then I left, fording the Buffalo river a mile north of the road. This was the last food pick up in Wyoming. The next – 108 miles ahead – would be in Montana.

7 Moran to West Yellowstone

Unlike Colorado – a confusion of peaks – my route through Wyoming was simple: part one – the Red Desert and South Pass; part two – The Wind Rivers and on to Moran; part three – the top left-hand corner, most of which was Yellowstone National Park. It seemed fortuitous that the Divide should run through it. I was thirty miles short of the boundary.

Heavy umbells of yampa – it resembles hogweed – swung like counterweights against my knees. Under the yampa were gentians, so many that they looked like a crop, and inside the gentians were ants, bees and wasps, and sometimes a lurking spider. It was difficult to appreciate that in less than two months all this would be deep in snow, but north country summers at 8000 feet are no more than commercial breaks. Visitors swarm in like midges from some time in May and by mid-September are gone. Even the first official survey of the area, in June 1859, was beaten back by the weather, and Yellowstone remained largely untouched for another ten years.

Why the region was unknown for so long is a mystery. Trappers seem to have avoided it. Perhaps the short summers put them off, beaver pelts being in prime condition during winter, when the whole area was cut off. Lewis and Clark, the first transcontinental explorers, missed it, though one of their men – his name was John Colter – scored a direct if accidental hit. He left the expedition in 1806 to trap the lower Yellowstone river, and turned up in St Louis four years later, his account of boiling hot springs and bubbling mud pools passed off as bad cabin fever. But he obviously convinced one man, an English naturalist who took the trouble to write down his story.

"This man," wrote the naturalist Bradbury, "reached St Louis in May 1810, in a small canoe, a distance of three thousand miles which he traversed in thirty days. I received from him an account of his adventures after he separated from the Lewis and Clark party, one of these, from its singularity, I shall relate." Which he does.

Colter, trapping the upper Missouri, is captured by six hundred Blackfeet. His companion is riddled with arrows. At first inclined to set Colter up as a mark too, the chief intervenes and leads him, stripped naked, a quarter-mile on to the prairie. A "horrid whoop" sounds and, catching on fast, Colter bolts through the prickly pear, "exciting himself to such a degree that the blood poured from his nostrils". Hard by the river, feet solid with thorns, he hears the sound of footsteps behind him – a lone indian ahead of the pack. Colter stops dead, grabs the indian's spear, and skewers him to the ground. Diving beneath a raft of drift timber he remains submerged all night. The indians eventually give up. Seven days later, still entirely naked, Colter turns up at a lone trading post. He is saved. He made me feel an absolute pansy.

At ten the next morning – August 26th – a cloud of deer flies went by. I caught them all up an hour later – a packtrain of twenty-one twitching mules, their three wranglers taking a break by a stream. Another elk-hunting outfit was setting up for September.

You could tell which one of them was the cook. While the other two laughed, shirtless and wet, Neil just sat under the brim of his hat, ignoring the cool water beside him. He popped a beer, took a sip, looked tough, wasn't. Neil was the sort of guy that believes in everything but himself. You could see that from the way he held his beer can. It was a prop. So was the way he talked about Vietnam, which was where he'd learnt to cook.

The other thing about Neil was that he only had one eye. This quite suited him. He'd lost it in a bar-room fight, and this quite suited him too.

"Drove eighty fucking miles," he said, "with the cocksucker hanging down my cheek."

I lobbed a teabag into the pot. Nothing like that had ever happened to me. Neil lit a joint, exhaled, and asked me if I'd come far.

"Fair way," I said.

He took another hit on the joint.

"You English?" he asked.

"Yeah."

"Thought so."

The stream divided a few miles further on to flow each side of a tree. A plank was nailed to the flaking trunk. "Parting of the Waters", it announced. "Atlantic Ocean 3488 miles. Pacific 1353". Two Ocean Creek drains into a boggy saddle right on the Divide from which rivulets flow both east and west. Otherwise it appears quite ordinary. About all that happened was that I dropped a lens cap into the water. I groped about for ages, a cursing Narcissus, but it was gone. To which ocean is anyone's guess.

I didn't bother to pitch the tent that night but lay back stargazing through the binoculars, millions of tiny headlights all weaving about like dodgems in my eyes. I put the binoculars down, the stars ceased to bounce, and I slept, though without my usual hog-like inertia. There were Grizzly Bears about. Not many – two or three hundred in north-western Wyoming – but one Grizzly is plenty. They weigh half a ton, do forty in top, and, as everyone knows, they love honey. I'd hung mine in a tree. Nightly lynchings of the food bags and the stove were to become routine from now on, though I tried to cut down the time I wasted next morning in trying to relocate the pine that I'd chosen. You needed to sleep far enough from your dangling food for the thus thwarted bear not to sense you, but near enough to remember where you'd put it. Mine was no more than a fifty-metre memory at best.

I can't honestly say that I took the bear threat at all seriously. People do get eaten, and horribly maimed, but they get killed in car crashes too. I hung up my food – put my safety belt on – and left it at that. I was to get my comeuppance, but not for several hundred miles. What I did take seriously, there on the park boundary, were the rangers.

I'd flown free as a bird now for close on two thousand miles, my only crime, if it was a crime, being the death of the grouse. Often it seemed that I had the whole west to myself, an illusion of course, but one I tried hard to maintain. I had carved neither hearts, names nor dates into trees, far less set the forests alight; I had polluted not a lake or a stream, had dropped not a scrap of litter. There was secret pleasure in a gentle passing – respect seemed to work both ways – so how odd it was that in Yellowstone Park, set aside expressly as a public pleasure ground, I should feel least pleasure of all. Nowhere else on the walk, not even on the most private ranch, did I feel as alienated as here. I followed the Divide for the next eighty miles like a guy at completely the wrong party, but then, I had no invitation.

I'd written to all three National Parks *en route*, but had received the same reply from each – that a Backcountry Use Permit could be issued no more than forty-eight hours in advance of a visit. In other words, you can't reserve campsites in National Parks for months ahead. This seems reasonable, unless, of course, you are approaching the park on foot, because Yellowstone – especially Yellowstone – is insulated by a good forty-eight hours of remote, uninhabited country, and having reached the park boundary you still have a forty-mile trek to the backcountry office at Old Faithful – a trek which I should not have been making: I couldn't enter the park to get a permit because I didn't already have one. Classic Catch–22.

The Rocky Mountain Park rangers back in Colorado had bent the rules and waved me through, but for some reason (perhaps because in response to a second enquiry I'd been sent just another copy of the regulations) I suspected this would not be the case in Yellowstone. I swung northeast along the Snake River with the hollow confidence of an escaped PoW; camped illegally; saw a moose; and, next morning, gave myself up. Camped illegally! You might as well say I'd farted illegally, but I'd seen a patrol cabin ahead and decided to call in as a pre-emptive measure.

I also wanted to report a stray horse. Neil and Co. had lost one and they thought it might be somewhere in the park, Yellowstone being an easy place to get lost in as T. C. Everts, a member of the 1870 survey party, quickly discovered. Negotiating a tract of fallen timber – flattened by earthquake or fire, he doesn't say which – he had become separated from his companions. A nearsighted man, he dismounted to examine the trail; whereupon his horse, and with it his guns, blankets and food, had bolted. Everts was left with two knives and his opera glasses, "alone", as he put it, "in an unexplored wilderness". Utterly bewildered, he wandered down the trail I was now on until he reached the expanse of Heart Lake, now blue under a perfect sky. Looking along the shoreline, I could see a girl in a green shirt. She was dragging an aluminium canoe up the beach. She lifted a string of wet trout from the bows and made her way up to the small cabin.

The cackle of a short-wave radio greeted me at the door.

"Hello," I said when the girl reappeared. "You must be the ranger."

"Yes," she said sharply. "Who are you?"

"I'm walking the Divide," I said, and gave her a brief account of the journey. She thawed very slightly. We weren't exactly in each other's arms, but at least the safety-catch was back on her voice. I mentioned the lost horse, admired the fish, and, when I reckoned she'd just about hung up her guns, told her I needed a permit. I might just have exposed myself. Perhaps I should have. The outrage, the squall of anger churning her face, was remarkable to behold.

"You don't have one?"

"No."

"Why not?"

"I, er . . . "

"Where did you sleep?" she cut in.

"Just here," I said, unfolding the map. She poked the grimy sheet with her finger.

"What're all these crosses for?"

The crosses, in biro, marked where I'd stopped for brew-ups.

"So what're all these numbers? 1300, 1600?"

"That's what time it was."

"Yeah? So where did you build your fire?"

Now this was the old knife-in-the-boot-trick, the derringer up the sleeve. Outside designated campsites, fires aren't allowed in Yellowstone. I had been outside a designated campsite. Then, "Did you bury your trash?"

Another backcountry no-no. I was reeling and, what's more, I was innocent. Why did she hate me? I never bury trash anywhere.

"No," I said. "I burnt it. Then I shot a moose."

Even the dead fish grinned at that, but Ms. Ranger didn't twitch. She eventually threatened to arrest me, thought better of it, and demanded some ID; for which I got what she called a courtesy tag in return. "For illegal camping," she snarled.

The courtesy tag was wired, with the backcountry use permit she finally issued, evacuee-style to my pack. It was, I suppose, the equivalent of a dunce's cap.

"Issued to encourage friendly co-operation," it said, "and good compliance with the regulations. Your co-operation helps to protect people, the park and the parkways, and to maintain safe, clean and convenient conditions for all."

Safety, cleanliness and convenience – the Father, the Son and the Holy goddamn Ghost – but you can't run a place like Yellowstone

without rules. Old Faithful gets two million visitors a year. I suppose I
was just the wrong guy in the wrong place at the wrong time. So was
poor T. C. Everts. Despite all the wildlife – he records otters in great
number, beaver and mink, deer, elk, and Rocky Mountain Sheep –
TC was starving to death. He was saved by a small green plant, a
thistle. "Eureka," he writes. "I'd found food."

His next meal was a raw bird. Drenched by the perpetual sleet he
had reached the hot spring beside which I now sat, and he made it his
home for a week. I had never seen a hot spring before, though I'd
known from the way the trees were thinning out that something was
up.

That the Yellowstone area is the world's best known kettle diminished the suspense not a bit. That, by local standards, the Heart
Lake springs were mere thimbles didn't matter. The furniture – those
crowded trees – had been moved back. A white carpet of gravel had
been laid, and there! – a faint whisp of steam teased the grass. Curious,
then, this vague disinclination to look down, this delicious reluctance
to see something for the very first time. When you are so close to a
new event, to a new experience, it often ceases to matter whether
anything actually happens at all.

This heresy fading, my eyes reached the edge of the pool. The water
was phenomenally clear – I thought fleetingly of glass-bottomed boats
– so what stopped me from jumping straight in? It wasn't the heat –
you didn't feel that till you physically touched the water, and then you
wondered what had stung you. It was, rather, the sterility. Sunlight
danced down there, but no fish. Small bones, tiny rocks, a tin can (A
TIN CAN!) lay at the bottom clean as napkins, each an individual
object – no ooze, no growths to pull them together.

But the moment passed. I had boiling water on tap! I pulled out the
pot, set up the camera, and made my first cup of instant tea. I was
tempted to dangle a teabag into the pool itself – look mum, no stove!
– and, sitting there in the sunshine, I grinned at the tiff with the ranger.
It had been my fault for winding her up. I would have loved her to
come by just then, to come over and have a laugh too, but she'd
probably seen hundreds of hot springs in her life, and in any case I
was too near the edge. T. C. Everts had actually fallen in.

Chilled to the bone he had fallen asleep on the heated encrustation,
enveloped in a perpetual steambath while the October storms raged.
Unfortunately he must have rolled over, and a scalded hip was added
to the pain of his already frost-bitten feet. By this time he'd lost both
his knives, but on the twelfth day it struck him that the opera glass

lenses could be used to kindle a fire – great for him, but bad, very bad, for the forest. Everts woke up the following night, his pine shelter ablaze, sheets of flame roaring up through the treetops. "It was wonderous," he wrote, "to witness the flash-like rapidity with which the flame spread. The trees shot forth streamers of arrowy fire, leaving an immense sweep of destruction."

By mid-afternoon I was back under the trees, a siberia of pines, following orange trail markers tacked – why so high? – ten feet off the ground. They looked like little bus stops. Otherwise I could see very little. There'd nearly always been an escape from forest so far – upwards to tundra, downwards to sage – but in Yellowstone the skyline was flat, the Divide on this plateau indistinguishable. I left it and headed directly for Old Faithful. Despite its 3500 square miles, Yellowstone, to the majority of visitors, is a long strip of tarmac through the trees – a 500–mile-long strip if you were to drive along every road; it is, or was, the famous bears, though contact is now discouraged; and it is, above all, the best known geyser in the world.

"What does she mean to the average American?" – the old man and I were standing in line for coffee – "Why, that's part of America, my boy! I was twenty-one years old when I came up here the first time, and that was in a model T Ford. Had to run her backwards to get up the hills. Now I'm here in a beautiful Buick 450, bringing my own daughter's kids."

What had been at first a faint hum in the forest had grown steadily louder all morning, and at midday I'd caught a flash of chrome through the trees. I'd smelt crawling traffic, and had stepped into what, for a hiker at least, was another world.

"Look at that," said Paul, an Alaskan I met in the car park. "The Winnebago. The big old motor-home. The guys with the polyester pants and the ladies with the blue-rinse hair. Been on their trail since April."

Paul had a large motorbike. This was his first trip to what he called the lower forty-eight.

"Ended up buzzing down to Phoenix. Had the address of a girl there – red hair, green eyes, biggest chest you've ever seen. Girls in Alaska're nothing like her."

"You do have girls in Alaska?"

"Ugly ones. Buffarillos we call them. They're outdoors women because when you get mad you can throw them outdoors and they'll generally live till the morning. But the girls in California! Man! Nearly crashed! Those must've been price tags they were wearing. The mosquitoes in Alaska would kill them!"

Old Faithful was an absolute treat. I didn't give a damn about the geyser itself, it was the people that were so delectable. There were hotels full; hundred-acre car parks full; coffee shops, lecture halls, even a small cinema full. It was as if, tramping through the wilds of Scotland, I'd just stumbled into Stratford-on-Avon. But to leave without seeing Anne Hathaway's cottage seemed silly, so I joined the trickle of visitors now quitting the restaurant for the treeless expanse outside.

Being safe (there were substantial benches to watch from), clean (as a whistle), and convenient (very – she blows like clockwork once an hour), Old Faithful seemed almost a microcosm of the nation itself, a place where a guy could walk proud and tall, credit cards slung at his side, though not everyone there was American. The woman next to me, for example, was Belgian, her husband busy with his camera.

"It's the fourth time we make a tour in America," she said, "but" – the crowd was thickening and her voice dropped dramatically – "really I don't like the people."

"Why not?"

"They are kind, but really a conversation about something interesting you can't do." She was interrupted as a first puff of steam drifted upward, the crowd now swelling to perhaps a thousand. More steam shot from the earth. People were laughing, excited, expectant. Loose children were grabbed by the hand. But the Belgian lady wasn't looking. "They have no personality," she said. "No culture. Today you can be a professor, tomorrow you are selling hot dogs. Maybe in one hundred or two hundred years . . ." but I was no longer listening. 5000 gallons of superheated water had shot twelve stories into the air, suspended by a tremendous cheer from the crowd. The enthusiasm was infectious. This was their culture – couldn't the old bag see that? A lot of people were actually clapping. What it all meant, what it symbolized, didn't in the end concern me. The joy of it all, the exquisite pleasure, was that everything was just as it was.

It took me another day and a half to walk out of the park, but first I tripped out along the boardwalks of the lower geyser basin – instant thermidor if you fell in because most of the springs were boiling. One fifth of all the geysers in the world lie within the square mile of Old Faithful and I was getting rather blasé about the whole thermal experience, but that evening, camped alone beside a pool called Ojo Caliente, Yellowstone began to sink in. It was, I thought, about as near to America as I was likely to get. I was wrong there. I still had seven hundred miles of it left.

Dark vapours, tinged by the sun, drifted over the open ground. From a wide clearing beyond the Firestone River came the gonging of Canada geese. One more day and I'd be out of the park too, though headed in the opposite direction. The geese were already on their way south, but tomorrow I would be in Montana, which is where, incidentally, T. C. Everts eventually wound up. He'd lost pretty well everything by now – his knives, his shoes, the opera glasses – and about all he had left was his life, when, groping his way round the side of a hill, he became, as he put it, "suddenly sensible of a reflection" – the astonished face of a trapper. Lost in the wilds for thirty-seven days, T. C. Everts was saved.

Statistical note:

> *Wyoming* – August 5th to 31st, no complete rest days at all. 509 miles, 26 nights on the trail. Used the tent 10 times, ate 3½ boxes of food, averaged 19 miles a day. Rained for a week in the Wind River Range, but only twice after that. Reached 11,000 feet once, otherwise ranging down to 6500 feet.
>
> *Montana* – August 31st to October 18th, less 4 complete rest days. 662 miles, 43 nights on the trail. Used the tent 14 times, but slept in many additional shelters. Ate 5 boxes of food but bought supplements. Averaged 15 miles a day. Rain and/or snow on 17 days, altitude generally low, hitting 10,000 feet once and ranging down to 4500 feet.

PART V

Montana

1 Route # 191

Montana was in many ways a fitting last act, though West Yellowstone, the small town on the northwestern boundary of the park, wasn't the greatest of opening scenes: the curtain rises. It is night, here on the edge of town. The used-condom zone. Garageless trucks stand deserted, white litter nuzzles the trees. Then – footsteps; a torch beam slashes the forest and I'm dazzled, caught half-crouching over my pack.

"You pitching a tent over there?"

"Yeah," I yell back. "Get your fucking torch out of my eyes."

"OK, OK, just didn't know what you was, is all. Motels ain't full in town."

I couldn't afford a motel.

"Then sleep on the sidewalk, but away from the garbage cans. Sanitation department has claws. One of them Mothers inside your tent and there ain't gonna be a lot left."

Bloody bears again. I ended up on the Information Centre roof.

At dawn I popped my head over the parapet. Mainstreet waved boisterously – Montana Meats, Montana Cheeses, Cameras, Curios, Montana Dentals, five motels and a church. And, by the Information Centre front door, this sign:

> THE 1959 EARTHQUAKE.
> On August 17th, 1959, at 11.37 pm this spectacularly
> scenic section of Montana became the focus of
> worldwide history. A heavy shock smashed the soft
> summer night . . .

Over breakfast in the Dairy Queen I decided it was more of a billboard than a sign: "In several mighty heaves Mother Earth reshaped her mountains in violent response to an agony of deepseated tensions no longer bearable . . . " I had much the same problem – too much Biscuits 'n' Gravy probably – and waddled over to a service station. Then I started walking again, out along route # 191. It ran west, straight as a sermon.

The very sound of hiking boots on hard asphalt rings false, at best an eccentricity, at worst the knell of the soft option. In the actual walking you could at least force the pace, chastising your muscles for the sin of taking to tarmac, but at food stops the guilt of those easy miles really hit you. Reviewing a completed stage I could, it is true, sometimes write down NO TAR!! in my diary; but then I'd remember the odd mile or two as I'd walked into the town. I'd check the map again. I'd measure off the exact distance, and wallowing in righteousness, jot down, say, FIVE MILES.

The total distances I'd walked on hard surfaced roads so far were, for New Mexico – 42 miles; for Colorado – 47 miles; for Wyoming, until Old Faithful at least – 0, not a single yard in nearly five hundred miles. But the diversion to West Yellowstone for food had rather spoilt the record, the one compensation being that tarmac always flew by very fast. Until those last miles of Wyoming I'd spent no more than six hours at a stretch on a road, though later, beyond the Bitteroots, I ate humble pie for a week.

That night I ate trout with the Hicks.

Various subtribes had passed me on route # 191 – bicyclists with wing mirrors on their spectacles; a flock of motorcycles; and, at about four that afternoon, a jogger. This was Mike Hicks. He drew ahead, became a blip, but didn't quite vanish. He'd stopped for me to catch up, his house one of a dozen A-frames newly built on the facing hillside.

"That's Helen, my wife, on the balcony," he said. She was waving energetically.

"Phone!" she yelled as we strolled nearer. Mike took the call, leapt into his car, and was gone before I'd unlaced my boots.

"Car wreck in the park," said Helen.

"Bad one," said Mike when he got back two hours later. He managed the West Yellowstone group practice. There was something remorselessly comical in the thought of the sluggish holiday traffic crashing. Roadside wildlife, it seemed, had an almost hypnotic effect.

"Buffalo?" I asked, very much the old hand.

"No," said Mike. "Just a couple of elk."

Meanwhile Justin-Joseph, aged ten, had taken me down to the small lake below the house. He was a phenomenal fisherman – he'd actually asked Helen how many she wanted him to catch.

"Dad goes to fly school," he said, flicking the line out. "I'm learning too, but I'm not ready to tie the hard ones."

I should have taken notes. JJ knew more about trout flies than I did about almost anything, though his brother, unfortunately, knew nothing about them at all. Shannon was four, very bored, and some minutes later dropped a large clod of earth in the water. So we ended up with just three trout and Helen got two more from the freezer.

Saying goodnight to kids is a laugh if they aren't your own. Shannon stumbled up the stairs in my boots screeching, "Look, I've got wings on my feet!"; JJ asked me to get his plastic record-player down and listen to "The Jungle Book" with him. Then I lay on the carpet and listened to "Rumores de la Caleta" by Albeniz and Tarrega's "Capricho Arabe". There was wine and chocolate, and stick after stick of raw celery. How amazing it was to be taken into people's homes like this.

2 The Centennials

The Hicks' linen was the first I'd slept in for what, next morning, took the first seven or eight miles to work out. While my legs – my now oddly professional legs – swung steadily forward, the countercurrent of memory drifted back, replaying Wyoming, camp after camp, replaying Colorado. It was good to sail upstream like this, away from the fathom-less present. That mystery I could leave to my feet. Let my boots extrude the actual, convert the not yet to the is. Meanwhile I'd enjoy river music. A journey is, after all, just a song. Someone plucks it out of the air, hums the tune for a while, writes it down. I was back to my diary. The last sheets had been in Creede.

It was late afternoon when I turned west off the road and began to climb, the shadows lengthening as I followed a dirt trail up through the trees. I was carrying water, I'd done twenty miles, I was tired, but there'd be no warm A-frame for me tonight; the unpleasant prospect of erecting the tent kept me walking deep into the twilight. I'd have to face the hassle of stopping fairly soon though, and was just about to go into my boy scout routine when reprieve in the shape of a tracked snow-cat beckoned from the clearing ahead. The vehicle was parked beside a sort of depot – a forestry installation perhaps. The building was locked, but – yippee! – the cab door of the snow-cat was not.

Dawn through the windscreen was as good as breakfast in bed, sunrise a yolky dribble down the distant shells of the Tetons. I'd followed the

Divide in a 120–mile semicircle round these unmistakable peaks, but now the watershed turned west, coinciding, for the next two weeks of the journey, with the Montana-Idaho state line. A short haul through the Centennial Range would bring me to food box fourteen at Monida, then I'd turn northwest to face the long haul up to Sula through the Bitteroot range, walking through hills so poignantly lonely that single, broken shacks became cities.

I emerged from the trees and for three days swept high above the Centennial valley, the sharp sting of sheep on the wind. There were few signs of elk about, but on the occasional dirt roads which attempted the watershed I saw camouflaged men driving pick-ups. The bow hunting season had begun.

When I came across them, Art, James and Mike were sitting round a campfire, farting. Their vehicles were parked under the trees, their beer parked under their vehicles. They were having a pretty good time. Ed, meanwhile, had fallen out of a tree. He picked himself up to a hail of derision and said, "Fuck it."

"The hooman bear trap," said James, at which point Danny roared up in what had once been a modest VW. He removed the door and got out.

"Danny's our Indian Scout," said Art. "Silent as a Buick V6, which is what he's put in that goddamn car."

"Wine?" said Mike, who wore glasses.

The evening progressed. I put the tent up inside out. Ed had another bash at the tree. By this time Danny had completely stripped down my stove. I'd mentioned that the jet was clogged and had asked to borrow his pliers.

"Don't look so worried," said Art. "That guy's really good with his hands. He'll fix it."

"Great," I said uncertainly, but he did.

We'd got on to warfare by now.

"You guys did real well in the Falklands," said Danny, still grunting over the stove. There was an awkward silence, then, "We've won fuck all for ages."

We discussed world affairs, we discussed camouflage, we discussed bar-b-que sauce; and, eventually, we discussed elk – specifically the elk which, to everyone's amazement, James had shot dead the previous year.

"Screwed up the whole trip," said Art. "A dead elk is a fucking hassle. Blood was running out of his garage door for the next three days in a row. His neighbours were counting their kids in at night."

These guys obviously went back a long way.

"Right back to our doctorates," said Mike. They were, all five of them, nuclear physicists. The National Reactor Testing Station was 120 miles down the road.

I met bow hunters the next night too, in more or less similar circumstances. The main ridge of the Centennial Mountains had dipped to another saddle – across which two ladies were pursuing a horse. I stepped confidently into its path. It ran straight past me. But I had the last laugh because the horse was trailing a head rope which I belatedly stamped on, jerking the animal to a halt. I was rewarded with a can of Coke and one end of a disgusting goat. Jennifer held down the other end, and Clara milked off two pints.

I liked Clara on sight, though the goat obviously loathed her which was rather unfair as this was the first time they'd met. It belonged to a guy called Tony. I was introduced to him an hour later, in which time I'd pitched the tent, lit a fire, and added a layer of clothes. Contorting myself in front of Clara's wing mirror, I had also combed out my hair. It had been very short when I'd started – neat for the talk in New York – but now it hung over my eyes. Clara got a pair of scissors from the camper and deftly converted what had become a lank balaclava into a snug-fitting cap. I was picking the last, snipped hairs off my tongue – how do they get into your mouth? – when Joe (Clara's husband), Peter (Jennifer's husband), and Tony (unmarried) turned up, their horses huge in the firelight.

Tony (unmarried) looked it. If his hands had ever been near a kitchen sink they'd probably been fixing the plumbing. He was, in fact, a trapper, though in summer he did a little prospecting. Gold-dust, muskrat and coyote fur were his stock-in-trade. *Gold-dust!* But what was that? A house? Oh. He had a house then, a day's walk west along the Divide in the ghost town of Monida.

Enter Joe, also from Monida, whose formative years had been spent in the used car trade – used for an hour or so that is, then put back. Then, not put back. Joe had the contacts, Tony the spray gun, and for a while they'd been the richest kids in town. But Monida, even then, was a small town, and when Joe got out of jail he didn't go back. When Tony got out of jail, Interstate–15 had bypassed the place and there was nothing to go back to. But he'd stayed. There'd been a car crash, a fatality, and a ghost town suited him fine.

Peter, by contrast, had no past – not one which showed anyway. His problem was handling the present. He had plonked himself down, beer can in hand, and was boring us with his day – the cam cream, the bow strings, the exact wind direction and strength. Not the smell of the wind, not the twang of the bow, not the luscious flight of even arrows that miss, but the facts, the black and white of it all. Tony and Joe had shot no elk either, but for them the bald facts were like paints. They could mix them, dilute them, elicit from them whole rainbows of truth. Peter could not. He was boring because he didn't know what painting really was.

There were no trees now, only hawks on the wind. The country, if anything, was bigger, swelling west in great downy waves; so big, it seemed, that nothing could ever change it. I forgot that soon these hills would be buried in snow, that this huge, dry land, with its brittle grasses and scattered cattle, would in a few weeks' time be smothered. There was so little out here to react to – the hills weren't awesomely rugged – but so much to simply take in, my body that day of no more account than thistledown blown on the wind.

A white dot, miles ahead, reappeared as the hillside dipped west; became a building, which even at this range looked deserted. A boarded-up saloon and the few shacks around it were all that was left of Monida. I got there just after midday, appeared to have the whole place to myself, and was startled by a shout from a pick-up.

It was Joe.

Long journeys tend to wear a bit thin, and you begin, towards the closing weeks, to seek substance in the miles you have walked; to cast nonsensical medals from the still-warm liquid of really rather mundane affairs. I was even beginning to ask myself if I had changed, though I knew perfectly well that I hadn't – that this journey was a celebration of things I already loved: the wind, the sky, the glorious nonsense of brief encounters. It was not a voyage of discovery, but there were times, nonetheless, when America knocked me right off my perch. Meeting Joe again was one of them. He'd been down the Interstate to get sinus pills for Tony and was waiting for me to come by.

"Wanted to speak with you anyway," he said, which struck me as vaguely ominous. He was leading me over to a nearby barn, a red barn, with a squad of white geese nibbling sky by the door.

"You can sleep in here if you want to," he said.

I still felt apprehensive. Joe hadn't let half the morning drift by just to tell me I could sleep in a barn. I was being set up for something.

But what the hell had I done? He'd flicked open his jacket. Oh shit. Where do I aim for if he hits me? I could see his lips moving. Eyes, throat and knees I reckoned – no point in pissing about. But he was trying to give me something. I risked a quick look down.

I was acutely conscious of the geese hissing outside.

There was a fifty-dollar note in Joe's hand.

Last night's conversation was already whirling back through my head. Money had come up – it often did – and I'd probably told Joe I didn't have much. Had I told him too loudly? I could have buried myself in the straw. I spluttered, prevaricated, slid inexorably towards confrontation.

"You're gonna need it," Joe urged. "I admire what you're doing and I want you to have it."

I was embarrassed from the barn roof down. I didn't admire what I was doing. In fact I didn't think of it as *doing* anything at all, and I wriggled on the sweet spike of compliment. But the money was something else. Though he didn't know it, Joe had scored a direct hit on the English, and in the matter of money I am very English indeed. You can be kind in England; benevolent; caring. You can be hopelessly charitable. What you cannot be, is generous. We English are far too symmetrical for that.

In the end Joe turned out to be right. I did need the fifty dollars. It was just enough for the Greyhound bus ticket which eventually saw me back to New York.

3 The Bitterroots

In the next ten days I walked 188 miles. I crossed three dirt roads and saw a total of seven people. None of them saw me.

On the first night I slept in a cabin at a place called Deep Cow Creek. The door was unlocked, there were three wooden beds, and I stretched myself out on the biggest. I felt just like Goldilocks, but no one came. Next morning I found a broom in the cupboard and swept the place by way of a thank you.

On the following night the dew froze on my tent. The sky was clear: Arcturus gleamed over black willows. I'd swung northwest – the Centennials had become the Bitterroots – but the country itself hadn't changed. The following morning I caught sight of a dozen cream-coloured specks way below me – birds, I thought – gliding in tight formation against the green fetch of the hills. It was only when they turned on a distant crest that I saw they were antelopes running. High on the watershed I was an antelope too. I found myself literally shouting for joy as I swept up and down on the wind. I could have carried almost anything that day. I wanted never to stop walking; to consume this huge, empty land for ever.

Days went by under my boots, the Divide rolling smoothly northwest. The only hiccup in southwestern Montana was lack of surface water – the underlying rock a permeable limestone. Not that I saw much of it. In the first sixty miles there was hardly a single outcrop. Sometimes the run of tilted strata showed like ribs through the thin dry turf, but even Elk Mountain, the last 10,000–foot peak on the journey, was almost wholly grassed over. The view from the top was colossal, no snow on the surrounding ranges but a sky greying over with watery cloud enough to suggest that there soon would be. Flocks of tiny pipits flew in staccato bursts against the wind. Kestrels, hardly betraying the strain, hovered over the nodding bunchgrass; a lone car sped like a dusty bullet along the dirt road far below.

The hills weren't entirely bare – whitebark pines were dotted about on the crests, here and there priestly spruce filled a swale – but the trees weren't seriously growing. They were, it seemed, just for show – like the bits of dark fluff that architects stick on their models. A lot of America was like that – so devoid of activity that you tended to forget it was real. There'd be no difficulty, you felt, in reshaping it however you wanted – shifting an unpleasing mountain here, widening a valley there – because apparently you'd affect no one. The lone car, for example, now miles away, could have veered off the road, rolled over six times, and carried on as though nothing had happened. That was the American way, goddamn it. That was democracy and freedom.

Actually it was nothing of the sort. What I had out here wasn't freedom at all, but liberty. Freedom sits in the head, a quality. Liberty is merely circumstantial. Few Americans I met understood this distinction, and in view of the country I'd walked through these past months I could see why. Space is a terrific luxury.

The landscape had changed abruptly. The trees which for days past had occupied only dark triangles, now massed to fill entire valleys. Where, for eighty miles, I'd been warbling on the wind, I now shouted to create an echo. For the first time in weeks the skyline was higher than I was. Rivers of stone poured down from the tops, whisps of forest gamely mounting the flanks. I felt suffocated by imminent horizons, and, at night, very lonely. In the southern Bitteroots I'd slept content, fifty miles of open country around me, but in these forested basins I felt threatened.

I still wore shorts and a T-shirt in the day, but by late afternoon would extract a crumpled top from my pack. At night I was sleeping with a hat pulled down over my ears. I hardly ever made a fire unless I had something to dry – partly sloth, mostly because I was alone. A fire for one seemed a waste.

Now a day short of Lost Trail Pass and a right turn into the Anaconda Range, I stopped on a sharp col for an afternoon brew. I was reaching the end of a long, weary stage; it was warm, I was tired, I slept.

I didn't exactly wake up with a start – I hardly ever did that – but I shot through the suburbs of drowsiness with more than usual speed. Something was climbing the talus below me – clink, clonk, plink, plonk – and I assumed it was an elk.

"Might as well get a picture," I thought, and stuck my head over the lip of the col to see if this was an elk worth changing lenses for.

Peril is hard to score. Let's just say that I didn't even get to remove the lens cap because, climbing purposefully towards me, was a fully grown female black bear; and behind her was the darlingest little black bear cub you ever could wish to see. I hadn't the slightest idea what to do.

But the bear still hadn't seen me. The last thing it expected was to run into some idiot in a West Virginia T-shirt. I wondered if I should cough – venture a discreet "ahem" – but in the end I did nothing: the bear changed course and eventually reached the saddle several hundred yards above me. She was magnificent. She just seemed to ripple upwards, unperturbed by the little clown behind her. Mother and cub vanished among the rocks.

This was one of the most beautiful moments of the journey. Within twenty-four hours I was to experience what was definitely the ugliest.

September 16th was a Friday. I followed an easy trail all day, seeing little because of the trees. Since I was in a hurry this quite suited me – I wanted to get to the post office at Sula before closing time. By four-thirty I realized that I probably wouldn't make it, but put on a late burst of speed and hit route # 93 over Lost Trail Pass at five. I stuck out my thumb and got a lift almost straight away. We sailed round a couple of hairpin bends then down into the forested valley. A strip of meadow either side of the road broadened out, and the forestry station – four or five bungalows and a cluster of sheds – appeared on the right.

"You wanna stop here or the store?"

I was miles away, stuck on a limerick.

"Er, the store please," I said. I'd spoken to no one for ten days so this was quite a speech. We drove on down the empty road. I abandoned the limerick and began to drool at the banquet coming up. I'd start with canned peaches if there were any. The car stopped, I said thank you and waved the back window goodbye.

Groceries, gas, gifts – Sula seemed pretty compact. I left the pack in the care of the full-sized Red Indian stationed by the door and went in, choosing a card from the rack as I went. "Sula store and campground," said the blurb on the back. "Just thirteen miles north of Lost Trail Pass and your first stop in Montana. Daryl and Alice Riggs bid you welcome."

"That's nice," I thought. I was used to bland courtesy by now and quite liked it. When someone calls me Sir in a shop I immediately assume he knows what he is talking about. But Daryl Riggs did not call me Sir. He didn't even uncross his arms – large arms, I noticed. Daryl was about six feet four. The store itself was unremarkable – just an isolated gas station and grocery, dependent on passing trade. I could have bought all my stuff in there blindfolded. It was, in a word, familiar, which made what happened next not just bizarre but surreal. Daryl Riggs reached behind the counter and levelled a black pistol right at me.

What sort of pistol was it? Things like this didn't happen every day and the details were precious. But a hefty shove had sent me careering into a shelf of junk paperbacks – perception, analysis, the plastic Indian all tumbling like laundry through my head; Riggs yelling loudly that he didn't like freaks and advancing as I picked myself up. I'd obviously met the first paranoid of the trip.

The gun by now was irrelevant. If I'd had one myself I wouldn't have used it. What Riggs needed wasn't a bullet but re-education. I'd have given him a Yellowstone courtesy tag and I'd have made him wear it for a week . . . but another shove had caught me off balance and this time I went flying through the door.

The plastic Indian – it was one of those gimmicky, Big Chief jobs – stared down impassively. God knows why, but I'd just been slung out of a two-bit grocery at gun point. I got up and stormed back inside.

"What the fuck're you doing?" I screamed at Riggs. "All I want is some food and my mail."

There was another brief tussle, I lost, and this time Riggs locked the door. I decided to ring the sheriff and ran across to the booth by the gas pumps, but not knowing the number slowed the action somewhat. So did the discovery – receiver in hand – that I had absolutely no change. I thought, fleetingly, of burning the whole place down and for the first of the three miles back to the forestry depot stretched Riggs on the rack of revenge. For the second mile I thought about the plastic Indian; for the third about my stomach. I was starving hungry, the depot was still open, and I dived into food box fifteen, to be rescued from the thickening drizzle by a forester called Carl Hensley. He'd seen me beginning to make a wet camp and had strolled over from his bungalow.

"You the guy who left the food here in June?"

"Yeah," I said.

"How's the trip been so far?"

"OK," I said. "Saw a bear cub yesterday."

"No problems then?" said Carl.

"Well . . ." I'd remembered my mail. Riggs in the shop tomorrow morning could well qualify as a problem. I described what had happened – though why it had was still a mystery.

"Shit," said Carl. "Come on back to the office."

A deputy took my statement over the phone – "You mind if we record what you say, Steve?" Riggs had, apparently, done this sort of thing before.

"He's some kinda redneck," said the deputy, "except he's from California. Sheriff'll go see him in the morning."

And that was that, except that the Hensleys stuffed so much food into me that the Riggs incident almost seemed worth it. They invited me to spend the night.

"Hey," said Carl, knocking on the shower door. "You wanna beer in there?"

I stretched out a wet arm.

4 The Anacondas

"Seen that?" asked the guy who dropped me back up on Lost Trail Pass. A sheet of paper was pinned conspicuously against the dark trees.

"To whom it may concern," it said. "A miner was lost somewhere in this area this past spring. Should anyone find a body or clues please contact your local sheriff . . . "

From a distance the hilltops looked like green cushions, coniferous horizons rolling smoothly one into the next, but what the western half of the Anaconda Range lacked in height it made up for in impenetrability. One day, perhaps, a logging crew might turn up the lost miner's bones, though I was hardly an hour into the forest before I realized this was very unlikely. The dim light fell in thin grey columns, the forest floor a silvery chaos of downed trunks. A new generation of trees, already mature, had sprouted through the stiffened deadfall – the trails long vanished, forward progress a grim steeplechase.

I had plunged lightheartedly into these forests, feeling, as a marathon runner must, that the stadium was getting closer. Only 400 miles to go, then five easy days – perhaps a week – of hitchhiking to look forward to. Getting back to New York should be fun: I'd had a beaded headband the first time I hitched across Canada, and (almost) a moustache, but I wasn't on the trans-Canada highway yet, and this wasn't the summer of '69. It was autumn in the Anaconda Range, equinoctal gales a near certainty and the Hensleys' breakfast wearing off fast. I camped in a clearing and woke up next morning with the tent half-buried in snow.

Kicking it off from inside was good fun. I didn't even have to get up. Through the front flap I could see more snow gently falling, the child-like flakes uncertain where they would land. I did only twelve miles that day, stumbling through the timber to reach a forestry hut at about six. It was getting dark earlier now.

The place was heavily shuttered, so I rigged up the tent on the porch. Things take so much longer when you're cold – I had four layers of clothes on but was shivering violently as I tried to light the stove. Snow kept blowing onto the burner; the flint was damp; a circle of blackened matches built up round my feet. My biro wouldn't work either and my diary entry for that day petered out in frustrated squiggles.

I was aware, in the night, of wind in the trees and felt the tent fabric flap loose, but, wedged between the minimum of discomfort I'd managed to establish and its certain loss if I moved, I remained zipped tight. Gathering up my things in the morning was a game, the exact shape of everything, including me, perfectly housed in what looked like white polystyrene. The air was cold – somewhere in the region of 5° Fahrenheit – and as I gained altitude it got even colder. It also got snowier. I was walking into the clouds, the trees which so neatly hid the view now obscured themselves. About the only thing I could see clearly were the tracks I'd just made through the snow. I'd not come far, and I followed them back down to the cabin.

Carl Hensley had warned me about this weather. "May snow quite a bit this time of year," he'd said, "but it doesn't usually stay long. Could have an Indian summer." To stick with the Divide right up to Canada I was going to need one. The last two hundred miles were through country I didn't want to miss – the Bob Marshall Wilderness and Glacier National Park – but a delay here in the Anaconda Range might confine me to a low-level route for the rest of the trip. I needed a bit of leeway. So back on the porch of the forestry hut I decided to write off central Montana (cheerfully – it consists largely of lodgepole pines) and spent the next six days walking 140 miles along roads. The time I saved by doing this turned out to be crucial, because, quite by chance, I was to cross the last high passes of Glacier Park in the storm which shut them for the winter. Odd that I should complete a walk of nearly six months' duration with less than twelve hours to spare.

5 Tarmac

I was welcomed to the lowlands by a dissident moose standing all on its own in a swamp. Moose always look as if they are suffering for theories which nobody else agrees with. This one hardly looked up as I passed but heaved itself out of the half-frozen muck to knock a moose-sized passage through the trees, the last trees, as it happened, for miles.

From the air the Big Hole valley is roughly the shape of a flatfish, fifty miles long, thirty broad, and surrounded by ranges of hills. At the end of the last ice age it was a flat-bottomed lake. I picked at it slowly at first, gathering momentum as I bowled along route # 43. A car whistled past, tail lights red in the murk. A hawk slid from a fence post ahead, skimming low over woebegone grasses. It was not an afternoon to be hunting, clouds whipping down from the north at such speed that comment became commentary – snow in half-volleys, block-buster squalls, angled backhanders sweeping down off the peaks. I looked like a mobile snowman, hosed in sleet as each squall swept south; breathing in sharply, I could freeze the hairs right up my nostrils. It didn't feel much like September.

I passed the Bighole National Battlefield on my left. It looked illogically ordinary. No half-way line or anything. Despite the museum the area had gone on being just ground. The attempt to make something more of it hadn't quite worked, though a pair of quotations on the wall of the small museum worked very well. The curator had been trying to get his car started as I passed – it was five and time to go home – but he kindly unlocked to show me round. There wasn't much to see – a few war bonnets, some maps – but it was warm in here and I squeezed out another five minutes by writing the quotations down. The first was from an Indian:

> You ask me to plow the ground! Shall I take a knife and tear my mother's bosom? You ask me to dig for stone! Shall I dig under her skin for her bones? You ask me to cut grass and make hay and sell it and be rich like white men! But how dare I cut off my mother's hair?
>
> Smohalla: Northwest Indian religious teacher.

The second quotation was from an army general:

> Toolhoolhoolzote had the usual long preliminary discussions about the earth being his mother, that she should not be disturbed, that men should subsist on what grows of itself etc., etc. He railed against the violence that would separate [the Nez Perce Indians] from lands that were theirs by inheritance . . .
>
> He was answered: "We do not wish to interfere with your religion, but you must talk about practicable things. Twenty

times over you repeat that the earth is your mother . . . Let
us hear no more, but come to business at once."
General O. O. Howard, US Army, 1877.

I'd done twenty-five miles that day – the first four or five blundering
around in the forests; twelve bailing out to the open valley; the rest
along route # 43. It was getting dark now but the road just seemed to
pull me along. On a walk like this the trick is to remember tomorrow
– to pace yourself over a week or a month, not just through a single
day. But roads are like a drug. They dilute responsibility. I knew I
was overstretching myself but I couldn't bring myself to stop. I eyed
the opportunity presented by the first haystack with more curiosity
than relief.

I was to see several more haystacks in the next few days, but this
was the first – the first of the whole trip. I'd walked 2000 miles through
the United States and had yet to cross an acre of farmland. Not that
this really was farmland – rough grass was the only crop – but it was
a whisper, in this empty heartland, of husbandry, deep soil and roots.
In the whistling snow I now recalled another – the name of a pastor
on a sun-blistered hoarding way back in the New Mexican desert. I'd
stopped in the shade of the peeling billboard and looked up. "Playas
Assembly of God," said the sign. "BLAIR OVERTURF, pastor."

It had been like bumping into a yeoman of England, a shire horse
among the mesquite and the cactus, a hobbit name there where no
leaf mould was, not a ploughshare for a thousand miles. Symbols are
wonderful things, the ultimate toys perhaps, and I'd slept in the deep,
deep shade of that name through the heat of an entire afternoon. I
needed my myths refreshed now and again, just as the Daryl Riggses
I met needed theirs.

I also needed shelter, and, rejecting the haystack, now turned left
off the road towards lights a mile off in the darkness – a low ranch
house, and behind it a row of sheds. It was nowhere near Christmas-
time yet, but the snow was indisputably crisp and even. I felt like the
when-a-poor-man-came-in-sight bloke from Good King Wenceslas as
I padded up to the door, wondering that there were no dogs. A yelp
from inside explained that – the thermometer on the porch already
showed fifteen below. A man in his sixties answered my knock.

"Er, good evening," I said. I'd forgotten the can-I-possibly-use-
your-barn-speech I'd been rehearsing and was feeling a little bit silly.

"You look pretty cold," said the man.

"Yeah," I said, glad of the prompt. "I was wondering if I could possibly . . . "

"Take the first bunkhouse over there," he said. "Stove's fired" – and with that he banged shut the door. He hadn't even asked me my name. His was Fred Rutledge.

The snow was trampled outside the first hut and I went in. I wasn't quite sure what to expect – saddles and lariats; a few "Wanted" posters perhaps? Not Arthur anyway. I could just see his head above the back of an ancient armchair, clouds of cigar smoke billowing up round the bare light bulb. Baseball was in progress on TV. The bald patch tilted back, a beer can was raised and, without looking round, Arthur growled out a single "Goddamn!" I realized I'd not shut the door. He said nothing but that one "Goddamn" all evening, though when I left next morning he came out with a classic "S'long". I'd helped him to hitch up a trailer.

Arthur had lived in the bunkhouse for a very long time and I tried hard not to intrude, though when Lee and Mike came clattering in I felt a little less inhibited. Something outside went "Clang, clang, clang, clang," which meant it was time for supper.

"You comin'?" said Mike.

"I've, er, got plenty of stuff right here," I said, hovering between good manners and affectation.

He came back five minutes later. "Fred 'n Vera say why aintcha there?"

There were eight men round the table, which for 60,000 acres and 4500 head of cattle seemed not overmany. Vera and her daughter-in-law hardly sat down the whole meal. It was way the best of the journey – melon, sweetcorn, grits; salad, milk, tea, coffee; spuds, bread rolls, cinnamon buns; pie, cream, and a bloody great platter of steaks. It wasn't cinnamon buns *or* cream and pie; not milk *or* tea or coffee. It was everything – whatever you wanted, firsts, seconds and afters all on the table at once. I easily ate the most.

Breakfast was at five.

"That's five ranch time," said Lee. "We work two hours ahead in the summer. Be changing back in a couple of days."

I loved this about America, this "Howdy stranger" – which really existed; this "Bed yourself down, we set our own clocks around here."

Fred not only owned thousands of cows, but he had his own buffalo herd. As I walked down the road the following morning I could see them pawing at the snow, their great, brown hulks dotted all over the range. It was a fabulous day – blazing sunshine and a freezing blue sky which made yesterday's weather seem psychotic. I reached the small town of Wisdom at ten, ate, and pounded on north. I was feeling extraordinarily lucky.

That night I trod on a skunk.

But my luck held and I emerged from the ruined cabin we'd shared unscathed. It must have been the only deodorized skunk in America.

My boots, by now, were beginning to show signs of strain. They looked like very old brothers, equal at birth but, despite identical and blameless lives, the living proof that nothing is fair, not even feet on the same pair of legs. I tread more heavily on the right. I don't mean to, but that's the way it is. My left boot, therefore, was still intact, a model of wrinkled content. But my right boot was finally taking revenge on the heel which had ruined its life. When a guy called John Palovitch stopped to offer me a lift I borrowed pliers and pulled all its poor old teeth out – corroded nails which were stabbing up at my foot every time I trod on a stone.

Several people stopped to chat that day. John Palovitch, for example, was obviously feeling liberated, his wife and mother-in-law away on a visit to Europe. A Mr Kelly, born in Roscommon, pulled up to ask through chewing tobacco if his dog was still in the back of his truck. It was. Someone else tried to give me a coat. Small kindnesses sped me onward – I'd done thirty miles by nightfall – and late the following afternoon I dropped the rucksack in a small town called Avon. I caught a bus down to Helena, picked up my food, and decided to take a day off. I'd not had one for ten weeks.

The day off, in fact, stretched to two, which I spent with a friend who had come to pick me up. Apart from Connie, Joe was the only person on the entire journey that I'd actually met before. We passed the time variously watching TV with forays to the kitchen for supplies – fluff-nutters mostly, which are peanut butter and marsh-mallows in bread. Thus transfixed we lay back to watch the Green Bay Packers and the New York Giants collide. I could have sworn the referees had toupees.

The following morning I went to the bank, had a half-hour wait, and passed the time watching Fred Flanders (his name in gold on the glass pannelled door), the Senior Executive Vice-President. It was only a very small bank. I could see Fred's mouth moving as he spoke over the phone. He was wearing a blue blazer and tie. I was trying to remember if I'd spoken to anyone in a tie the whole way. Possibly, but I couldn't recall it. I'd certainly not met a bank manager. Or a

black man come to that. Or walked through much more than a village-
sized town, outside of which I could have been anywhere. In Europe
you know which country you're in almost without having to look. In
the American west you can walk two hundred miles and not have the
slightest clue. No wonder the post offices have flag-poles. The Divide,
I realized, had shown me far more of a continent than it had of an
actual country. For which I was beginning to be grateful. Forty-eight
hours in the mainstream was just about enough. Joe drove me back
up to Avon next day, I squeezed sixteen miles from a grey afternoon
and slept off the fluff-nutters in a cowshed.

I'd hiked, so far, through very few settlements I didn't actually need.
For the purposes of the walk, towns had been just widely spaced fuel
dumps, but having taken to roads for the past few days, I'd had the
luxury every thirty miles or so of coffee and doughnuts, a comfortable
shit, and hot air to blow-dry my hands. I would generally push the
blow-drier button twice, the boredom of reading the labels again – all
those world patents pending – relieved by a delectable second helping
of air.

But roadwalking has its disadvantages. Rolling north alongside the
interminable highways I was drawn, somehow, into every windscreen
that flashed past, like a dog constantly fooled by a barrage of phantom
sticks. I'd become used to saying hallo to people – contact in the hills
was almost always direct – but for the past few days I'd had to relearn
the art of ignoring them. Down here I was an idiot, a colonial coming
home to find he doesn't quite fit. Feelings like this at the end of a walk
usually take a few weeks to subside, though this had been such a long
and solitary trip that readjustment might take rather longer. I
wondered if one day I might go too far and end up a hermit.

6 Lincoln to East Glacier

The morning – Thursday September 29th, twenty-two weeks since
Antelope Wells – was heavily overcast. The whole sky it seemed was
loaded on to the pack. I could usually tell within the first mile or so
how each new day would go, and for no obvious reason felt today
would be a bad one. Even the flat bits seemed steep.

Ahead of me was the largest stretch of official wilderness in the lower forty-eight states. It was, in fact, four contiguous wildernesses within a vast outfield of National Forest, with, at the pavilion end, the further million acres of Glacier National Park. It didn't look much on the whole map of Montana (the fourth largest state in the Union) but this was an area, in both size and shape, comparable to the four south-eastern counties of England. What lay ahead, in British terms, was a walk from Broadstairs (Lincoln, Montana) to Southampton (Waterton, Alberta).

How jolly that sounded. A good stout cane, an old haversack, and off we go along the North Downs. It might be a bit wintery, but there'd be plenty to see – iron-age forts, Saxon field patterns, Roman roads and Norman castles. Chaucer had probably come this way – Nazi bombers certainly had – but this sheer density of experience was inconceivable here in America, the tight net of European history replaced by a few thin lines. The one I was following – a forestry trail two feet wide – led by midafternoon to a pine-shrouded lake. I could hear people yelling, saw bobble caps through the trees, and decided to stop for a chat.

There was gear strewn all over the place. I dumped mine and got out the stove. A guy called Scott had rolled up his jeans and was paddling into the lake.

"Hey, Dean!" he yelled. "You wanna get Becky and help me?"

The first flurry of snow caught them wading out of the shallows with half a dozen big stones in their arms.

"What're they for?" I asked as Scott stumbled by, his bare legs blue with cold.

"A steam house," he said. "We've brought a plastic tarp especially for it."

So that night I had a sauna. Getting the red-hot stones from the fire to the tarpaulin shelter was tricky, but Dean did it with a collapsible shovel, a trail of embers sizzling behind him in the darkness. Ten of us piled in, stripped to the nick-nocks in temperatures well below freezing. Someone held a torch, Scott yelled, "Here we go!" and tipped his canteen over the hot rocks. Giggles, screams, a pandemonium of steam, Scott yelling for more water and for someone to shut the flap. A couple of the girls had bailed out and someone else was crawling in. The heat was intense. So was the crush of young bodies. Things could have got distinctly exotic – I was rather hoping they would – but they didn't and we all ended up rosy and clean singing hymns round the fire in the snow.

The Montana Wilderness Bible College was fifteen miles over the hill, not too far out of my way, and, invited to give a short talk on the hike, I stayed two nights and a day. I can't remember what I said, but everyone cheered and made me feel tremendously welcome. Facing the snow again was an effort.

Cloud, endlessly shifting, drifted across the bleak mountains, the thin dark firs, solemn as dolls, dressed in white by the blizzard. Only the larches, paradoxically bare, made anything of this sombre landscape, teasing the sleet as it howled past, each twig a shimmer of rime. For the next thirty miles the Divide ran along a feature called the Chinese Wall, an escarpment whose height – a sheer nine hundred feet – was perhaps less awesome than its regularity, an apparent sea-cliff towering out of the trees, broken at its southern end into mountains that resembled vast liners, deck upon deck of sheer grey limestone, the talus alone dwarfing the forest.

I was above the timber now, fresh snow squeaking under my boots. The heels were virtually worn flat and compacted wedges kept building up under my insteps. Painful walking. I was stopping every few yards to kick hard against the rocks; painful too, because the toe caps had started to fray. I was stupidly proud of my boots. They were worse than useless by now, but if they really had fallen apart I'd have been heartbroken. I would never throw them away. In years to come they'd turn up in the attic, all withered and stiff and my brother's kids would shout down that they'd found a pair of dead rats. When they were older they'd laugh at the memory.

The peak of Scapegoat mountain ahead had vanished into the clouds. Things were happening up there I had no part in – alliances, schisms, grey fleets under sail, blind empires of cloud streaming south. The wind hurled itself off the cliff face, whirling pillows of snow from the high ledges. Dead timber creaked in the forested basin below. It was time to get off the ridge.

Despite the intimidating weather, trails through the Bob Marshall Wilderness were good, though with the limestone rearing continuously to the west it would have been hard to get lost. The escarpment ran north as a series of colossal embayments, white-capped forest surging right to the foot of the talus. This entire region of north-central Montana was, geologically, a bit like a loose deck of cards, tilted and pushed sideways *en bloc* against the western margin of the Great Plains. Walking directly east I could have been through the flanking escarpments in less than two days. Though elevations were lower here (the wall barely scraped 8000 feet above sea level), the peaks, when I saw them, were as rugged as anything I'd yet walked through. But it was the combination of appalling weather and swiftly shortening days that most cut down my mileage in these last two weeks of the journey, and that night – October 3rd – was a howler. I spent it tucked up in a cook tent.

I'd heard a dog barking ahead, seen a fluorescent jacket through the snowbound trees and smelt wood smoke curling over the timber. An outfitter's camp: four canvas tents; mud in the snow; and even a cat, its basket packed in on the mules, because Ray, splitting wood, said he'd rather see paw marks on the table than mouse shit. The dog's job was to keep away bears.

The cook tent was deliciously warm, a radio dangling from one of the poles, wooden palettes on the boggy floor. Ray pulled down his cuffs to lift a steaming ham from the stove. "Nothin' fancy," he said. "Our Nimrods're meat and potatoes men. Case of having to be with me doing the cooking. Sounds like them coming now."

We had supper under the hiss of a tilly lamp. Ham, beans, spuds, tinned rice. Mike belched and said it had hit the fuckin' spot. Young Joe said it was the cat's arse – the best meal Ray had cooked in the four days they'd been there. Old Joe had sore eyes and said goodnight. The others soon followed. They only had two more days to get their elk. Good God. I'd almost forgotten that there were people out there with jobs. They went to work in the morning, came back at night, they got paid, they went on vacation. I hardly recognized my own culture – a telling flash of forgetfulness, like coming home from a few weeks in France as a kid and saying "Oui" by mistake instead of "Yes". Ray plonked down a pot of coffee.

"Chester come up today about twelve."

"Any mail?"

"He missed it."

"Old Chester. Ask him to dig a trench round a tent and you end up with a moat. Remember last season? Clear fells half a mountainside for a camp and the forestry nearly cancels my licence."

Ron was the outfitter – the white hunter, out after elk with the Nimrods all day . . . what was this Nimrods business?

"Clients," said Ron. "Got a bible?"

I had two bibles, courtesy of the Wilderness Bible College.

"Genesis somewhere . . . " Ron was flicking through the pages. "There you go – 'And Cush begat Nimrod bla bla, a mighty hunter before the Lord.' Old Chester always calls them that."

There wasn't a scrap of light until seven-fifteen next morning. Ray had staggered in from his own tent at five, switched on the radio and started breakfast. By the time Young Joe and Mike appeared he had last night's football results and the weather forecast off pat. So had I. Ohio had kicked the shit out of Michigan and we were in for another storm. Old Joe's eyes were still bloodshot and he stayed behind with a pack of cards and the coffee pot, but the other two saddled up, fetched their rifles and followed Ron up the trail.

Elk hunting was the local industry, October the height of the season. Hence the fluorescent clothing – nobody wanted to get shot by mistake – and the mule-churned state of the trails. I squelched on alongside the Sun River to reach a trailhead at midday. Bob, Joe and Bill – big, fleshy men – were leaning against big, fleshy cars.

"Workin' out how rich we are," said Bill. "This time of year you get grain prices three times a day. Four on some stations. Spend the summer growin' it and the winter decidin' when to sell."

Three fat farmers – a window on to the plains. But I didn't really want to look. I didn't want playtime to end. The physical comfort of returning home was something I looked forward to; and I wondered too, in these last few hundred miles, what I'd eventually make of this walk – how it would all come out in the book I was going to write; but reaching Canada, actually finishing, was as difficult to imagine as death. There would be an end, I accepted that, but it would only be an excuse, something to thank for giving me a beginning.

Under the trees now the past few days' snow was gone, the forest floor rotting and damp. Sunbeams penetrated here and there, falling like bright coins on the dark humus, a pungent jungle of fungus and moss and spiders and tiny white mites. The trails were black ribbons of mud. Whenever I saw bear tracks pressed into the goo I'd shout as loudly as I could. I didn't want any chance encounters. Spruce grouse peered down through the trees, the females tranquil, the males like bantams, their combs puce with desire. The elk were rutting too, and as the trail wound back under the cliff I heard what sounded like Bette Midler on bugle. Bull elk straining to produce this sound looked ridiculous – though aggression and sex, which I'm sure are first cousins, usually do. The cow elk hardly looked up.

That night there was another storm, the wind like a goods train howling through the trees, me fervently hoping that no branches would fall on the tent. I was camped on the Divide at a place called Spotted Bear Pass, and got disoriented next morning as I came down through the dense timber, thinking I'd done at least five miles when in fact I'd only done one. I was actually less lost than entangled, and extremely fed up with seeing nothing but pines, though just before I stumbled onto the trail I found the remains of an elk – bits of skin and hair scattered about, the jaw bone still violently red. The Bob Marshall Wilderness is one of the last haunts of the Rocky Mountain Wolf, though this kill was more likely to have been made by a bear.

Grizzlies actually kill very little. They live much as hunter-gathers do, three-quarters of their diet roots and berries, a proportion of carrion, and only the occasional swipe at anything moving. But a hefty swipe. The paw marks in the mud were as big as my face.

The trail became stonier, the bear tracks faded out, and for the first time in a week I was staring down on the timber not through it. I could have done with an armband. The sieg heil of trees swaying below was hypnotic, troughs of green forest dipping under each escarpment to rise high on the back of the next, the tilted limestone riding east in tumultuous waves.

I still had three more days of forest to go, and made the most of my reprieve by remaining on Kevan Mountain for the rest of the afternoon, watching the sky, three storms at once; watching the wind far below in the trees; refitting fragments of original blueprint as I tried to link the overthrust strata. What had happened was shockingly clear – perfect horizons, thousands of feet thick, tossed casually into the clouds, the ice-gouged peaks white horses in a gale. Some of them, far to the north, were in Canada.

The eighth, the ninth, the tenth of October: rain, pine forests and mud; wading the south fork of the Medicine River eight times in a morning; grey stones, grey cloud, stinking grey ragamuffin feet. I'd not crossed a road for ten days – not for 150 miles – and had hardly washed in a week, my T-shirts and pants in threadbare ruins, everything rank with old sweat. One more food pick up to go. It wasn't far ahead.

I passed a beaver pond, aspens golden among pines; then, pines green among aspens and Calf Robe Mountain falling away as I marched down the road. A valley, widening now; box cars of the Burlington Northern Line rolling east at a steady thirty and painted yellow as the autumn itself; a fenceless station; a hotel. Strange to see a hotel. It was built in the style of a Swiss chalet, the mountain backdrop alpine. East Glacier itself was a few scattered dots on the map. Looking east there were no trees at all. Just a hint of an endless horizon where the dun coloured plains met the sky. Geography can be very abrupt.

7 The End

I picked up the food from the Conoco gas station and wandered across the rail tracks to the National Park depot. A helicopter clattered overhead, bringing in the body of a climber who'd fallen off a glacier. It seemed odd that people could be dying in climbing accidents only minutes removed from here. I'd called in to ask which trails in the park were still open and ended up staying the night. The ranger I stayed with – his name was Bill – asked how I'd got on in Yellowstone.

"Not the highlight of the trip," I said.

He laughed. "Ranger trouble?"

"Yes," I said.

"Known for it throughout the service," said Bill. "We have as many public as they do but we try to leave them alone. Here on in through you wanna be careful. Got more bears per square mile in Glacier than anywhere in the lower forty-eight and right now they're all eating like crazy. They've got about two weeks feeding-time left, then the whole park'll be snowed out till spring."

I'd not seen myself in a full-length mirror for months and, stripped off that night for a shower, I realized I'd completely changed shape. The wisp that had set out from Antelope Wells now looked distinctly squat, the chest and shoulders unrecognizably huge, the bean-pole legs bulging with muscle. Bears didn't worry me much. But Bill had asked me to ring back when I got through to Waterton and I said that I would. He reckoned I had about seven days' walking to go.

The park had been shut for a month already, trail bridges over the larger streams dismantled for winter because of the snow load on the cables. I was going to get wet feet. The park handout for hikers wasn't very encouraging either.

"A few groups," it said, "have successfully travelled the proposed Continental Divide Trail through Glacier after September, but all have experienced very close calls and near tragedy."

But no one listens to reason during the last week of term. Canada here I come. I roared out of East Glacier, whipped up and over the flanks of Mount Henry and dropped down to Two Medicine Lake – a grimy afternoon, the high fell fields a gravelly mosaic, the plains cold under a leaden sky. There was little to suggest that looming ahead was a classic glacial landscape. Studying the map it had been difficult to think of the Park as anything other than a classroom model: look, kids – a hanging valley; look, kids – a pyramid peak, look, kids – a horse. Horses aren't glacial features, sir. So they aren't. Approaching the lake I had made my second capture of the trip. The guy that owned the horse looked a little embarrassed as he burst through the trees. His name was Gordon Sullivan. We spent the night on the veranda of the deserted tourist facility at the Two Medicine Lake trail-head.

It was extremely cold. Gordon got up to check on Dust who was stomping around in the horse box he had trailed up from his home in Great Falls. He was a professional photographer.

"First came here to do a commercial book," he said, "but I'll be photographing these mountains till I die. I've chosen to have my ashes spread on Triple Divide Peak . . . "

"God help the undertaker," I said.

"Yeah," said Gordon. "He'd better be healthy. First thing that grabs you about Glacier is the vertical lift. Cuts you down to nothing at all. That's where these Rocky Mountain High guys miss the story, because you're not really trying to be at one with nature out here – you're trying to be at one with yourself. You're trying to get your own shit together. Doesn't matter if you're walking down 10th Avenue South or up the trail to Siyeh – if you're not walking with yourself, you're not walking. See, we are these mountains. Without us they aren't. Without our interpretation of them they don't exist. Is that hard to understand?"

Eventually we got on to bears.

"This is going to sound psychological," Gordon said, "but you watch a cat with a mouse. The game isn't on till the mouse takes off. Same with a Grizzly. He wants to intimidate you into moving across the timber so he can pick you out. So if you don't move you've knocked the ball into his court. Rather than giving him a reason to pursue, he's gotta make up his own mind to do it. But if he's coming at you anyway and you have to run drop your glove or something on the trail. Ten to one he'll slow down to give it a sniff. Myself when I'm scared I have a natural impulse to throw up which would probably do just as well."

My first contact came the following morning. I was humming the

"Banana Boat Song" at the time, wishing, as I ploughed up to Piti-maken Pass, that the clouds would either drop into the valleys or bugger off altogether. There was a rustle in the krumholtz, I stopped humming, and a pair of bruins fled down the path. This was ludicrous. My first two Grizzlies had behaved like a couple of rabbits. I almost shouted at them to come back.

The park that afternoon was a smudge, a chessboard of new snow above timberline, below it grey lakes and black trees. Holes in the cloud gave porthole views down, and the fleeting illusion of flying. What you needed in Glacier was a parachute. The headwall to my left was twice the height of the Empire State. Window cleaners appeared to be at work on the face – tiny white dots moving slowly from left to right. They were mountain goats, the thin silver rope dangling beyond them a stream. The main valleys, however, were gentle – long, half-rounded troughs, most containing a ribbon of lake.

I stuffed the food bags into a clump of dwarf fir that night, hoping that if a bear came across them he'd leave me and the tent alone. At 6800 feet, I'd camped just below Triple Divide Peak, a sharp pyramid now lost in the gloom, which splits falling water three ways – to the Pacific and Atlantic as usual, but northeastward now to Hudson Bay. For the last sixty miles the streams on my right would all drain into Canada. I snuggled down with the torch and the map.

The mountains in Glacier had three sorts of names. Some were dreadful – Peril Peak, Citadel, The Guardhouse; some were commemorative – Mount Logan, Mount Jackson and so on; but by far the best were translations, probably from the Blackfoot language – Almost-a-dog Mountain, Running Crane Lake, and, dominating the valley which almost splits the park in two, Going-to-the-Sun Mountain. Probably quite erroneously, I imagined the Blackfeet moving up through here in the spring, under the crags of Heavy Runner Mountain and across Logan Pass to descend on the Flatheads in the west. Not, however, the present-day Blackfeet. Bill had driven me out to Browning, a reservation town on the plains. Five minutes there had been enough to see that nowadays the Blackfeet weren't going anywhere. I thought of the fireworks, back in Wamsutter. All those Happy Lamps and Artist's Dreams. It seemed a travesty that a people who could name a mountain Going-to-the-Sun, or a lake Falling Leaf Lake, could have been so degenerated by the Peril Peak culture. I had no right to weep for the Blackfeet, but I was ashamed sometimes of a culture – my culture – which so mirrors everything in terms of itself; which celebrates not what it sees but what it conquers.

Snow had drifted into the tent during the night. By the time I'd dug myself out I was starving. I ate, and, feeling too full, followed the trail down Hudson Bay Creek. I couldn't see much through the trees and was letting out a precautionary yell every few hundred yards – yesterday's bears may have looked like rabbits, but they'd been big ones. I didn't actually shout recognizable words. It was more the sort of Hey-up nonsense you use to get cows in, the sort of noise you only make when you're on your own. But I wasn't. At midday I had the shock of hearing somebody else shouting too. The first backpacker for 600 miles was trudging up the trail towards me. Not, I thought, a week-ender. His gear was too good. It looked new. It was new. Randy Hessony had done just fifty-five miles. He was heading for Mexico.

In October? He was going to walk the Divide in mid-winter? He must be absolutely insane.

". . . er, great," I was saying. "Great trip."

He'd asked me how I'd got on and I was racking my brains for things to say. How do you tell a guy who's already set out that he isn't going to make it? You don't. You give him all the advice and information you can, then you shut your mouth. And for the next couple of days you thank him for the lesson.

There was a postcard from Randy waiting for me when I got home. This is what it said.

> Dear Stephen,
>   It was good to run into you on the trail in Glacier. Congratulations on completing the walk. I returned home at East Glacier. My ankle didn't get better, but really my heart wasn't into continuing. It takes a special attitude to push on into unknown experience. I didn't have the self-confidence to go it alone. I am still dreaming of the Divide in the winter – maybe I'll return with somebody. Hope you had a good trip home. Take care,
>   Randy.

I really admired him for admitting all that.

St Mary Lake is roughly the size and shape of Lake Windermere. In places the trail along the southern shore had been dynamited out of the rock, and, stopping for a late-afternoon brew, I accidentally knocked the rucksack over the edge. I had to walk back a mile before

I could descend to retrieve it, and spent the night on the beach. The sun had set and darkness was creeping across the water. There were holes in the tips of my gloves, and my fingers showed through, pale as the sky between the black banks of cloud. I made supper, sipped tea and thought. I was always sipping tea and thinking, but lately the colour of my thoughts was changing, the green – the go, go, go of a relentless journey – mellowing to orange. In a few days' time I'd be hitch hiking east, going back home to write a book. Then what? I remembered the bullshit I'd heard at the Explorers Club dinner. All that risk nonsense. Journeys aren't a risk at all. It's the in-betweens that find you out.

Though the tourist facility on Logan Pass was closed, the car park was surprisingly full, vehicles slushing off the road to halt in the midday sunshine. This was a popular spot – accessible and dramatic, the Divide a stupendous shark's fin of rock a full vertical mile above the McDonald valley. A good place to come with a day sack and a thermos. A sign pointed off to the Highline Trail, a scratch across the rock face which I'd follow for the next twenty miles before dropping into the northbound trough of the Waterton Valley. The possibility that I might finish, might cross the border the day after tomorrow suddenly hit me. One more night after tonight. It was as if, having run through a sizeable inheritance, a brown envelope had just hit the mat. Should I blow what was left – do it all in a day – or spin it out for as long as I could? I had no plans and lingered in the car park, watching people rummaging around for coats and hats and cameras in the backs of their cars. I no longer had a car. I'd sold it. Shit. I'd forgotten all about that.

"You comin' or goin'?"

John, twenty-five, and Joe, twenty-six, looked like off-duty sherpas, their faded jeans almost exotic against otherwise standard hiking gear. I leaned against their van.

"Good question," I said. "Probably both."

"Right! You're comin' *and* goin'! Same as us."

The eight miles north to Granite Park Chalet was, they said, the furthest they'd hiked in their lives. They kept running their hands along the cliff face overhanging the path. A small cascade splashed across the narrow trail, the water cold enough to shatter your teeth.

"You drinkin' that stuff?"

I gargled a yes.

"You are? Here – " Joe was holding out his canteen. He'd never tasted wild water before. Nor had John. They were from Brooklyn.

After a summer out west in the van they were heading slowly for home.

"Gotta be able to say we used the tent once though," said John. "We'll pack out again tomorrow."

Snarling grizzlies were shown on conspicuous orange posters wherever bears frequented the trail, and that afternoon the warnings had sprouted thickly. These bare, upper slopes looked unlikely feeding grounds, but the season's crop of roots and tubers lay close under the surface. We slept on the terrace of the locked chalet, barricading ourselves with heavy wooden benches against possible intrusion.

I woke John and Joe with a cup of tea at dawn and said goodbye. They were the last people I saw for thirty-six hours, by which time the walk was over.

I'd never seen ground ice before, but during the night the bare earth round the cabin had been lifted two or three inches – the long delicate crystals like whiskers of glass, each tipped with a crumb of soil. I spotted a bear, way upslope, but it took no notice of me, and by ten I was picking my way across the Ahern drift, a permanent steep snow bank that I'd been warned might force me off the hillside. The path curled in immense half-circles round these high, lonely basins – real She'll-be-coming-round-the-mountain-when-she-comes stuff – but it was the next loop of the trail, round Cattle Queen Basin, that so very nearly stopped me. Drifting snow completely blocked the path, the cliff sheer above and below. I dropped the rucksack and started to bore my way through. It was snowing heavily, but I'd give it a couple of hours and see how far I got. I was clear in forty-five minutes, by which time the diggings behind me were already refilling.

The Divide spilt off Mount Kipp, dropping out of the clouds to the break of slope across the glacial bench ahead, and, at 7400 feet, I crossed it for the last time. I sat on a rock, staring down into the Waterton valley, an artificial horizon of cloud slicing off the tops of the peaks. The southern end of Waterton Lake was now just twelve miles away – an hour or so of wintery hillside to cross, then downhill all the way. At just over 4000 feet above sea level, I'd be ending the walk at roughly the altitude I'd started. Otherwise there was little to stitch the two ends together – a pocketbook full of notes, some beaten-up gear, a long project drawing to a close. I felt slightly lost at this thought, a tendril running out of tree, though I still had the writing – a year's work, perhaps two – before I'd need something to twine round again. I wondered what it would be. Perhaps I'd become a real tramp, wrap a bottle of meths in a spotted handkerchief and sleep under the hedges for a while. Or tranquilize myself with a salary? Become our-man-in-the-wetproofs for some magazine. One day I'd have to leave this Divide, come down on one side or the other; but fuck it, I thought, as snow started to fall, I'd spend at least one last night up here. The afternoon was drawing in anyway, the snow, the far peaks, merging with the wintery sky.

My eyes began their practised examination of likely spots for the tent, flicking expertly among the frosted clumps of dwarf fir. Upslope, three hundred yards to my left, isolated boulders announced a scree slope swooping into the clouds. The bare ground between had been ripped through and rooted for edibles by snuffling bears, though the whole fell-field looked deserted now. But the grainy light was deceptive. It smoothed out the bumps, obscured the dead ground, and I should have been concentrating.

I wasn't. Though my boots, less than twelve miles from retirement, remained faithfully on duty, the pack, worn and stained, bearing uncomplainingly the first of the evening snowfall I, dog-like, was indoors, lost in the flickering shadows cast by the embers of a journey – a warm hearth, and deep, deep contentment. Suddenly the door burst open. Stark lights, cold air flooding the room. I'd chanced to look up through the thickening snow and I was sixteen yards from a bear. Pacing that distance, taking it home with me, was about the best souvenir of the trip.

The bear was on its hind legs, sniffing the air. I was on my hind legs too, but I'd gone entirely rigid. I couldn't even shut my mouth, though all sorts of things were happening in my head – delegates from a dozen different conferences all shouting loudly at once, with a memorable idiot from photography who kept popping up from his seat and grin-ning. I even heard a suggestion that the bear wasn't there at all. But it was, the last valley a dark trough below and behind it. My stomach flopped down through my knees. I'd come all this bloody way, and quite suddenly I wasn't going to make it. My toy had been taken away. Caught on completely open ground what the hell was I supposed to do? Fuck all the stupid advice I'd been given – fuck dropping a glove, fuck vomiting – this was a real bear breathing at me now and a real journey I'd so nearly done. Frustration unthawed my lungs. I heard myself screaming abuse at the bear, a full-blown, spittle on the lips temper-tantrum. So much for bowing out gracefully. This was a ten-men-in-white-coats job, three of them quite badly bitten. But my pathetic raging had worked. I was out of swear words and nearly of breath when the horrible, questing nostrils turned away and I was presented with the bear's shaggy back. The animal had dropped to all fours and sloped into the hollow ahead, to reappear seconds later, galloping up the far hillside with three much smaller bears behind it. I stood tight and watched them go. Then I paced out the distance: sixteen yards. And then I started to run. I hardly noticed the pack. I ran, and I ran, and I ran. Down through the krumholtz, down through the forest, down from the high, stoney mountain trail to a muddy track along the Waterton river. I did ten miles in just over two hours, though by the time I reached the deserted jetty at the south end of Waterton Lake it was dark.

In summer a pleasure boat makes regular trips from the Canadian end of the lake, but the whole place was abandoned now. I unrolled my sleeping bag for the last time on the concrete floor of the disembarkation shed and drank tea by candlelight. I felt mildly humiliated. The bear had punctured whatever balloons I'd inflated over the past six months, bringing them down sharply to a world so much larger than I. This feeling didn't last long though as I'm not by nature all that humble. In fact I'm a bit of a snob, at least as far as commemorative plaques are concerned. The one on the shed wall was immense, hemmed, Greek-temple-style, in plastic laurel.

"No fences," it said, "no wall, only a pencil-thin line of clear-cut forest from the Atlantic to the Pacific marks the border between these two nations . . . "

Propaganda always makes me feel smug, but the plaque was absolutely right. It was only a pencil-thin line through the forest. I crossed it at ten the next morning.

Epilogue

The trip back was eventful – Canada is the world's second biggest country, but rather stupidly I succeeded in setting fire to it. The prairie grasses were tinder dry, the wind incessant, and I was a day short of Winnipeg, brewing up between lifts, when I knocked over the stove. I just had time to hurl the rucksack and the camera bag into the road, but the food bags were already melting. Canada lost a couple of miles of verge. I lost a bit of my past.

Appendix

1 ROUTE

A Continental Divide Trail through the United States is not yet (1986) an established fact, though it probably soon will be. I made up my own route as I went along, choosing to go northbound for aesthetic as well as climatic reasons.

2 MAPS

A hassle. The US equivalent of the British Ordnance Survey is the US Geological Survey (USGS), now in the process of metrification. The National Cartographic Information Centre (507, National Centre, Reston, Virginia 22092) will send indexes and order forms. Where available I used National Forest Service (NFS) maps, regional headquarters at 11177 W 8th Av., Lakewood, Denver, Colorado 80225. Colorado is covered by an excellent privately produced series – ripproof, contoured, and showerproof – available from Trails Illustrated (TI), Box 2374, Littleton, Colorado 80161. The following list of the maps I found most useful runs south to north:

Antelope Wells	1"	USGS
Walnut Wells	1"	USGS
Playas	1"	USGS
Coyote Park	2½"	USGS
Silver City	1:250,000	USGS
Gila NF	½"	NFS
Black Range PA	1"	NFS
Quemado	1:100,000	USGS
Fence Lake	1:100,000	USGS
Zuni	1:100,000	USGS
Cibola NF-Mt Taylor Ranger District(RD)	½"	NFS
Hosta Butte	2½"	USGS
Casmero Lake	2½"	USGS
Chaco Mesa	1:100,000	USGS
Chaco Canyon	1:100,000	USGS

Santa Fé NF West	½"	NFS
Boulder Lake	1"	USGS
Lumbarton	1"	USGS
Chama	1"	USGS
Rio Grande NF	½"	USGS
Chama Peak	1"	USGS
Platoro	1"	USGS
Wolf Creek Pass	1"	USGS
Spar City	1"	USGS
Creede	1"	USGS
Sargents Mesa	2½"	USGS
Chester	2½"	USGS
Pahlone Peak	2½"	USGS
Bonanaza	1"	USGS
San Isabel NF	½"	USGS
Garfield	2½"	USGS
Shavano Peak	1½"	TI
Collegiate Peaks	1½"	TI
Independence Pass	1½"	TI
Leadville South	1½"	TI
Arapaho NF	½"	NFS
Breckenridge South	1½"	TI
Loveland Pass	1½"	TI
Rollins Pass	1½"	USGS
Indian Peaks	1½"	USGS
Rocky Mt NP	1½"	USGS
Routt NF	½"	NFS
Medicine Bow NF	½"	NFS
Rand	1½"	TI
Steamboat Springs S.	1½"	TI
Steamboat Springs N.	1½"	TI
Hahn's Peak	1½"	TI
Solomon Creek	2½"	USGS
Wyoming State road map		Rand McNally
Rawlins	1:250,000	USGS
Lander	1:250,000	USGS
Bridger-Teton NF- Buffalo, etc. RDs	½"	NFS
Bridger Teton NF- Bridger Wilderness	½"	NFS
Temple Peak	2½"	USGS

Lizard Head Peak	2½"	USGS
Mount Bonneville	2½"	USGS
Halls Mt	2½"	USGS
Fremont Peak	2½"	USGS
Gannet Peak	2½"	USGS
Union Peak	2½"	USGS
Yellowstone NP	1:125,000	USGS
Gallatin NF-Hegben RD	½"	NFS
Beaverhead NF-Madison RD	½"	NFS
Targhee NF-Dubois and Island Park RD	½"	NFS
Upper Red Rock Lake	1"	USGS
Antelope Valley	2½"	USGS
Lower Red Rock Lake	1"	USGS
Big Table Mt	2½"	USGS
Beaverhead NF-Wisdom and Dillon RD	½"	NFS
Salmon NF-N.Fork RD	½"	NFS
Salmon NF-Leadore RD	½"	NFS
Interagency Travel Plan	½"	NFS
Goat Mt	2½"	USGS
Goldstone Mt	1"	USGS
Shewag Lake	2½"	USGS
Beaverhead NF-Wisdom and Wise RD	½"	NFS
Deerlodge NF-Philipsburg & Deerlodge RD	½"	NFS
Helena NF-Lincoln and Helena RD	½"	NFS
Anaconda Pintlar Wilderness	1:50,000	NFS
Lewis and Clark NF-Sun River and Teton RD	½"	NFS
Scapegoate Mt	2½"	USGS
Flint Mt	2½"	USGS
Prairie Reef	2½"	USGS
Amphitheatre Mt	2½"	USGS
Pentagon Mt	2½"	USGS
Glacier National Park	1:100,000	USGS

3 TIMING

In an average year, southern New Mexico is snow free by April. I started on May 5th. Northern Montana is not usually clear until late June. Low-level routes are, of course, clear earlier and later.

4 DISTANCES

Specific mileages given in this book were measured with a wheel on a map and tend to be understated. I covered approximately 2350 miles at an overall average, including half days, of sixteen miles a day. I reached Canada on October 18th.

5 FOOD

Pre-purchased, almost entirely from supermarket shelves. I prepared eighteen ten-day ration boxes, and, before I started, left them at cafés, shops, forestry offices, etc., at roughly 150–mile intervals. The shortest hop was 75 miles, the longest 193 miles. A typical food box would contain the following items:

Instant Potato	Granola Bars
Instant Rice	Nuts, Dates, Raisins
Instant Oats	Orange Drink Powder
Instant Noodles	Vitamin Pills
Dried Vegetables	Cigarettes
Retextured Vegetable Protein	Matches
Bacon Bits	Kerosene
Beef Jerky	Polythene bags
Soup Powder	J-cloths
Boullion Cubes	Candles
Tea Bags	Soap
Dried Milk	Batteries
Sugar	Lighter
Jam	Firelighter
Honey	Boot Wax
Peanut Butter	Paper
Biscuit	Biro
Snicker Bars	Footpowder, Maps, Films, Tapes.

6 EQUIPMENT

(i) The idea of receiving large sums of money, even free gear from a sponsor, is not unattractive, but this was a purely private walk. Where I have made them, my recommendations are voluntary.

Six months' continuous wear is more than most gear is designed for, and I bought the best I could afford. Conditions varied from hot, dry desert to high-altitude blizzards. I got by without ice axe and crampons, but could have done with them in Colorado and the Wind Rivers. Decent snow shoes or crosscountry skis would have made southern Colorado a less arduous experience, but again, I got by without them.

(ii) Rucksack – Berghaus AB–65. Internal frame. Well designed, accessible and excellent for loads up to seventy pounds.
Stove – MSR XGR. Expensive. The only one to use. Sigg fuel bottles.
Tent – Robert Saunders Jet Packer. Good, but prone to condensation.
Sleeping Bag – Karrimor Salewa. 3–season. Excellent.
Knife – Opinel No.7.
Compass – Silva type 1.
Binoculars – Pentax 7 x 20. 9 x 20 would have been better.
Torch – Tekna Lite. Excellent.
Spoon, 2 cups, Whistle, thin foam mattress, seam sealant, nylon cord, nylon pack cover, needles, safety-pins, spare buttons, sticky tape.

(iii) T-shirts (2), pants (2), shorts (1) – all cotton.
Socks (6) – mixture of man-made and wool fibres.
The rest were all man-made fibres:
  Ultimate padded waistcoat. Excellent.
  Helly Hanson reverse-fibre pile jacket. Excellent.
  Helly Hanson lifa longjohns and gloves. Excellent.
  North Cape polo-neck vest. Excellent.
  Rohan bags (light summer trousers). Excellent.
  Rohan breeches. Excellent.
  Troll neoprene coated overtrousers. Excellent.
  Berghaus Sirocco Gortex jacket. Superb.
  Gaiters, woolly hat, flip-flops.
  Scarpa Bronzo Boots. Superb.

(iv) First aid: Melolin dressings; Spenco second skin; knee socks; elastoplast; Steristrips; gauze; bandage; footpowder; Dettol; antiseptic ointment and powder; eye-drops; painkillers; lip salve; skin cream; Muskol insect repellant (superb); Mycota; mirror, comb; toothpaste; razor blade; scissors; tweezers.

(v) Camera Bag. Olympus OM2 – good but flimsy. Zuiko 24mm, 50mm, 85mm, 135mm lenses. Polarizing and skylight filters. Kodachrome–64 slide film. Close up lenses, tripod, cable release, spare lens caps, cleaning kit. Sony TCM–600 tape recorder. Alwych all-weather notebook. Pens. Pencil. Tin whistle.

(vi) Books: Geology – The *Roadside Geology* series from Mountain Press, Missoula, Montana, is admirable.

Plants – *A Field Guide to Rocky Mountain Wildflowers* by Craighead and Davis, Houghton Mifflin Co., Boston.

The Audubon Field Guide to North American Trees (Western Region), Alfred A. Knopf Co., New York.

Birds – *A Field Guide to the Birds of North America*, National Geographic Society, Washington.

7 PROBLEMS

(i) Animals: Moose can get a bit aggressive but generally mind their own business. Rattlesnakes bite but I didn't see any. Mountain Lions ditto. Prairie dogs can carry plague, buffalo shouldn't be patted. The only real dangers are bears – to be avoided at all costs – and *giardia*, a microscopic bug that can make the bottom fall out of your world, or vice versa.

(ii) Water. Should be boiled, purified and held up to the light (see *giardia*) but I didn't bother. The longest gap without water was 32 miles. This was in Wyoming, but New Mexico was pretty dry too. If you know how to switch on a wind pump you'll be OK.

(iii) Heat-stroke and Hypothermia. Be prepared to avoid both.

(iv) People. Very friendly, but avoid Sula, Montana. Also, wear something fluorescent in the hunting season.

(v) Temptation. I walked the whole way.